THE HUMANIZING BRAIN

THE HUMANIZING BRAIN

WHERE RELIGION AND NEUROSCIENCE MEET

———

JAMES B. ASHBROOK

AND CAROL RAUSCH ALBRIGHT

FOREWORD BY

ANNE HARRINGTON

The Pilgrim Press
Cleveland, Ohio

The Pilgrim Press, Cleveland, Ohio 44115
© 1997 by James B. Ashbrook and Carol Rausch Albright

Biblical quotations are from the New Revised Standard Version of the Bible, © 1989 by the Division of Christian Education of the National Council of the Churches of Christ in the U.S.A., and are used by permission

We have made every effort to trace copyrights on the materials included in this publication. If any copyrighted material has nevertheless been included without permission and due acknowledgment, proper credit will be inserted in future printings after receipt of notice.

Printed in the United States of America on acid-free paper

02   01   00   99   98   97   5   4   3   2   1

Library of Congress Cataloging-in-Publication Data

Ashbrook, James B., 1925–
    The humanizing brain : where religion and neuroscience meet / James B. Ashbrook and
Carol Rausch Albright ; foreword by Anne Harrington.
        p.   cm.
    Includes bibliographical references (p.   ) and indexes.
    ISBN 0-8298-1200-8 (paper : alk. paper)
    1. Brain—Religious aspects—Christianity.   2. Man (Christian theology)   3. Christianity—Philosophy.   4. Knowledge, Theory of (Religion)   I. Albright, Carol Rausch.
II. Title.
BT702.A844   1997
261.5'5—dc21   97-25730
                                                                                    CIP

To
PHILIP HEFNER,
theologian, mentor, friend

PAUL D. MACLEAN,
neurophysiologist, friend, encourager

JOHN R. ALBRIGHT,
physicist, friend, spouse

– Contents –

– Illustrations –

FIGURES

TABLES

– FOREWORD –

The Jewish philosopher Martin Buber once wrote: "Man cannot approach the divine by reaching beyond the human: he can approach it through becoming human. To become human is what he, the individual man, has been created for."[1] In *The Humanizing Brain*, Ashbrook and Albright have traveled a different conceptual road from Buber's; nevertheless the spirit of Buber's words resonates powerfully throughout their explorations. For them too, our questions of "ultimate concern," our hopes of grasping something we name with words like "God" and "the divine," must begin by engaging the subtlety and profundity of our humanness.

It was Buber also who insisted on an ideal of dialogue as the most authentic form of both spiritual and human encounter. Ashbrook and Albright share this commitment, arguing here for the possibility of a sophisticated and respectful rapprochement between neuroscience and religion that is prudent yet tenacious. If we would probe our humanness, the authors assert, we must begin with the brain, because it is the brain—and all that it does—that defines us most clearly as human. The brain is also a liminal object for us, demanding on the one side a reckoning of the ways in which we are material, biologically constrained creatures; on the other side arming us with capacities to imagine and hope for realities beyond the material. In this sense, our fractured understandings of ourselves, both secular and spiritual, meet and jostle uneasily here. The question of this book is whether here, too—in our understandings of the brain—might be found material and insights for a "reinvention of the sacred" in terms our age can hear and believe.

We are biased in our culture today to suppose that any appeal to the authority of fields like brain science and evolutionary theory is an inevitably reductionistic move, one that is destined to blow apart any lingering hopes we might have that words like "divinity" and "the sacred" can still have meaning for us. This bias is understandable. As a rule, when brain science has taken it upon itself to pronounce on the continuing credibility of cherished religious ideals, the news has indeed been gloomy. One of the most familiar—and still widely proclaimed—renditions of the usual message was dubbed the philosophy of "Nothing But" by the psychologist Wolfgang Köhler. According to this philosophy, the collective evidence of physiology, evolutionary theory, and brain science led to the conclusion that we humans are "nothing but" products of chemistry and mechanics. Our existential hopes and ethical passions are epiphenomenal irrelevancies; indeed, our very lives have no inherent worth beyond some calculus of expediency, since, viewed from the reductionizing perspective of "Nothing But," "the corpse and the living adult have the same value."[2]

Writing in 1938, Köhler himself had come, not to praise the philosophy of "Nothing But," but to bury it. He felt that it was both demonstrably fallacious (in the face of new developments in both physics and the life sciences) and morally dangerous (in the face of the frightening appeal of the fascist doctrines of his time for a spiritually starved populace). Ashbrook and Albright have staked out a similar project for themselves,[3] reconfiguring it for the intellectual and ethical temper of our own time, and drawing on sciences that men like Köhler did not have at their disposal: not only modern, evolutionarily grounded understandings of the brain, but insights as well from new fields like complexity theory.

Looking at ourselves in the mirrors held up by brain science helps us rediscover a fruitful sense of strangeness, of noninevitability about the most familiar dimensions of our being: our exploratory curiosities, our aesthetic orientations toward order and pattern, our primal needs to connect to other human beings, our penchant for violence, even cruelty, our imaginative capacity to discover meaning and purpose in the ambiguous realities of our existence.

But that is not all. For Ashbrook and Albright, mapping the dimensions of our humanness in this way is not just an end in itself, but a prelude to a more radical inquiry: whether these deep structures of our humanness, as we have come to understand them, can guide us in our efforts to figure out the underlying deep structure of the universe—that we may symbolize using a word like "God."

The argument here begins with an epistemological assertion (about the nature of knowledge) and ends with an ontological provocation (about the possible nature of reality). It runs like this: the human brain is set up in such a way that we are incorrigibly anthropomorphic in our efforts to make sense of reality. Wired to want and seek ordered patterns, emotional connection, and larger personal meaning in the world, we cannot help but discover a "human face" in our encounter with the cosmos too. But what is the status of this discovered "face"? One answer with a hoary history is that it is delusional—a lie that we cling to, because the real truth about the "really real" would be too difficult for most of us to bear: namely, that it is a cold, meaningless place that does not know of our existence and did not want or need us to happen.

Ashbrook and Albright push back hard against the pessimism that favors this message of disenchantment. "An anthropocentric perspective is unavoidable," they admit, *but* this "does not automatically negate the validity of what is perceived." On the contrary, they dare to suggest that our habit of humanizing the universe may in fact be our ticket to understanding something very important about that same universe: "the brain of *Homo sapiens* reflects something basic to the setting in which we find ourselves . . . mirrors the universe that births us."

The "voice" of this book, more often than not, speaks using the imagery and idioms of the Judeo-Christian tradition. The authors are clear, however, that this is because they are most comfortable negotiating their understandings in the cultural currency of that tradition—not because they suppose that their local map does full justice to the larger territory.

In fact, as the authors proceed in their explorations, they end up posing as many challenges to more traditional Christian assumptions about God as they do to more traditional scientific assumptions about humanity. Theirs is no Christian god in the familiar biblical sense—a creator who stands outside creation, at best intervening in response to a petition, or with the occasional spontaneous thunderbolt or miracle. Instead, we are invited to contemplate an idea of a god so buried inside the processes this deity sustains that distinctions between creator and creation must be rethought. Back in the early nineteenth century, the German philosopher and poet Goethe insisted: "*Was waer' ein Gott, der nur von aussen stiesse?*"—"what kind of a god would it be, who only pushed the world from the outside?" This is the view of Ashbrook and Albright too, as they draw for us a picture of a god who is frame and ground of a larger reality that we parse into the material, the human, and the sacred only because we do not know how to speak a language sufficiently integrated to show how it is all of these things and none of them.

Toward the end of their book, Ashbrook and Albright quote a line from a poem by Emily Dickinson—"The Brain is just the weight of God."[4] Buried within that quiet assertion is a challenge to our understanding that still remains very much undigested. Can we do better justice today than in the past to that challenge—and what larger undigested business of our time is likely to get triggered if we were to venture on a rigorous effort to find out?

Anne Harrington
Harvard University

– PREFACE –

In this book we explore the possibility of a neurobiology of meaning. To that end we use the mind-producing brain as the primary lens with which to understand clues to God's ways of being God. We call this working brain a humanizing brain. It reflects the trajectory of evolution and the perspective of a transcendent cosmos.

This is a story of something lost and something found. The modern era lost a sense of the sacred, a deep sense of the wondrous deep order of life itself. At the end of the modern era people are searching for a rediscovery of that at-homeness in themselves and in the universe.

Beginning with Descartes in the early seventeenth century, the Baconian tradition of science—with its drive for prediction and control—shoved aside awe and wonder. Pieces swallowed up the whole. The simple strangled the complex.

With the end of the twentieth century and the questioning of the assumptions of scientific Enlightenment, people are rediscovering the realm of the sacred. Scientists and visionaries alike are identifying "a spiritual hunger." On every side we hear calls to "reinvent the sacred"—to recover the "sense of our own deep worth" as the core of life itself.[1] The religious fervor that powered the civil rights movement reflected this resurgence.

We understand the sacred to refer to the "whole" of life. The "whole of life" means that which makes life possible, that which brings life into being, that which nurtures and sustains a liberating future.

That power of making whole gained ascendancy with the political fervor that brought down the Berlin Wall. It is regaining its personal anchoring with the yearning for spiritual renewal. It is regaining its cosmic anchoring with the discerning of ecosystem relatedness. People are rediscovering meaning. In this book we undertake the task of making that rediscovery accessible, understandable, and viable.

Neuroscientist Antonio R. Damasio contends that in separating body and soul the Cartesian split of emotion and reason led to a breakdown of rationality itself. Furthermore, he concludes, "It should be clear . . . that the secrets of the neural basis of mind cannot be discovered by unraveling all the mysteries of one single neuron, . . . or by unraveling all the intricate patterns of local activity in a typical neuron circuit."[2] In its reductionistic form, Western medicine has "amputated" the concept of humanity, eliminating emotion and feeling and the primacy of subjective experience in viable knowing and acting. As Damasio observed,

> Versions of Descartes's error obscure the roots of the human mind in a biologically complex but fragile, finite, and unique organism; they obscure the tragedy implicit in the knowledge of that fragility, finiteness, and uniqueness. And where humans fail to see the inherent tragedy of conscious existence, they feel far less called upon to do something about minimizing it, and may have less respect for the value of life.[3]

A purely biological model of the human person fails to deal with the complexity of human suffering. It equally fails to engage the creativity of human significance. "The truly embodied mind," Damasio insists, "does not relinquish *its most refined levels of operation, those constituting its soul and spirit.*" For here is the dignity, the complexity, the uniqueness, the "human scale" that is basic to our being the human beings that we are.[4] In the evolutionary record, life emerges, "not simple, but complex and whole."[5] There is no such thing as a single and simple living thing. Far less does simplicity characterize the human; instead we embody the complexity and interrelatedness of the universe that sustains us.

We add our view to those committed to reinventing the sacred. Awe and wonder come in response to the deep order inherent in life itself, to that whole-making and meaning-discerning that the humanizing brain exhibits. The task of recovering the sacred is more complex than any one discipline or person can embrace. Yet the task is central to every discipline and every person. In this book we explore the neural underpinnings of meaning-seeking, of the complex whole and the elegant parts. They constitute differentiating yet integrating operations of ourselves as biological organisms.

The United States Congress and President George Bush called the 1990s the Decade of the Brain. This emphasis highlights the centrality of the brain for understanding ourselves and for living our lives. The centrality of meaning-seeking dramatizes the social and political upheavals of the last quarter century. It underscores the personal and private agonies of millions. In direct ways the political arena focuses on these forces. In a less direct way religion in the era of the brain provides a parallel concern for renewing humanity.

Since the early 1970s, the first author, James Barbour Ashbrook, has explored implications of brain research for issues related to faith and meaning and ministry. He, more than anyone else in these intervening years, has persisted in working out what a neurotheological approach might consist of. In recent times he has found, through the Chicago Center for Religion and Science, conversational collaborators who have accelerated the process of exploration and understanding.

Since 1989, the second author, Carol Rausch Albright, has served as executive editor of *Zygon: Journal of Religion and Science.* This publication, and its related association with the Institute on Religion in an Age of Science, has provided "an invisible college for scientific study of values and religion."[6] In addition, she has been associate for programs for the Chicago Center for Religion and Science, and codirector of the John Templeton Foundation Science and Religion Teaching Program, Southern Region. Thus, she has been at the intersection of the ongoing dialogue between scientists and religionists, both in facilitating the conversation and in being privy to the issues of the dialogue.

Together, Ashbrook's knowledge of neuroscience and theology and Albright's knowledge of the religion and science dialogue bring a unique background to understanding where religion and neuroscience meet. Our collaboration excites us. We welcome the privilege of contributing to the wider dialogue for the sake of a better and more humane world.

So many people have contributed to our thinking—too many to name. However, in academic language, they constitute a community of scholars and students without whom no learning and conversation could have occurred. In biblical imagery, we regard them as "a great cloud of witnesses" surrounding us (Hebrews 12:1a) with their wisdom and their work. We would be remiss, however, if we did not mention Philip Hefner, Karl Peters, and Ralph Wendell Burhoe. In a multitude of ways these three have provided thoughtful encouragement and regular access to forums in which the religion and science dialogue can occur. Without them this work in neurotheology would not be as developed as it is nor as refined as it is becoming.

Others have made specific input: neurophysiologist Rodney Holmes and physicist John Albright have been part of continual conversations. Psychologist Forrest Vance, theologians Philip Hefner and James Will, and neurophysiologist Paul D. MacLean have read all or part of the manuscript with their critical appreciative eyes. Historian of science Anne Harrington has graciously lent her encouragement with a foreword. Joan Svenningsen, administrator of the Department of Pastoral Psychology and Counseling, Garrett-Evangelical Theological Seminary, provided efficient and gracious secretarial support. Editor Timothy Staveteig has nurtured the idea of this book over the years. We are grateful to him for his continued interest and for guiding it into print. We are also grateful to Kelley Baker and Ed Huddleston at Pilgrim Press, who assisted us in so many ways, and to Wayne Moquin, who tackled the indexing with expertise.

We live in a universe that gives birth to humanizing, to the making of meaning, to making whole and enhancing parts. Because of that, we believe that God gives grace and we respond in faith. Religion mediates the reciprocal integration of grace and faith, of God and humanity. To live in a state of grace is to live in faith. To live in faith is to be whole, to have goals, to love. The integrity of such whole-making Reality is salvation: "For by grace you have been saved through faith" (Ephesians 2:8).

– INTRODUCTION –

TOWARD A NEUROBIOLOGY
OF MEANING

In a surprising turn of events, people are calling for a rediscovery of the sacred. The pieces of life lie scattered across the landscape of existence. Only a recovery of a deep sense of inherent order and wonder can bind up the brokenhearted.

We join that rediscovery process, but with a unique approach. We explore the neural underpinnings of our human need for meaning. These brains of ours make us unique in the world—yet their operation also demonstrates our kinship with the rest of the universe.

Aldous Huxley once observed that we "ought to be able to talk about a mystical experience simultaneously in terms of theology, of psychology, and of biochemistry."[1] We assume there are correlates among physiological activity, cognitive processes, and symbolic cultural expressions.[2] We explore possible cultural parallels, symbolic affinities, and central tendencies in relation to neurophysiological processes.

To this task we also bring insights contributed by the emerging discipline of complexity studies. *Complexity* in this context does not mean "complication." Complexity here refers to the insight—across the spectrum of the sciences—that a tendency toward *adaptive self-organization* is inherent in the way the universe is put together. A complex system is organized within itself and adapts continually to its environment.

The human brain is the most complex entity, for its size, that we know of in the universe, and for that reason we see it as a premiere expression of the central tendency toward complexification in our universe. We believe that explorations of the nature of our brain can help us better to understand "the ways things really are"—in our brain and in our world.

In this exploration, we keep in mind that there are many ways to describe reality, and no one way is privileged to the exclusion of other ways. Perhaps, in the end, the languages people use are the languages with which they are most comfortable and in which they are most competent. Our own most comfortable language is religious, in accents of the Judeo-Christian tradition that has shaped our life experiences. Our secondary languages are those of the sciences, particularly cognitive neuroscience. The languages of other religious traditions and other disciplines are the "native tongues" spoken by some. We believe that these many languages are basic to knowing what matters to us as human beings, and we use them in our exploration here.

For us, religion expresses human meaning and human meaning seeking. Religion expresses humanity's drive to make sense of its changing, challenging, confusing world. The era of the brain opens up a fresh perspective on this seeking of meaning. New imaging technology is now catching the brain in the very act of thinking; new analytical techniques provide a better picture of how it all operates. Historian of science Anne Harrington refers to this as "the neurobiology of meaning."[3]

We write with the conviction that humanity is finding ways to heal the disruptions in its midst. The splits between religion and science, between inner experience and objective observation, between imaginative interpretation and empirical explanation have been the curse and the grandeur of the modern era. But we believe these splits are at last on the threshold of being modified. The rediscovery of the sacred carries a new wealth of possibilities.

BRAIN RESEARCH AND RELIGIOUS UNDERSTANDINGS

In this book we explore ways in which the workings of the brain correspond with people's understanding of the divine. People have described God as ever present, God as nurturing, God as meaningful, God as purposeful. We correlate these perceptions with various features of the brain's operation. Some would take these correlations as evidence that the concept of God is a mere projection of human experience. We readily acknowledge that the brain necessarily "humanizes" all perceptions, indeed all cognition. The brain transforms raw stimuli into recognizable patterns. It does so because we humans have an inborn need to make sense of experience, to look for relationships, to identify causes and effects. (Figuring these things out has, of course, helped the species survive and multiply.)

Along with a constructionist view of reality, we also take the stance of a realist. We argue that the brain's perceptions do tend to have referents in reality, and this also applies to our religious perceptions. Further, believing that our universe has evolved, we place our speculations in a framework of evolution. We claim that human thought and our ideas about religion and God are there because they have survival value, and that they have this value because they contain elements of truth.

In what follows we relate various images of God and religion to the evolution of the brain and the varied ways in which it works. Our approach, therefore, is one of convergence and overlap among technical disciplines. We combine the languages of religion, whether understood in broad cultural terms or in narrower theological categories, with neuroscience talk to make sense of religion. As an additional help, we draw on the insights of the new discipline of complexity. We are not out to convert anyone. Rather, we use these various languages to help seekers and believers like ourselves understand the mystery of meaning more fully.

Neurophysiologist Rodney Holmes points out that we must think of the human being as *Homo religiosus*. We are, and apparently always have been, creatures who respond to a larger meaning-making universe than we ourselves can create. Archeological evidence of religious observances indicates that we have been religious for as long as we have been *Homo sapiens*, perhaps longer—even in the clouded past of our pre–*Homo sapiens* ancestors.[4]

God-talk is really human-talk, since it is we who are conversing. In another sense, though, we can distinguish human-talk. Human-talk focuses on the mechanisms, the motives, and the meanings of human persons and human communities. We use it to explore the ramifications and implications of the human context for religious meaning.

Despite insistence to the contrary, all theology uses other languages in order to express the mystery of the universe. No talk of God can be without reference to that which we know directly. What we know directly is always inseparable from the culture of which we are a part. We cannot know or speak of God as something—a Being, even Being itself—without connection to human consciousness. That makes the issue of God and religion an interpretive one—a matter of framing experience and evidence in meaningful ways.

In technical terms, theology is a hermeneutical discipline. It uses whatever data are available to describe God and what God is about. Those data come from nature, from human relationships, and from historical events. The data people choose are somewhat arbitrary. They grow out of people's own particular interests, background, and competencies. Even so, everyone attempts to make sense of as much data as possible. In short, everyone interprets experience. We ourselves have been molded and taught by the Judeo-Christian tradition—its historical accounts, reflections, metaphors, and myths. In our discussion we will refer particularly to key accounts from this tradition because of the weight they have inevitably assumed in our own "humanizing" of experience. Without them, *we* could not be ourselves.

We assume that the human brain bridges the imaginative and the physical realms in ways that are uniquely personal. Therefore, we believe neuroscience deserves more attention in this task of "making sense of God" than physics or philosophy. Physics is more physical and rational but less personal; philosophy is more rational and personal but less physical. Only studies of the brain-mind require us to explore both the physical and the personal simultaneously. The phrase "making sense" embraces both symbolic thought and the apparatus for processing that thought. We make sense with our mind and we make sense with our body, particularly its brain. Neither mind nor body makes sense by itself!

We believe that the brain reveals a basic and universal structure that underlies all belief systems. It matters not whether those systems and worldviews are explicitly religious. The "new brain"—technically the neocortex—found in primates, especially humans, creates culture. Culture is the system of information passed from one generation to the next, not by genetic inheritance but by teaching. We ourselves find it clarifying to distinguish between that deep and necessary subcortical structure undergirding meaning seeking—technically the old brain—and the surface and necessary cortical expressions of culture with which we surround ourselves.

UNRULY MYSTERY

Despite ancient and widespread perceptions of the divine, the reality of God remains elusive. Humans seek God's presence even as they fear God's absence. We see religion as attempting to bridge this gulf, to hold us steady even if God seems unavailable. Religious practices provide useful guidance. They represent the "well-winnowed wisdom" that has evolved through eons of time.[5] Religion presents ways of behaving and relating that enable people to live together in relative harmony and productivity. (The exception comes when people confuse *their* understanding of God with *God*, thereby engaging in such fanatical behavior as heresy hunts, political persecutions, *and* assassinations.)

We believe an expanded religious understanding can hold promise for the future. From the farther reaches of the globe to the most intimate alleys of the neighborhood people shudder with the violence of extremism. Religious fanaticism saturates that extremism even as political ideology justifies it. At the same time—from a growing commitment to nurturing nature to the intense longing for personal centering—people search for spiritual roots. The forces of disruption struggle with the drive to connect. Religion, like the city of Jerusalem itself, both tears people apart and draws people together. While the outcome is uncertain, the dynamic is clear. We must rediscover the sacred if we are to deal constructively with the politico-religious issues of our time.

LINKING THE EXPERIENTIAL AND THE EMPIRICAL

Starting with the Whole

We start with the whole. Think of the whole as the gestalt of grace, the universe in which we find ourselves, the universe of influences of which we are a part and with which we interact. That means we start with religion and that with which religion deals, namely, God. This is an orientation, varied as its expressions are, that assumes the relatedness of regularities and a relatability of emerging possibilities. We live in an open system, self-organizing in its creative processing.[6] Looking to the past, we draw upon the religious traditions we have inherited. Looking to the future, we see religion affirming the venturing, the risking, the yet-to-be-realized surprises of life itself.

We want to be up-front about our own vantage point. We resist the religious forces of ideological restriction. Such restriction interprets religion in a doctrinaire way. Its propositions are absolute. It designates who and what are "right" and who and what are "wrong." It obsesses over what is "orthodox" and what is "heretical."

We ourselves have been shaped by the time-tested character of the more generative aspects of the Judeo-Christian tradition. While we take the empirical evidence of the neurosciences with utmost seriousness, we recognize that our orientation is derived from this religious tradition. In contrast to an absolutist view of tradition, we want to reenliven religion. We conceive of this reenlivening as shifting from religious ideas back into human experience. Most of all, we hope to return to religion's sensibility by means of the explanatory evidence of the neurosciences, enriched by emerging insights into complexity and self-organizing systems. We believe such evidence can bring a sense of humanity's place in the web that holds the universe together in fragile elegance.

Russian neurophysiologist A. R. Luria rejects reducing "the whole wealth of human behaviour [i.e., the phenomenon of human consciousness] to associations of separate elementary events . . . rather [the explanation lies] in its inclusion in a rich net of essential relations."[7] At the level of the individual, this net forms the many facets of character and activity. In groups, complexity increases geometrically, drawing upon coincidences of time, place, and ideas. At a high level of complexity, symbolic affinities mark periods in history with culturally significant styles. We speak of the High Middle Ages or the Enlightenment. These styles are found in a period's architecture, sculpture, painting, literature, music, and ideas.[8]

For us, starting with religion—with a sense of the whole, a sense of the sacred rather than the parts—takes account of more facets of human experience than a reductionistic analytic process. The awareness of the parts provides focus for the sense of the whole, yet by themselves the parts never add up to a sense of the whole.

Between the atomic particles of the microcosm and the astronomical possibilities of the macrocosm we discover ourselves as human creatures. We are personal beings in a physical universe. The biological information carried by the complexity of molecules contains vital information about life as a whole. As philosopher of science Holmes Rolston, III, writes, "The whole organic program is inlaid into nearly every cell. . . . The whole script perfuses all the parts, but the secret is a secret of the whole, not of any mere part, even if it is stored in all the parts."[9]

In citing this scientific perspective, we are equally conscious of the religious perspective of an Augustine:

> You [O God] are not scattered but reassemble us. In filling all things, you fill them all with the whole of yourself.
>
> Is it that because all things cannot contain the whole of you, they contain part of you, and that all things contain the same part of you simultaneously? Or does each part contain a different part of you, the larger containing the greater part, the lesser parts the smaller? Does that imply that there is some part of you which is greater, another part smaller? Or is *the whole of you everywhere, yet without anything that contains you entire?*[10]

We find this reflection of Augustine an experiential window on the same reality that Rolston describes through an empirical window. The part carries the secret and specific ordering of the whole even though the secret ordering is more of the whole than of any particular part.

In holding together scientific causality and religious meaning we propose that the humanizing brain mediates between them. More specifically, we understand the brain-mind as an information system that operates both bottom-up—from molecules to neurons to personalities—and top-down—from culture to values to consciousness. Such a view allows us to consider information processing as a way to make sense of biochemical, cognitive, and cultural affinities and differences. Explanation and experience are complementary perspectives.

In a generally accurate depiction, historian Lancelot Whyte claimed European thinkers fall into two camps: "the one seeking order, similarities, and unity (often called 'mystical' or 'religious') and the other seeking differences among particulars (the 'tough' thinkers or scientists). The first seek comfort in feeling a unifying order, the second in defining particulars."[11]

There are, however, many exceptions to this generalization, notably among theoretical physicists, who often appreciate the particulars while also seeking order and theoretical beauty in ways reminiscent of mysticism. To Albert Einstein, for example, "The aim of science . . . is a comprehension, as *complete as possible*, of the connection between the sense experiences in their totality, and, on the other hand, the accomplishment of this aim *by use of a minimum of primary concepts and relations* (seeking, as far as possible, logical unity in the world picture)."[12]

To explore a neurobiology of religion puts us on the side of those "seeking . . . a unifying order." At the same time we take seriously those "defining particulars."

UNITING WITH NATURE

In its larger ramifications, such an approach shares an affinity with an ecologically based ethics. Cultural geographer I. G. Simmons points the way to this valuing when he writes:

> The core of the new environmental behaviour then becomes an awareness of self in which we no longer stop at the boundary of our skins nor indeed perhaps at the limit of our tentacular reach for resources. Instead we are to *see ourselves as united with the rest of the universe in a ground of being.*[13]

What environmentalists are espousing in relation to the natural environment, we are espousing in yoking religion's meaning and neuroscience's investigations. That is, *theo* refers to God, and God refers to mystery and meaning, the ground of humanity itself. At the same time, *logos* refers to an understanding, an ordering, an intelligibility in that mystery.[14] In this sense, our conviction about religion is a conviction that this universe, while mysterious, also possesses an inner logic. While we make this as a statement of faith, scientists and religionists alike make similar statements of faith.[15]

THE LOGIC OF MYSTERY

We propose that humanity can key in to this inner logic of mystery through the brain and its mind! We agree with physicist Paul Davies's insistence that our human "presence in the universe represents a *fundamental* rather than an *incidental* feature of existence."[16] For the human brain-mind is the most highly developed known expression of the increase of self-organization and complexification toward which the entire universe seems to tend.[17] We humans represent the implicit oneness of a self-organizing system.[18] The self-organizing system operates both in ourselves and in the universe. That is why the religious concept of God most fully expresses what this exploration is about. It points to—hints at—some ultimate significance beyond that which the vocabulary of self and society or of nature and history can capture.

SYMBOLIZING THE INACCESSIBLE AND INEXPRESSIBLE

We cannot put the dimension of depth—the gestalt of grace and the elegance of the whole—into words. It simply is inaccessible to adequate conceptualization. Further, it is inexpressible in that it is beyond description. Our only recourse is to express that "depth" in symbol and metaphor.[19] The word *God* refers to a "depth" and "wholeness" *unlike anything that we humans know or can know.* Certainly it is beyond our ability to discriminate and label.

Through the centuries, people have reported a sense of the presence of a supreme being. Yet to describe that being stretches human capacities beyond their limits. So people have had to resort to analogy to describe God. We draw on everything that we know through lived experience. All that is built into our very being, into our soul, discloses our knowledge of God.

We understand religion as a means of humanizing the mysterious "Ground of Being," to use Tillich's phrase. That brings God within human understanding. In turn, new understandings of the brain provide new awareness of the structure, the processes, the activity of seeking for meaning and for the ultimate. So, in the era of the brain, religion finds its logos, its inner logic, in terms of the accumulating evidence of neuroscience.

The human brain specializes in humanizing the context in which it emerges. It interprets the world in human terms. Everything that matters in life arises from this orientation. Humanity finds itself in the world. That means personal relatedness, personal pain, personal aspirations, personal observations, personal memories. Out of this raw material, the meaning-seeking brain constructs meaning. Religion in its basic sense means concern with the whole of things—with God.

The concept of the humanizing brain[20] offers a perspective for integrating notions of ourselves and our place in the universe. This perspective deals with *nature as the context* of life, *history as the content* of humanity, and *God as the criterion* of what matters in the life of humanity. It provides explanatory support for the wisdom of the ages, primarily as we have received that understanding through the religious traditions. Increasingly we humans can specify what goes into making sense of God.

As people know more "of what" life consists, so they learn more "how" to live that life. In understanding the humanizing brain, they can discern clues to more genuine human community. Like the universe that fostered it, the brain is organized through patterns of complexity and interdependence. Knowledge of the brain's development demonstrates that relatedness is the primary reality that liberates rather than constricts. We now know that the universe does not consist of independent and discrete entities. Instead, the universe exists as an ever more intricate network of interdependence, a differentiating complexity in an ever expanding self-organization of possibilities.

For us, the Godlike and the humanlike are not substantial, demonstrable entities. We do not equate either with any specific physical reality. That would be a literal reductionism, contrary to all that we understand about God, ourselves, and the universe in which we live. Reality itself is not a static entity. Rather, reality is a dynamic process, a process of differentiating and integrating at every level of complexity, from subatomic particles to the cosmos— including mental processing. We believe God to be integral to these processes while, also, in the language of gestalt psychology, providing their supporting context.

THE SELF-EVIDENT DYNAMIC SOURCE OF ALL

In understanding God and religion, we align ourselves with the experiential tradition of Augustine. Its truthfulness has stood the test of experience. "Where then," he asked in his *Confessions,* "did I find you [O God] to be able to learn of you? ... *There is no place,* whether we go backwards or forwards; there can be no question of place. O Truth, *everywhere you preside over all* who ask counsel of you."[21]

In a footnote to this reflection, editor and translator Albert C. Outler added: "When [God] is known at all, God is known as the Self-evident. This is, of course, not a doctrine of innate ideas but rather of the necessity, and reality, of divine illumination as the *dynamic source* of all our knowledge of divine reality."[22]

In developing this assumption of God being the dynamic source of all, Augustine provides a classic expression. He refused to confuse the parts with the whole, the figure with the ground:

> And what is the object of my love? I asked the earth, and it said: "It is not I." I asked all that is in it; they make the same confession. . . "We are not your God, look beyond us." . . . And I said to all these things in my external environment: "Tell me of my God who you are not . . ." And with a great voice they cried out: "He made us" (Ps. 99:3).[23]

Here, then, is the basic assumption in understanding God. God is the "self-evident" and "dynamic source" of *all reality* as experienced and expressed by human beings. There is *no* place, *no* entity, *no* tangible reality that encompasses all that the concept of God represents. Yet the dynamic differentiating and integrating process is active in every place, in every entity, in every tangible reality.

We believe that "in God all holds together," to use the language of the Letter to the Colossians (1:16–18). We describe how that reality is evident in what we know of the universe and of ourselves as part of that universe.

In the brain's materiality—its physical matter, its anatomical structures, its biochemical processes—the brain provides the most empirical anchor of intentionality, or what many take as "higher-order consciousness." Intentionality involves learning and memory, anticipating and evaluating, consciousness of being conscious. This empirical anchor does not make the brain a computer nor the world "a piece of computer tape." Rather, this empirical view takes "intentionality into the picture," as neuroscientist and Nobel laureate Gerald M. Edelman argues.[24]

At the same time, in the brain's cognitive representations—its perceptual processes and pattern making, its imaginative constructing and symbolizing—the mind presents the most experiential source of meaning seeking. Further, in the integrating core of the old cortex—the limbic system—the brain balances what is novel and creative with what is necessary and adaptive. And the still older brain that we share with reptiles propels us toward behaviors necessary to sustain this materiality. These behaviors involve food seeking, safety seeking, and mate seeking. We humans are made to create a niche for ourselves in a universe not of our own making. We live in a reality in which "all holds together." And we are even cocreators of the social and cognitive structures that hold all together.

With that conviction that "all holds together," this book presents evidence of how the brain works to make sense of religion and God. God is that ultimate reality with which religion deals. Faith takes on new clarity when informed by knowledge of how we make meaning and how we maintain and enhance that meaning. In understanding the brain, we seekers may come to understand how we become the human beings that we are—our genetic inheritance, our cultural variations, and our divine destiny.

Now, with the sophisticated tools of neuroscience, inner experience is more accessible to empirical investigation. New technologies are catching the mind in the very act of processing and thinking. This in no way reduces its mystery; it only enhances how awesome human-centeredness really is. The very brain seen in the PET scan has a "subjective value-belief system" that shapes culture and events and even its own biochemistry, according to Nobel laureate Roger W. Sperry.[25]

We humans are embedded in the universe. We depend on it for our every breath. The rules that govern its operation govern our own functioning as well. Thus the mystery of the brain reflects the mystery of the universe. Such was the conviction of Santiago Ramon y Cajal, the "maestro" of the microscopic study of the brain.[26] The mystery of the universe inevitably leads us to speculate about the mystery of God. But we speculate about the mystery of God only because our minds are oriented to the making of meaning with one another. We constantly search for what makes sense of our reality.

Because we are humanizing creatures, ultimate concern about God requires ultimate concern about humanity. In like manner, ultimate concern about humanity leads to ultimate concern about God. *It is the humanness of our brain that shapes all that matters to us, whether we call that God or Nature or Life or History or Fate or Destiny or Evolution.*

In the past, the relationship between religion and science has focused on the context of nature and the working of God.[27] As the human sciences have joined the conversation, that conversation now includes discussions of the significance of humanity.[28] Within the last two decades neuroscience has emerged as a bridge between the physical and the human sciences.[29] This bridge provides new possibilities for exploring and understanding religion.

The bridge may be examined through the concept of mind. When neuroscience refers to the *cortical* and to the *subcortical* structures, the *mental* contents being discussed are the *conscious* and *nonconscious*, respectively. Both kinds of mental content have correlates in the brain. These terms parallel religion's reference to "the *experience of the numinous*," that is, the consciousness of the nonconscious, the holy mystery at the heart of a world that we experience, in the first instance, as material.

At the conscious level people put experience into words. Such conceptualizing reflects cultural conditioning. We make explicit what is beyond the capacity of language to capture. At the nonconscious, subcortical level we take in and transform stimuli into an infinite range of possibilities.

Recognition of subcortical processing reminds us of the "inexhaustible depth" of human experiencing. So, too, recognition of the whole brain and its neocortex emphasizes humanity's humanizing intentionality. Through our brain's activities, we humans become cocreators of a universal context of relationality.

To symbolize God in personal language does not make "God" into an object about which to argue. In Tillich's words, objects taken from a realm that is lower than the personal cannot symbolize "the depth of being." Lower than the personal means

> from the realm of things or sub-personal living beings [including reptiles and other mammals]. . . . [Instead, God] is a symbol, not an object, and it never should be interpreted as an object . . . it is one symbol beside others indicating that our personal center is grasped by the manifestation of the inaccessible ground and abyss of being.[30]

A commitment to God, thereby, construes ultimate mystery "as human-affirming, human-sustaining, and human-enhancing," to cite theologian Gordon Kaufman.[31] We align ourselves with those who find that humanizing focus in the Christian tradition. Because of that humanizing focus, we always understand God "in the light of Christ—the paradigmatic image of the human." Christ provides a principal "clue to what is really going on in the world (what 'God is doing') that is of ultimate importance to men and women."[32] As Kaufman puts it:

> By invoking the name "God," then, we mean to be focusing our consciousness on that process of or pattern in events (whatever it may be) which is at once creative and directional and unifying, which brings all that is into being and binds it into a *uni*verse—an ordered world that can sustain the web of life as a whole, and human historical existence within that web.[33]

With Kaufman we believe that the symbol "God" expresses "the ultimate mystery of the cosmic ecosystem of which we are part (God's 'transcendence') and the cosmic evolutionary-historical trajectory toward humanization (God's 'humanness')." The reality of living in a meaning-making universe is that it *is* "creative and directional and unifying."[34]

In subsequent chapters we will set about making sense of mystery, of religion's God in terms of where and how religion and neuroscience meet. Lest we appear to be innocents abroad, uncomprehending of a world that inflicts suffering and tragedy, we acknowledge that pain is part of the picture. Here we sketch how we develop these ideas in more detail.

OVERVIEW

Part 1 of this book lays out a possible neurobiology of faith by linking the physical and the experiential. The brain is a humanized brain in two respects: it seeks out and responds to the human face; and it pulls together and organizes a variety of perceptions and memories. Humanity is oriented to human reality and motivated to make sense of what it observes. Thus, we suggest that the humanized brain is necessarily a humanizing brain. The mind-producing brain compels us to deal with our universe as a humanlike reality. To aid the reader a glossary of technical terms can be found at the end of the book.

In the past, the idea that the universe is humanlike (as well as physical) has had a bad press. People ridiculed it as "anthropomorphism"—the creation of a universe—even of a God—in our own image. Isaiah attacked the House of Jacob for filling the land with idols and bowing "down to the work of their hands, to what their own fingers have made" (2:8). Enlightenment thinkers—influenced by scientific discoveries like Isaac Newton's (1642–1727), the rationalism of René Descartes (1596–1650), the empiricism of Francis Bacon (1561–1626) and John Locke (1632–1704), and such writings as David Hume's (1711–76) and Ludwig Feuerbach's (1804–72)—rejected conceiving everything in terms of ourselves.[35] Modern iconoclasts such as Friedrich Nietzsche (1844–1900), Karl Marx (1818–83), and Sigmund Freud (1856–1939) mocked the position. Today, postmodern perspectives remind us of the constraints of contexts, the pluralism of perspectives, and the constructions of the mind. Even so, all theories of projection must account for that screen upon which the projection is directed. Meaning embraces meaning making as well as meaning discovery!

When we refer to the brain as expressing the origin and destiny of reality, we assert that the evolutionary emergence of the brain reflects a basic dynamic within the physical universe. In its exquisite complexity the brain is the product of basic trends, basic forces of *what is*. That implies the evolutionary tendency is to ever greater complexification as part of a meaning-discovering process. We discern change from a universe "without form and void" to the formation of stars, heavy elements, molecules, planets. The appearance of life heralded a shift from stellar and planetary evolution to *adaptive systems* able to respond to their environment in ways that further their survival and that of their progeny.

We propose that the concept of "mind" bridges the complexities of the physical universe and the complexities of the human world. The brain-mind is by far the most elegant and complex adaptive system (for its size) that we know of in the universe. In that sense, the destiny of evolving reality—so far—could be the humanizing brain. Because of that brain, we humans carry the responsibility and the burden of contributing to the outcome of the evolution still to come; *we have become cocreators*.[36] Thus the brain of *Homo sapiens* reflects something basic to the setting in which it finds itself. It seems that, in an important sense, the humanizing brain mirrors the universe that births it.

It appears that the brain-mind evolved as it did because the world in which we humans find ourselves evolved as it did. Our brain equips us—imperfectly, but amazingly well, considering the options—to perceive our world in its important dimensions. We can discern its tangibleness, its wondrous order, its emotionality and directionality, even its unpredictability. In turn, we have important impacts on our world. Further, we and our world share a certain directionality that points to a shared and open future. The overarching reality of the world we perceive, and with which we interact, may thus be perceived as God's world.

In part 2 we set forth our constructive attempt at connecting neuroscience and religion. We draw on neurophysiologist Paul D. MacLean's classic view of a triune brain, with three anatomical and functional sectors—three minds, if you will—as clearly suggestive of various ways of understanding God's ways of being God. While we are cognizant of recent findings that whole brain interaction helps to support the various functions that MacLean describes, we still find his design to be an extremely helpful heuristic. And while we acknowledge that the brain necessarily humanizes all of its perceptions, we suggest that these perceptions of the nature of God are worth taking seriously. The elegant human brain interfaces with the world on many fronts, and the experiencing mind provides people with both the pain and the grandeur of being human. We suggest that the accuracy of its perceptions is to be taken seriously, and those perceptions include not only scientific findings but also the religious intuitions that have characterized our species from the beginning.

The sensory-based "reptilian brain," found in reptiles, birds, and mammals, attends to what matters for surviving and thriving. It is "present" in its environment without qualification. It reminds us of perceptions of God expressed through the structures of concrete reality, of a God whose "eye is on the sparrow."

The personal attachments, emotional responsiveness, and meaningful memory enabled by the "old mammalian brain" are consistent with the widely expressed views of God as nurturer, as love, as provider of meaning for our lives.

The new brain—the neocortex—seems to employ an ordering and organizing power that uncannily resembles the order in the universe. The pattern-making consciousness of the cognitive brain suggests God's creative power in ordering a universe whose vastness exceeds our comprehension. Its linguistic abilities interpret the "Word of God."

The frontal lobes of the new brain support the ability to empathize with others. They also have the capacity to construct scenarios, to prioritize, and to guide us toward our goals. They suggest a God who knows our needs better than we do ourselves—and has a purpose with intentions for the universe and for the individuals within it.

We trace the emotional impetus for meaning making to the mammalian cry of separation.[37] Either mothers or infants voice that cry upon finding themselves at an uncomfortable distance from each other. Infants must learn to comfort themselves in such times of separation. Beginning in infancy, we learn to live in an intermediate realm between what we need and what we find responds to that need. According to British psychiatrist D. W. Winnicott,[38] we learn to fill that space with "transitional objects" and symbols. Beginning with toys and blankets, progressing to other possessions and to productive and creative activity, we find and construct substitute symbol-objects. Humans find meaning through attachment to their loved ones, and also to these potentially valuable substitutes.

Because no love is perfect, transitional objects become the raw material of meaning making and meaning discovery. As with the significant caregiver, so with God—we are both separated and connected. So we learn to use transitional objects to hold the world together when God seems absent. Because of these we come to know that we live by faith and not by sight!

Males and females tend to experience meaning making differently. Both their brains and their upbringing differ in characteristic ways. Other genetic and temperamental factors also color experience. These characteristics influence the ways humans seek for meaning. Thus, different genes and experiences make for different realities. These different realities help to explain the difficulties people have in connecting with each other and comprehending each other's experience. At the same time these differences contribute to a richness in human ways of perceiving and construing reality.

Life exists on the cusp between order and disorder. This is a state of tumultuous potential necessary for new order to emerge. Even "the best and the brightest" cannot manage the powerful forces of life and death, or the contingencies of planetary evolution. We are partners, not owners, in an unfolding drama. While we believe in a loving, gracious, and beneficent context for human life, we also recognize the presence and threat of that which is not loving, not gracious, and not beneficent. For a host of reasons the brain can lose its adaptability, turning integrative cooperation into destructive dysfunction.

In this era of the brain, religion finally rests on the fact that we humans in our own ways embody and express the presence of that which is greater than ourselves. God is other than anything we can imagine. We live in a universe that gives birth to humanizing. This is why religion and neuroscience meet. In the meeting we discern clues to the "really real."

PART ONE

LINKING THE PHYSICAL AND THE IMAGINATIVE

ONE

A NEUROBIOLOGY OF FAITH

THE PRIMAL URGE TO KNOW

AND THE PRIMAL URGE TO RELATE

The human brain is puzzling, to say the least. By itself—separated from a body and a person—it appears unimpressive, though strange. Slightly larger than a melon, walnutlike in its wrinkles and grooves, putty or playdough in appearance, its immediate features are evident (see figure 1.1).

The tissue that we see is the *neocortex*—evolutionarily the newest part of the brain. In humans it is so large that it must be intricately folded so as to fit within the skull. Viewed from the top, the neocortex is divided into two halves or hemispheres, left and right. Deep grooves, called *sulci,* divide each half into four sectors, or lobes. The paired *frontal lobes* lie behind the forehead and occupy most of the front half of the brain; they deal with intentionality and help coordinate the functions of the other cortical areas.

Behind the frontal lobes, across the top of the head, are the *parietal lobes.* These deal with general sensory information. On the sides of the head and behind the frontal lobes are the *temporal lobes.* These process sounds and, in humans, speech. The *occipital lobes,* in the back of the head, are the center for processing visual information. It should be noted that these specializations are not absolute; the various parts of the brain contribute to each of these complex functions.

Hidden under the wrinkled cap of the neocortex are other parts of the brain. If we were to flip our specimen brain upside down, the part on top would now be the *brain stem.* It connects the brain to the spinal cord and also is responsible for various functions critical to the maintenance of life, such as circulation, respiration, and temperature control. The brain stem also activates behaviors related to the basic survival of the individual and of the species: reflexes;

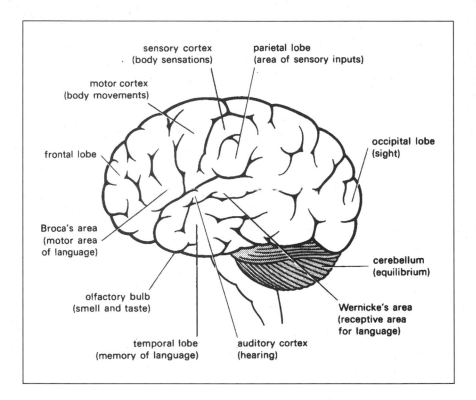

Figure 1.1——Main features of the cerebral cortex. *From* The Brain Book *by Peter Russell. Copyright © 1979 by Peter Russell. Used by permission of Dutton Signet, a division of Penguin Books USA Inc.*

movement patterns; fight, flight, or freeze responses to danger; and seeking a mate. Next to the stem is the *bulbous cerebellum,* the area that primarily coordinates motor activity. All vertebrates have brain sectors much like this one.

Sandwiched between the neocortex and the brain stem and hidden beneath the surface is a portion of the cortex evolutionarily older than the neocortex. Found not only in humans but in all mammals, it is primarily responsible for emotion, caretaking, and memory. This portion of the cortex, along with some parts of the brain stem that collaborate with it, is collectively referred to as the *limbic system.*

The inner part of the brain includes several *commissures,* or nerve-tissue bridges that carry information from one part of the brain to another. The most important of these is the *corpus callosum,* which connects the right and left cerebral hemispheres. Cells called *glia* provide support and nourishment to various parts of the brain but do not transmit information.

BRAIN DEVELOPMENT

At birth, the human brain contains billions of nerve cells, or neurons, but they are largely unconnected with each other. Some connections, like those that enable a toddler to walk, develop on their own natural timetable; for example, even children who are blind learn to walk without ever observing anyone else doing so. Although much of a brain's basic architecture is genetic, the structure and connectivity of the brain are also molded to a very significant extent by each individual's experiences—by interaction with people and physical conditions in the environment.

Although most of the brain's neurons are present at birth, the brain multiplies in size and weight several times over as a child matures. This growth is due to the proliferation of *axons* and *dendrites*.

Axons are "branches" that carry messages out from a neuron; an axon may be several inches long. Dendrites are bushy structures to which axons from other neurons connect; dendrites are the receivers of messages. An axon comes into contact with a dendrite from another neuron at an area called a synapse (see figures 1.2 and 1.3).

Messages pass from axons to dendrites through activity mediated by chemicals called *neurotransmitters*.

Learning calls forth new axons and dendrites, and the brain's weight thus multiplies several times over during childhood. Throughout life, new connections form new networks of neurons; old networks may, in time, lose power from lack of use. Thus, learning is lifelong, and, in general, the more one continues to learn, the better the brain continues to function through the years.[1]

In fact, it seems that people who are dissatisfied with parts of their mental organization—old "hangups"—can deliberately work to modify that neural organization through certain forms of psychotherapy. Various powerful experiences, including religious experiences, can be transformative. There is a striking parallel here with the early formation of neural networks. As we will see in chapter 4, to develop into a normally functioning human being, a small child must live amid interactions of love. Deprived of such interactions, a child will not develop normally. Similarly, the "remodeling" of neural networks also seems to require interaction with a loving "other." That "other" may be a therapist, a wise friend, someone mediating the presence of a loving God, or mystically

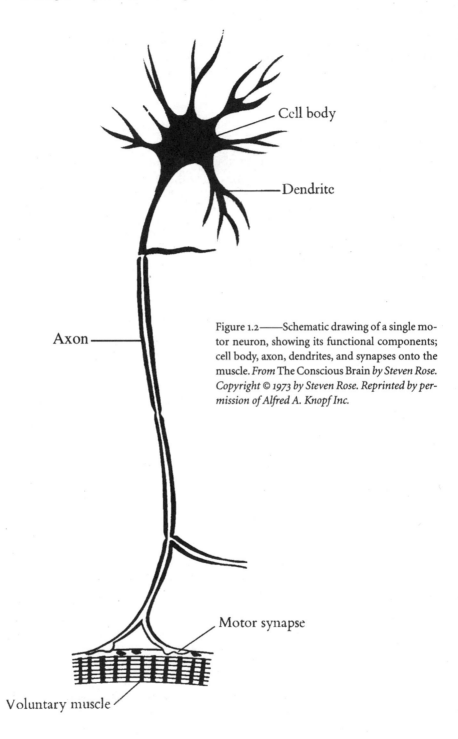

Cell body

Dendrite

Axon

Figure 1.2——Schematic drawing of a single motor neuron, showing its functional components; cell body, axon, dendrites, and synapses onto the muscle. *From* The Conscious Brain *by Steven Rose. Copyright © 1973 by Steven Rose. Reprinted by permission of Alfred A. Knopf Inc.*

Motor synapse

Voluntary muscle

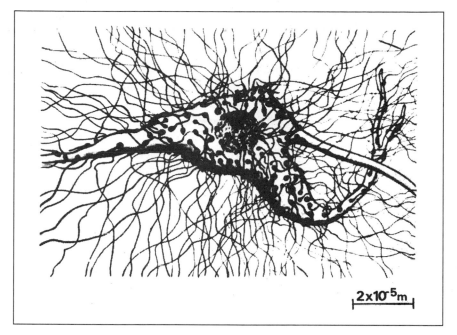

Figure 1.3——Drawing of a single neuron and synapses upon it by Ramon y Cajal. *From* The Conscious Brain *by Steven Rose. Copyright © 1973 by Steven Rose. Reprinted by permission of Alfred A. Knopf Inc.*

experienced transcendence. To call forth deep, positive change requires the presence of deep wisdom and love.

While this description of features and functions is accurate, it oversimplifies both the complexity *and* the specificity of the human brain. This odd-appearing mass of matter turns out to be the most compelling, the most powerful, the most intriguing matter in the known universe. Nothing can match its majesty; nothing can approach its complexity; nothing can detract from its sophistication. It, and it alone, provides entrance to all that is human and humane, yes and all that is distorted and dysfunctional, in our known world.

In these two opening chapters we set forth our understanding of the humanizing brain and its humanizing activity. In doing so we intertwine brain evidence and God-talk.

We propose that the concept "mind" denotes the *human* meaning of the brain. The genetic brain shapes the developing mind. In turn, the developing mind reshapes the physical brain. The result is an emergent mosaic of meaning seeking and meaning making as to what matters to the survival and thriving of the human species. It is our brain-mind that marks our human grandeur and our all-too-pervasive misery.

Two features are basic to our brain and its working. They can be interpreted in either nonreligious or religious ways, because we humans live in two worlds—the everyday world of time and space and the extraordinary world of meaning and ultimate concern:

- Our brains are "hardwired" to seek out and respond to the human face. This propensity keeps us humans oriented to what is human. It also makes us basically relational in our stance in the world.
- We humans keeping trying to make sense of what we experience. As a result, we keep organizing the random and disorganized—both things and ideas. This propensity contributes to what matters to our survival—and to what is significant for who we are.

In short, our brain orients us to the basically human, to what is complex and whole. In technical language, these features mean we are object-seeking/meaning-making creatures. Like Siamese twins, the seeking and the meaning processes intertwine. We separate them only for purposes of analysis and understanding.

The 1981 Nobel Prizes awarded in "physiology or medicine" dramatically symbolize the intersection between the physical environment and the world of meaning. One prize went to Roger W. Sperry for his work in identifying "some effects of disconnecting the cerebral hemispheres." This is known more popularly as "split-brain research." The other laurel went to David H. Hubel and Torsten N. Wiesel for their work on "the primary visual cortex and the influence of environment."

For us, a meeting between religion and neuroscience focuses on the issue of how we humans hold together *sensory* processing and *symbolic* processing. This connects perceptual realism and psychic meaningfulness. Sperry's work lifts up two streams of conscious organization; Hubel's and Wiesel's work identifies highly specific visual response patterns. Together these researchers provide clues to the way our brain humanizes what we encounter.

MAKING SENSE OF EXPERIENCE:
THE PRIMAL URGE TO KNOW

Consider first Sperry's work on split-brain patients. Behind the discovery of two streams of consciousness lies a more basic capacity—specifically, the drive to make sense of what we experience. We regard this drive as the inquiring, meaning-seeking capacity of the human brain. The empirical evidence supports a human bias for order.

How do people put things together cognitively? To answer that we turn to a clinical study of a sixteen-year-old boy named Paul. The case illustrates the way we make sense of the world whether we are brain injured or have a normally functioning brain.

What Do You See and What Does It Mean?

Paul was one of about fifty patients operated on for uncontrollable epileptic seizures. The surgery consisted of opening the skull and cutting the main fiber tract that sends messages back and forth between the left and right hemispheres (see figure 1.4). That tract is called the corpus callosum. Different sections of it

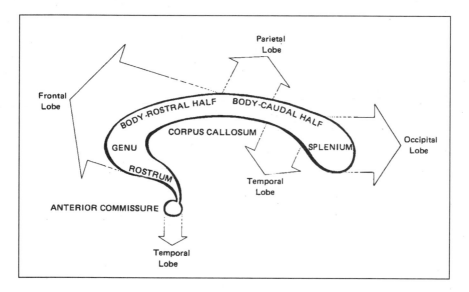

Figure 1.4——The corpus callosum and other bands of nerves (commissures) connecting parts of the forebrain. The corpus callosum is known to be functionally divided in a manner that finds the interhemispheric fibers coursing through the posterior (back) area, or splenium, to be projected primarily to the occipital lobe. As shown, the body of the callosum projects to the parietal lobe, and the anterior (front) regions interconnect the frontal lobes. The temporal lobe is interconnected via the anterior (front) commissure and the caudal (tail) parts of the body of the callosum. *From Michael S. Gazzaniga and Joseph E. LeDoux,* The Integrated Mind *(New York: Plenum Press, 1978), 2. Reprinted by permission of Plenum Publishing Corporation.*

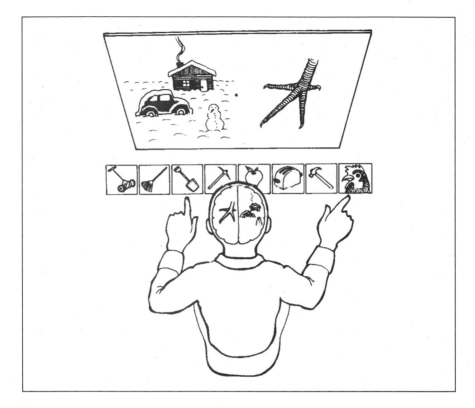

Figure 1.5——Study of right and left brain functions. Two different cognitive tasks were presented simultaneously, one to each hemisphere. The left hemisphere was required to process the answer to the chicken claw, while the right dealt with the implications of being presented with a snow scene. After each hemisphere responded, the left hemisphere was asked to explains its choice. See text for implications. *From Michael S. Gazzaniga and Joseph LeDoux,* The Integrated Mind *(New York: Plenum, 1978), 90. Reprinted by permission of Plenum Publishing Corporation.*

connect with different areas of the cortex. Researchers hoped this would stop the spread of the electrical thunderstorm flashing from one side of the brain to the other. In controlling the seizures, the operations proved successful. However, more subtle problems arose. We say more about this in chapter 6. Here we point to the way Paul handled the task of identifying objects.

Researchers asked him to sit at a table and look at a single point in the center of a blank screen directly in front of him (see figure 1.5).[2] They flashed pictures of objects to either side of the fixation point. Then they asked him to identify what he saw. The speed of the flash allowed only the hemisphere to which the stimulus was directed to "see" what was on the screen. That is, the left hemisphere would see only what was in the right visual field and the right hemisphere only what was in the left visual field.

Almost our entire nervous system works in this crossover way. The left brain controls the right side of the body, and the right brain controls the left side of the body. This is true of what we take in as well as what we put out. Since the connecting fiber tract of the corpus callosum had been cut, neither hemisphere knew what the other hemisphere knew.

To the right of the fixation point the researchers flashed a chicken claw. Therefore, Paul's left hemisphere received the picture. To the left of the point they flashed a snow scene with a snowman, a car covered with snow, and smoke rising from the chimney of a house blanketed in snow. His right hemisphere processed that picture.

On the table they had spread out eight cards, each with a different object: a lawnmower, a rake, a shovel, an ax, an apple, a toaster, a hammer, and a chicken head. They asked Paul to point to the card that went with what he had seen on the screen. His left hemisphere directed his right hand to pick the chicken head; it went with the claw. His right hemisphere directed his left hand to pick the shovel; it was associated with the snow scene.

When the fiber tract is cut, neither hemisphere knows what the other hemisphere knows. The information cannot get through to the other side. Thus, each half makes a different association to what it has seen. Each half is unaware of the fact that the other half is responding to an altogether different scene.

After Paul had selected the shovel and claw, a researcher asked him, "Why did you do that?" meaning, Why did he pick the different pictures? Without a moment's hesitation Paul looked at him and said, "Oh, that's easy. The chicken goes with the chicken head and you need a shovel to clean out the chicken shed."

What had happened?

Because the left brain handles the right side, both input and output, we can understand how the claw went with the head. Because the right brain handles the left side, both input and output, we can understand how the snow scene got linked with the shovel. How, though, did the shovel—the right hemisphere's association to snow—end up being needed to clean out the chicken shed? How did the chicken—the left hemisphere's pairing of claw and head—end up representing a chicken shed that needed cleaning out?

What happened to the snow? Where did the shed come from? Why was the shed dirty? How did a snow shovel become a shovel for a chicken coop?

The Interpretive Left Hemisphere

Patients like Paul help answer such questions. In most people the left hemisphere is the talking half of the brain. It is the source of active speech and words. If it is damaged, active speech is affected.

From the mid-1800s to the mid-1900s scientists called the left brain the "major" hemisphere. It could talk. All that mattered was the ability to speak. They thought of the right hemisphere as "minor." It was silent. Later we say more about this unexamined assumption about what is important in human experience.

For now the important fact is this: When the fiber tract is cut, the right hemisphere cannot say what it knows, nor does the left hemisphere know what the right hemisphere knows. The main communication line is down. Hardly any inside information passes between them.

The right brain could not let the left brain know about the snow scene directly. Even so, by pointing with the left hand it could still associate the scene in the slide with a card on the table. The act showed that the right hemisphere knew what it saw. At the same time, although the left brain did not have access to what the right brain knew, it could still handle the task of explaining why the hands behaved as they did. The left hemisphere knew why the right hand picked the head—because of the claw. Although ignorant of the snow scene, it did observe that the left hand picked the shovel.

To answer the question, "Why did you do that?"—referring ambiguously to the two different cards—the talking hemisphere had to make sense of two sources of information. First, there was the information it knew directly. Second, there was what it observed and thereby knew only indirectly. At the same time the silent hemisphere knew that it had seen a snow scene because it used the left hand to select the shovel. Although the researchers kept the two hemispheres in the dark about this little trick, they knew what was going on because they had set up the experiment.

The snow scene/shovel connection is a relatively neutral one. It may trigger a feeling of being warm, snug, cozy, relaxed in the midst of a gentle winter day. The shovel may lead one to think of needing to shovel the walk. Taken together, the paired pictures are not likely to work one up into a state of excitement nor throw one into a state of despair. They are simply there as objects of information—connecting stimuli with responses.

From an emotional point of view the shovel was merely a tool for which Paul had to account. The explanation was cognitive, rational, logical. No significant amount of feeling was evident. Even so, Paul's response suggests that the brain—most particularly the talking left hemisphere—acts in a meaning-making way. It observes what is going on, and in the very act of observing it assumes there is some relationship—some reasonable connection—among the separate items of information at its disposal. A meaningful connection constructs an explanation—creates a story—even if that explanation is faulty. In short, the left hemisphere is the interpreter of our experienced world, but from a vantage point that observes from the outside.

The Hunger for Pattern

It seems that nothing can be innocuous enough to abort that explanatory process. Asked to figure how a series of random numbers go together, people agonize over the task. They arrive at a solution, explain it, and when informed that these are random numbers, they still insist there is meaning in the order. Unless especially trained to do so, our brain simply does not allow for the possibility of unconnected or random experience.

George Johnson, science writer for *The New York Times*, describes our brain's ability to detect elusive patterns as a "hunger for pattern . . . even when it isn't there."[3] In the mid-nineties, astronomers cautiously announced evidence of regular pulses of radio waves, which subsequent research showed were not always so regular. Similarly, giant accelerators send beams of particles—protons and antiprotons—crashing into each other in order to sift the resulting debris for patterns. The issue, according to Johnson, "is separating order from randomness, weeding out false positives—the patterns that leap by chance from the background noise." This hunger for pattern calls forth such ideas as "canals of Mars" or "the man in the moon," or "the shovel is to clean out the chicken shed." Our human brain—with its imaginative symbolizing predisposition—is constantly sifting the messy world of randomness for the "tiniest hints of order."

If meaning seeking is present in ordinary experience, what does an emotionally laden element add to the experiment? Is the resulting explanation as straightforward as *"Oh, that's easy* [which means easy for the talking brain]. [The left brain saw the claw; it knew that. Therefore,] *the chicken claw goes with the chicken head* [which the right hand picked.] *And* [because the left brain saw the left hand pick the shovel it knew the shovel had something to do with what was happening. Therefore] *you need a shovel to clean out the chicken shed."* The inference allows one to make up a perfectly sensible scenario if one knows about a claw, a head, and a shovel and does not know about a snow scene. Does emotion affect the explanation?

A similar experiment with a woman split-brain patient suggests an answer.[4] In the midst of a series of rather dull items being flashed on the screen, the researcher showed a picture of a nude woman to her right hemisphere. When asked what she had seen, she reported, "nothing." Her left hemisphere, of course, had no knowledge of what its counterpart was seeing, so it had nothing to say. At the same time she blushed, squirmed, smiled, looked confused and uncomfortable. Her right hemisphere was reacting emotionally to the nude picture.

Just as Paul's left hemisphere saw his left hand pick the shovel, so her left hemisphere only *knew about* those uncomfortable feelings because it observed them. It did not *know* them directly. Her talking brain realized that something was going on in her body. She had to account for that observation. As a way of explaining her discomfort and confusion to the researcher and to herself, she exclaimed, "Oh, what a funny machine!" Here, again, we come upon the human tendency to put things together by making sense of experience.

The talking hemisphere is the brain's interpreter, as neuroscientist Michael Gazzaniga labels it.[5] It explains why things are the way they are. It attributes causes to actions.[6] It gives everything a sense of coherence, making life reasonable, sensible, comprehensible. Insofar as it can express that in words, it lets others know what's what—with us and with the world around us. The left hemisphere creates the illusion of mental unity.

The silent hemisphere, in contrast, is the brain's experiencer. It is the source of inside information. By "inside" is meant perceptions and feelings and impressions that come before words. A person glimpses these apart from words, as in sensations. They are discerned in more than words, as in creating a frame of reference that eludes words.

Interpreted Experience

We need to say more about the left hemisphere's being the interpreter and the right hemisphere's being the experiencer. These ways of describing what they do are oversimplified and somewhat misleading. Even in split-brain patients, the two halves communicate with each other by means of other connections, especially in the older levels of the brain.

We can distinguish interpretive and experiential features of brain activity, yet all complex activity—and making sense of life is the most complex activity of all—requires and draws upon every part of the brain. Everything people do activates both hemispheres, although they are not activated equally.[7]

These experiments with split-brain patients are cited to make a single point, namely, that *we human beings are meaning-seeking animals. Faith—our most basic life-orientation—is the pivotal expression of meaning seeking. As such, faith is built into the activity of our biology, our nervous system, our neurocognitive processes, our humanizing brain. Reciprocally, faith reflects the grace of the context of meaning in which we find ourselves. We receive our meaning-seeking capacity before we develop that capacity. We are "at home in the universe"*[8] rather than being strangers in a strange reality.

Experience, observation, explanation—these processes are present simultaneously in everything we do and in everything we are. There is no such thing as an uninterpreted life. We humans make sense of what we experience in ourselves and of what we meet in the world. We put things together. That's just the way we are. This process integrates what catches our attention, the emotion elicited by the stimulus, and the way we represent that as a symbol and/or an idea.

"Putting things together" refers to more than simply connecting one idea with another, as a claw with a chicken head or a visible shovel with an imaginary shed. Putting things together includes all that we are. That means body and mind, feeling and thought, experience and interpretation, even embarrassment as a visceral experience with a slide projector that has no necessary relationship with a person watching it. Even these distinctions simplify the whole-making process that goes on in our brain all the time.

The right hemisphere is mostly silent, yet researchers find its contribution to meaning seeking crucial.[9] Its silence does not mean lack of consciousness or that the left hemisphere is the only source of conscious experience. Rather, the right hemisphere contributes a sense of pattern, a leap of imagination, nuances of feeling. The left hemisphere, in contrast, specializes in details and particulars. Together the two hemispheres are the source of our experience of ourselves. This experience is a reflective consciousness. It finds its fullest expressions in the phenomenology of experience—the symbolic process, language, and culture in all its forms.

Thus, "putting things together" is related to religion. For we humans fashion a meaningful world by an ongoing process of adaptation. The prospect of a meaning-seeking brain in a nonhuman setting, therefore, lies in our balancing that inner consolidation of self and soul with an external accommodation to reality as it opens before us. We regard the self as the socialized identity of a person and the soul as that person's unique integrating of the sensory and the symbolic processes of meaning making. Human beings are self-organizing organisms in a self-organizing universe. God created a world where electrons and photons, mathematics and meaning combine in wondrous ways.

The origin of such meaning seeking lies in our relatedness with others. That relatedness may be immediately with the mother or other caregivers or ultimately with the relational universe in which we find ourselves.

RESPONDING TO THE HUMAN: THE PRIMAL URGE TO RELATE

Consider now Hubel and Wiesel's work on identifying specific visual response patterns. A basic capacity underlies specific visual patterns. That capacity is the drive to relate to the human and the humanlike. The humanized brain resonates with that which gives it birth.

We do not live in a vacuum. In order to develop, we require the influence of an environment. We are born into a particular context. That context contains key signals designed to activate our developing brain.[10] Without that interaction between the environmental stimulus and our response, normal neural connections do not develop.[11] The most crucial of those key signals is the presence of the human caregiver. The face of another human being calls forth who we are. We are created to relate.

In identifying human relatedness, we turn to evidence about the visual system—what we see and how we see. Hubel and Wiesel have pioneered this area. We point to their research to argue that human beings respond to human presence. Their work is built on the technique of the recording of cortical neurons by microelectrodes, as epitomized in 1959 by J. Y. Lettvin, H. R. Maturana, W. S. McCullock, and W. H. Pitts's article "What the Frog's Eye Tells the Frog's Brain."[12]

What the Frog's Eye Tells the Frog's Brain

The frog's brain responds to only four visual stimuli. These are: a moving object; a moving object that enters the frog's field of vision and stops; a decrease in overall illumination; and a small, rounded object that moves erratically in the field of vision. The first three cells are known as "predator-detectors": movement triggers a general alarm; stopped movement means potential danger from a predator; and a general darkening signals a stalking predator. The fourth cell sends a "black-spot" message, the "bug-alert," which signals a dark spot against a shifting background of light and dark.[13]

Similar research has shown that the European toad's brain is wired as a "worm detector." As shown in figure 1.6, a moving spot only elicits a moderate

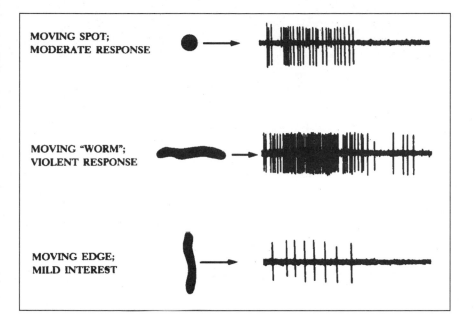

MOVING SPOT;
MODERATE RESPONSE

MOVING "WORM";
VIOLENT RESPONSE

MOVING EDGE;
MILD INTEREST

Figure 1.6——The toad's worm detector. *Reprinted with the permission of Simon & Schuster from* The Enchanted Loom: Mind in the Universe *by Robert Jastrow. Copyright © 1981 by Readers Library, Inc.*

response from the computing cell located behind the toad's eye. The electrical signals shown at the right of figure 1.6 were recorded when a small probe was placed in a "computing" cell behind the toad's eye. They indicate the messages sent from the toad's eye to its brain as the eye caught sight of various kinds of objects. The signals are in the form of pulses. A rapid burst of pulses means an intense response.

In the illustration in figure 1.6, the arrows represent the direction of motion of a moving object. A moving spot elicits some interest, and the toad's eye sends a moderately intense signal to the brain (*top*). A line moving in the direction of its length triggers the "worm" response, and an intense burst of pulses goes to the brain (*middle*). A line moving perpendicular to its length is not wormlike, and a weak signal goes to the brain (*bottom*).

Toads and frogs can only see moving objects with extremely simple shapes. They never see a tree or the pattern on a butterfly's wings. From a human perspective, frogs and toads live in "a visually impoverished world."[14]

Work on the visual cortex raises "the question of how the brain builds a picture of the external world on the basis of information originating in this same world." Hubel and Wiesel, according to Luciano Mecacci, professor of physiology at the University of Rome, demonstrated that "information enters *an organized network of neurons whose functions are established according to a logical system* and is not entangled in a confusion or random mass of nerve cells." In contrast to the earlier understanding, we now know that information is carried to various areas spread throughout the cerebral cortex. Information is probably processed in parallel as well as autonomous ways, with no one association area "dominant" over other sensory areas. The areas that "map" the external world consist of "integrated blocks of neurons with specific functional properties."[15]

Sensory windows indicate what the brain "sees" and "senses." These windows differ among species. "Different sensory windows and, therefore, different 'worlds' correspond to the brains of different animals," according to Mecacci. These different windows and worlds "are in part superimposed over each other because the various sensory windows are partly open to the same portions of external reality." This range of stimuli varies among various animal species and humans. What is "seen," therefore, is a transformation of "reality" according to the neuronal structure of the organism. In brief, the results of the last thirty years of neurosciences clearly indicate that the brain explores the world through a grid defined by its neuron structure: what it sees is a transformation of what has passed through that grid.[16]

Different species "see" and thereby "live in" different worlds. When Paul MacLean anchors knowledge in the subjective brain, he is identifying this transformation of external stimuli into an internal map. We might say that the *humanizing* brain is actually the evolutionary result of a *humanized* brain.

From that earlier work on the retina of the frog and the visual systems of arthropods, researchers had identified the idea of "feature detectors." Specific cells would exhibit patterns of excitation depending on specific stimuli. Frogs and other animals, for instance, are wired to respond to moving bugs. For frogs, small moving objects mean food and large moving objects mean predators. If an object does not move, the frog does not respond. Thus, small moving objects trigger flicks of the tongue, while large moving objects trigger leaps into water.[17] Brain cells are quite selective. They respond to certain specific stimuli and not to others.

Researchers knew about "feature detectors" in the retina of frogs and the visual systems of arthropods. Hubel and Wiesel, however, first demonstrated examples in the mammalian nervous system. Each cell of the primary visual cortex becomes active only in response to its own specific stimulus requirements. Subsequent research has modified this more radical view of specific feature detectors, but neuroscience literature has taken in the basic idea of pattern selectivity.

In the late 1960s researchers reported finding in monkey brains "a cell selective for the shape of a monkey hand."[18] Subsequent investigation disclosed cells that were "selective for photographs of faces." By the 1980s and 1990s many researchers were investigating and identifying a variety of face-selective cells.[19] Some cells respond best to a straight-on view of the face; others to various other facial orientations.

What has emerged is not the simple firing of a single cell in response to a specific stimulus. A single cell that fires in recognition of some stimulus has popularly been referred to as the "grandmother" cell. This is misleading. Rather, there is a pattern of neural activity across groups of cells. Some cells are capable of receiving higher-order details and matching these details with previous patterns of detail. The abstracting process, therefore, allows us to handle "an almost infinite variety of objects."[20] Initially, cells of a primary order attend to stimuli and select what is relevant to the person. Then cells of a higher order combine various features and integrate them into a pattern. The lack of evidence for selective visual responses to objects such as fruit, tree branches, and other objects is intriguing. *Only the face and hand provide evidence of selective cell ensemble activity.*[21]

The work of Hubel and Wiesel has achieved its greatest success in identifying the anatomical arrangement of cortical cells. There is an orderly arrangement of cortical neurons, an unsuspected microstructure. Initially, the eye that takes the lead in processing information organizes the neurons. So, too, in our orientation to the environment. The preferred orientation of successively recorded cells shifts regularly through a small angle as a recording electrode moves across the cortex.

Figure 1.7, for instance, shows a complex cell responding best to a black horizontally oriented rectangle and the same cell responding to a moving horizontal bar. A downward movement elicits more response than an upward one. A moving vertical bar produces no response. In sum, cells are biased to a particular spatial size. These cells are also clustered. The arrangement of cells according to their selective response remains an open issue. However, *research establishes the givens of selective preference.*

By 1963, Hubel and Wiesel had demonstrated a "critical" or sensitive "period" for the development of visual experience.[22] If deprived of visual experience up to about six weeks of age, a newborn kitten shows a marked reduction

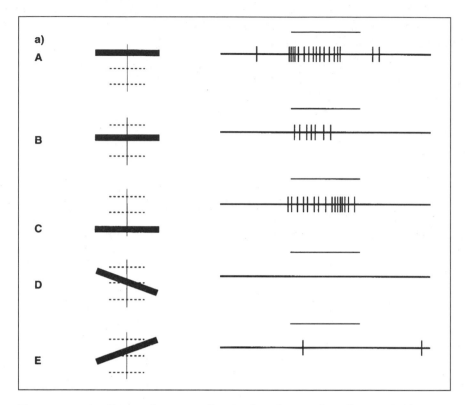

Figure 1.7——A cell responds to a specific stimulus. This complex cell responded best to a black horizontally oriented rectangle placed anywhere in the receptive field (A–C). Tilting the stimulus rendered it ineffective (D, E). *From David H. Hubel, "Evolution of Ideas on the Primary Visual Cortex, 1955–1978: A Biased Historical Account." In* Les Prix Nobel, *224–48. Reprinted by permission.*

in the number of cells that receive connections from both eyes. In short, potential neural connections can be—and *are*—altered by visual experience. The critical time period varies among species, but the result of deprivation is permanent blindness.

We now take a speculative leap from feature detectors in various species for specific stimuli and visual bias in humans. Survival in humans, as in other mammals, depends on our innate capacity to establish a working relationship with a caregiver.[23] Both the newborn's cry and the adult's responding with caregiving accomplish this connection. More specific for our point about our human predisposition to the human environment is research on infant preference.

Infant Preference

The young infant responds to the human voice, particularly the high-pitched female voice, as "the most preferred auditory stimulus."[24] It also responds to the face; a smile generates a biological and social bonding between mother and child. Of the forty-four separate facial muscles, four involve chewing and forty involve facial expression. "No other species has such capacity for making faces!"[25] The face serves to communicate feelings to others and also helps its owner to experience emotion. The combination of face and voice elicits the strongest following response in the infant. The child invariably attends to the face-voice of the mother.

In an early study of the social capacities of the young infant, C. Jirari examined the head-following behavior of infants aged twenty-four hours or less.[26] She used four stimuli: "a schematic face, a scrambled symmetrical face, an unsymmetrical face, and a blank card." From responses of thirty-six newborns a distinct order emerged: the face was stronger than the moderately scrambled symmetrical stimuli; and the moderately scrambled symmetrical stimuli were stronger than the blank card. She repeated this experiment with forty other infants whose age averaged ten minutes. Although there were no statistically significant differences between the moderately scrambled and the scrambled stimuli, the infants followed the face significantly more and the blank card significantly less.

Researchers Mark H. Johnson and John Morton have studied "the case of face recognition" extensively. Replicated findings show that "a face-like pattern elicits a greater extent of tracking behaviour than does a non-face-like pattern."[27] They wonder whether such behavior is "cognitive" rather than "merely . . . a sensory motor reflex." Based on their empirical studies they argue for "a *primal* mechanism" that preferentially orients the newborn when a face appears outside the central visual field.[28]

Other research demonstrated two different continua of head following. The first continuum related to the human face. For "given a face, it is the eyes which are salient for the infant."[29] The second continuum related to checkerboard complexity. Human infants, for instance, responded initially to the more complex figures on the right in figure 1.8 than to the simpler ones on the left.[30] Evidence supports the contention that *newborns prefer "faceness" and complexity.*[31]

In another experiment, monkeys learned a discrimination problem. The only reward was being able to open a window that permitted them to look out and watch the comings and goings at the entrance of the lab.[32] Sheer curiosity—striving for specific stimulation, information, knowledge, or understand-

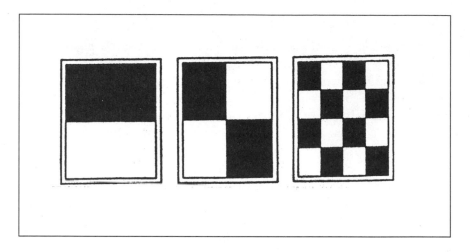

Figure 1.8———Simple and complex figures. *From Daniel E. Berlyne, "The Influence of Complexity and Novelty in Visual Figures in Orienting Responses,"* Journal of Experimental Psychology *55:289–96.*

ing—seems universal among primates, and especially us humans. We attend more to what is complex—within limits—than to what is simple.

Perceptions of complex visual patterns—faces, geometric designs, and the like—depend on the specialized processing of the right hemisphere. This processing is localized most probably in the back (posterior) part[33] as well as the visual-temporal regions. However, appreciation of facial expression, in contrast to facial recognition, requires activity of the frontal cortex as well.[34] The capacity to process complex visuo-spatial stimuli has given *Homo sapiens* a distinct evolutionary advantage. We are capable of recognizing and "sizing up" other humans in a very detailed way, in addition to being flexible enough to process other complexities.[35]

Without minimizing the influence of the environment on the human organism, the evidence here supports the assumption that the brain is not a passive receptor in an active environment. Instead, the brain actively shapes experience according to its inner purposes of human orientation.

FAITH AS THE BASIC HUMAN ATTRIBUTE

It seems that this cumulating evidence from neuroscience has two religious correlates. One, the pattern-making capacity reflects human experience of God as Logos, or Word. Think of this as a pattern of ordering. Two, the object-seeking capacity reflects human experience of God as Love, or a Thou-oriented relating in reality. Curiosity and complexity find their fullest expressions in the human context.

The Ambiguous Human Context

Ambiguity and ambivalence mark the human context. It is ambiguous because so much of what goes on among us arises from internal motivation and meaning. We *interpret* the significance of what is taking place, making inferences from incomplete information.[36] So, much that goes on inside us arises from contrasting and conflicting information. The result makes us uncertain and ambivalent about the world. We struggle to *prioritize* the values we value.

An environment saturated with ambiguity and ambivalence requires highly specialized skill in extracting information necessary for survival.[37] Our brain specializes in reducing ambiguity, ambivalence, and complication. Even though attracted to intricacy, we humans actively shape it into sensible schema. We are hardwired to construct patterns of the highest organization in order to determine and respond to what affects us.

The Human Animal

Whether we humans sniff with our noses like mammals or search with our eyes like birds, we are curious. We snoop around, we listen, we feel, we explore. Quite simply, we are oriented to the outside world.

At the same time, we become aware of what goes on inside us. Unlike other animals, we cultivate where we are and nurture who we are. We dream dreams; we imagine possibilities; we construct new ways of being where we are. In other words, we organize our "nesting and resting" for larger and longer-term purposes.

The myth of the Garden of Eden portrays this curious cultivating capacity. It describes how we name what we encounter (Genesis 2:19–20a), and how we are to cultivate the setting in which we find ourselves (Genesis 2:15). The phenomenon of breathing "the breath of life" (Genesis 2:7) involves the interaction of life with its supporting environment. That interaction is necessary for life. The interaction with the world also marks the advent of complex behavior. With living things there is a level of complexity below which it is impossible to go and still remain alive.[38]

Thus breathing symbolized, and continues to symbolize, the dawn of *some-*thing from *no-*thing, the crossing of the thresholds of complexity. That complexity ranges from the inorganic to the organic, from the organic to cells, from cells to consciousness. To physicist Paul Davies "something like a law of increasing complexity" exists on every scale.[39] These thresholds of complexity appear and evolve in a context of cosmic connectedness. Humanity is not the improbable. Rather, "we are the expected," as complexity theorist Stuart Kauffman puts it.[40]

Our God-Given Dignity

In celebrating God's glory and humanity's God-given dignity, Psalm 8 voices the pivotal, somewhat privileged position of humanity:

> O God, our Sovereign,
>   how majestic is your name in all the earth! . . . .
> When I look at your heavens, the work of your fingers
>   the moon and the stars that you have established;
>   what are human beings that you are mindful of them,
>   mortals that you care for them?
> Yet you have made them a little lower than God,
>   and crowned them with glory and honor.
> You have given them dominion over the works of your hands;
>   you have put all things under their feet . . .
> O God, our Sovereign,
>   how majestic is your name in all the earth!

We suggest that the pivotal position the psalmist describes for humanity is analogous to the pivotal position of neuroscience in mediating between the physical and the human. The psalmist refuses to license human beings trampling the rest of creation "under their feet." Rather, the psalmist declares our responsibility to mediate between God and "the works of [God's] hands."

Ordering and God as Logos

The Gospel of John opens with this magnificent poetic vision:

> In the beginning was the Word, and the Word was with God, and the Word was God. He was in the beginning with God. All things came into being through him, and without him not one thing came into being. What has come into being in him was life, and the life was the light of all people. (John 1:1–4)

In Greek, the word for *word* is *logos*. God is known as "The Word" (Genesis 1:1; John 1:1). The term has a rich history with varied emphases.[41]

In a religious context, *Word* or *Logos* refers to two forces at work in the universe: the one order creating and the other meaning making. People have known this by such various terms as Law or Purpose or Power or Intelligence or Principle. Christian theologians have linked the Old Testament meaning of *Word* as God's self-disclosure with the philosophical meaning of *Logos* as controlling principle. In doing so, they have referred particularly to Jesus as the Christ, the Logos and Wisdom of God.

Word also has linguistic connotations. In that context, it conveys a different meaning. Linguists who work with a "transformational grammar" model of language identify two levels of language activity.[42] There are the surface structures and the deep structure. Particular cultures shape surface structures. These structures, for instance, determine how the parts of a sentence go together. Deep structure gives a complete representation of the meaning of a sentence. Its complete meaning is its intended reference(s).[43] Surface structures are culture specific; deep structure is biological regardless of culture.[44] Further, it is species specific. That means these structures are general and unique only to humans.[45]

All surface words—actually, language itself—are transformations of the deep structure of reality as found in the inner working of the brain. In transforming deep structure to surface structures, we delete information, we distort information, and we generalize information. As a result, words are actually "maps" or "models" or "representations" of the territory of deep structure. They never are the territory itself.[46]

We suggest that both the religious and the linguistic perspectives reflect this basic humanizing drive to make sense of what we experience. Each points to our meaning-seeking capacity. That capacity comes with the emergence of the large neocortex, or "new brain." The subcortical region lies below the level of consciousness. Here the brain brings together an outer world of sensory stimuli with an inner world of imaginative symbolizing. Here is the locus of spontaneous intuitive integration.

RELATING AND GOD AS LOVE

As the psalmist has identified humanity's privileged position in the cosmos, so he voices that key signal of our being predisposed to relating:

> Hear, O God, when I cry aloud,
>> be gracious to me and answer me!

> "Come," my heart says, "seek [God's] face!"
> Your face, God, do I seek.
> Do not hide your face from me. (Psalm 27:7–9)

We would interpret that phrase "my heart says" as the genetic predisposition to respond in a species-specific way to the environment in which one finds oneself. That means most specifically to the presence of the human face and voice. Human presence is our perceptual and experiential anchor. Human presence provides orientation to the world around us. Human presence organizes and interprets what we encounter and construct.

God's face is a poetic way of generalizing from our experiences of human faces to that reality that gives birth to who we are. When the faces of reality (actually and metaphorically) turn from us, we wither and die. When the faces of reality (speaking metaphorically) are turned toward us, we blossom and live (cf. Psalms 104:27–30).

Philosopher Martin Buber has epitomized this phenomenon of the personal quality of the universe in his classic discussion of our relationship with God as *I and Thou*. The eternal Thou is a symbolic personification of ourselves and reality. That personifying capacity is, according to religious studies professor and clinical psychologist James Jones, "what makes us human."[47] The universe in which we live reflects our aspiring selves.

People experience and express their relatedness to the physical world as well as to the social world in terms that convey personal meaning. That is why all language ultimately rests on human experience. We transform subjective experience into more objective language. The seemingly objective meaning rises out of the metaphorical. Metaphorical meaning rests on an elusive realm of unvoiced meaning-making experiencing.

When we lose the ability to personify, to experience and express the human and humane dimensions of our reality, then "we have lost part of our humanity." That essentially human part is the origin of transforming experience.[48] The symbolizing capacity frees us from the constraints of a totally deterministic environment. This capacity to imagine, to construct, to play, which comes with the emergence of our new brain—the neocortex—is a central ingredient in religion.

Faith as the Ultimate Human Category

Having affirmed a faith stance, we find further support in the conviction of the comparative religion scholar Wilfred Cantwell Smith. He contends that "faith" is more basic to human nature than "belief." For him, belief has come to "resemble the descriptive propositionalism of a modern theorist's reporting on the current state of his opinions." Such reporting misses faith as "the primary religious category, and the final human category."[49] Faith denotes the basic directionality that guides the "pilgrim's progress." Faith is the path, sometimes clear, sometimes obscure, upon which we beat our way through the thickets of life decisions toward goals we regard as good.

Faith is evident in our humanizing brain even in a nonhuman environment. Anthropologist Richard Leakey provides an intriguing anecdote of the seeking brain. He reports finding a circle of 700-pound stones seven miles from the place they had been formed. He wondered, What would have led a mammal, the human mammal, to have dragged such weight such a distance for no utilitarian purpose? From whence came that symbolic gesture, he asked? Some need other than immediate necessity must have been at work, according to Leakey.

It seems that in such activity there is evidence of imaginative consciousness seeking a relatedness to reality, even by hominids earlier than *Homo sapiens*. Early burial customs inaugurated by Neanderthal hominids about 80,000 years ago suggest an awareness of death and loss of relatedness.[50] The circle of stones and the burial customs each reflect meaning-seeking activity. These symbolic acts suggest the separation/connection call. We reach out to make contact with the invisible power that holds us.

Neurophysiologist Rodney Holmes reflects on such evolutionary evidence and the emergence of the "*human* realities of intellect, consciousness, and religiosity."[51] These attributes depend on the full emergence of the cerebral cortex. Holmes is arguing against any theory of localizing complex human activity in any single specific part of the brain, a position that the authors share. But he is, and we are, also suggesting that "there are realities that are not material: they include social reality, psychological reality, and metaphysical reality."

Evolutionary biology is joining humanistic positions in establishing the fact that we humans are meaning-seeking creatures. We now "look at the text of human natural history," writes Holmes, "and interpret it in terms of Ultimate Reality." Our brain-mind enables us to construe the world differently than, say, bird brains or frog brains do.

The particular form a faith orientation takes varies tremendously. Variability and pluralism are facts of life. When people take any single position as ultimate, the result is disaster for the human community. The myth of the tower of Babel (Genesis 11:1–9) reflects the hubris—the arrogance—of a monolithic cultural-linguistic hegemony and the confusion of multiple tongues and cultures.

The basic fact of our humanized brain is clear. We cannot *not* make sense of what we experience. We translate sensory-symbolic interaction in every level of our brain-mind into intentional activity. Such activity creates a more meaningful environment, a milieu that "fits" the universe in which we live and move and have our being.

Only in the experienced reality of a Pentecost and Pentecost-like reality can people maintain the human paradox: on the one hand, retain their own cultural-linguistic identities, and on the other transcend these limited identities by understanding the larger reality in which we all participate. That larger reality finds expression in the phrase "each hearing [the wonders of God] in our own language" (Acts 2:6, 11).

CONCLUSION

We have drawn upon the work of Nobel laureates Roger Sperry in split-brain research and Torsten Wiesel and David Hubel in visual processing to represent focal issues related to the humanizing brain. Taken together, their findings provide glimpses of the impressive body of knowledge that neuroscience is accumulating about the human brain. They encourage our exploring humanity's destiny in God. The evolutionary *humanized* brain opens before us an emerging future generated, in part, by our *humanizing* brain.

"MIND" AS BRIDGE BETWEEN RELIGION AND NEUROSCIENCE

THE BRAIN AS PHYSICAL AND RELATIONAL

The *humanizing* brain reflects *and* expresses both what is outside us—what we receive through perception and sensation—and what is inside us—what we experience and interpret. The human brain, in short, is "the ultimate receiver and analyzer"[1] of what matters to us. This chapter explores implications of that anthropomorphic position.

As used here, the concept "mind" refers to the human and the humanlike features of the brain, whether in humans or in animals. The primary features of mind (especially in human brains) are intentionality and subjective consciousness, reinforced by empathy, rationality, imagination, memory, and adaptability. Whenever the concept "mind" is used in relation to brain, it "humanizes" the meaning of "brain"; and whenever the concept "brain" is used in relation to mind it "concretizes" the meaning of "mind." "Mind," therefore, can serve as a bridge between religious convictions and neuroscience investigations. While not dichotomizing brain and mind, physicist Paul Davies observes that

> mind—i.e., conscious awareness of the world—is not a meaningless and incidental quirk of nature, but an absolutely fundamental facet of reality. . . . We human beings are built into the scheme of things in a very basic way.
>
> Our mental processes have evolved as they have precisely because they reflect something of the nature of the physical world we inhabit.[2]

The humanizing brain potentially carries the most privileged information about the nature of reality to which we have access.

In understanding what matters most in the universe—that is, in our religious thought—we rely on the humanizing brain. Along with anthropologist Stewart Elliott Guthrie, we submit that "religion consists of seeing the world as humanlike."[3] Because the world is ambiguous and undeveloped, says Guthrie, we are constantly needing to interpret it. Because of our mind-brain, our interpretations of what matters most are necessarily humanlike: that is, our humanized brain creates a humanizing and humanlike universe.

A CONNECTION BETWEEN BRAIN AND UNIVERSE

Origen, the great Christian third-century theologian of Alexandria, and Bernard of Clairvaux in the twelfth century spoke of the mystical marriage of the Logos and the soul.[4] Logos points to the ordering and orderly structure of the universe. Soul identifies the core of human dignity. In some mysterious way, such thinkers believed that the universe reveals itself in humanity, the macrocosm-in-the microcosm. So we, too, believe.

In a slightly different way, William James (1842–1910) raised the similar issue of the connection of brain and universe:

> Is the Kosmos an expression of intelligence, rational in its inward nature, or a brute external fact pure and simple? If we find ourselves, in contemplating it, unable to banish the impression that it is a realm of final purposes, that it exists for the sake of something, we place intelligence at the heart of it and have a religion. If, on the contrary, in surveying its irremediable flux, we can think of the present only as so much mere mechanical sprouting from the past, occurring with no reference to the future, we are atheists and materialists.[5]

The biblical narrative of the tower of Babel (Genesis 9:1–11) points to the fragmentation that follows in the wake of a single language, a single viewpoint, a single hegemony. A single perspective generates competing perspectives. But hierarchical power marginalizes others and so distorts the depth of reality, the deep structure of what matters most. People then live in a universe that is *not* "an expression of intelligence, rational in its inward nature."

In contrast, the biblical narrative of Pentecost (Acts 2:1–13) points to the differentiating that comes with multiple languages, multiple points of view, multiple possibilities. In that situation every culture carries something of all cultures. No culture expresses the whole of reality. Instead, we live in a universe that *is* "an expression of intelligence, rational in its inward nature." (That is not to say that the universe is paradise. Moral decisions by moral agents inject good and evil into human history.)

Pentecost reminds us that we can hear each other speaking of the really real "in our own languages." From a nontheological, biological perspective, linguist Steven Pinker speaks movingly of the same universal reality of the really real. He summarizes his convictions about the "language instinct."

Most of the differences among races, he argues,

> are adaptations to climate: melanin protects skin against the tropical sun, eyelid folds insulate eyes from dry cold and snow. But the skin, the part of the body seen by the weather, is also the part of the body seen by other people. Race is, quite literally, skin-deep, but to the extent that perceivers generalize from external to internal differences, nature has duped them into thinking that race is important [and that certain cultures are more advanced than other cultures]. The X-ray vision of the molecular geneticist reveals the unity of the species.[6]

Then Pinker highlights the "X-ray vision of the cognitive scientist":

> "Not speaking the same language" is a virtual synonym for incommensurability [not having any common quality], but to a psycholinguist, it is a superficial difference. *Knowing about the ubiquity of complex language across individuals and cultures and the single mental design underlying them all, no speech seems foreign to me, even when I cannot understand a word.* The banter among New Guinean highlanders in the film of their first contact with the rest of the world, the motions of a sign language interpreter, the prattle of little girls in a Tokyo playground—*I imagine seeing through the rhythms to the structures underneath, and sense that we all have the same mind.*[7]

Whether people use religious language or nonreligious language, what they say expresses humanity's capacity to make sense of the sensory and the symbolic. Every culture exhibits that capacity. Likewise, our actions are inescapably relational, regardless of how they are motivated or understood. Here, in truth, is the mystical marriage of the Logos and the soul! We all engage in humanizing reality!

BETWEEN NATURE AND MEANING

Because we are human we find ourselves in a unique position in nature. Like frogs and cats and monkeys and plants and rocks, we are *part of* a natural setting. It is physical, an extension of both time and space. But unlike frogs and cats and monkeys and plants and rocks, we are *apart from* this natural setting. Because of our cognitive ability, we create and imagine new relationships, new possibilities—for ourselves and our world.

By virtue of living in a human universe, humans experience both the realism of being *part of* the natural order and the meaningfulness of being *apart from this natural order.* The nervous system differentiates experience and integrates it at the same time. It combines multiple inputs with imagined scenarios. This dialectic makes for unsuspected possibilities—and also accounts for predicted actualities. The combination both *reflects* an orderly environment and *creates* a recognizable world. We make sense of reality in terms of our own sensibility.

The human brain embodies two evolutionary pushes: the one toward complexification and the other toward adaptation. In turn, the human brain exerts the emerging pull of human aspirations. Together, the evolutionary push *and* the emergent pull make us unique among creatures.

In other words, our brain is the *physical* anchor that immerses us in the natural environment. At the same time its *human* capacities orbit us into an emerging world of culture. Culture has the potential to develop beyond anything we can imagine. The physical brain orients us to the physical environment in specific ways; so, too, the cognitive brain orients us to the human world in specific ways.

Neuroscience is in a pivotal, somewhat privileged position between the most specific chemical and physical processes and the most sweeping cosmic and psychically significant processes. To use the language of traditional disciplinary concerns, neuroscience resides between physics and metaphysics. Neuroscience is disclosing how the brain works, in health and disease. New therapeutic interventions can prevent disorders or enhance creativity. Finally, neuroscience is helping us know who we are as human beings and whether the humanizing brain has survival value. Thus neuroscience deals with both the most particular and the most inclusive.

Many scientists remain skeptical of a yoking of science and religion; others believe deeply in a God-oriented universe. For instance, Ilya Prigogine, awarded a Nobel Prize in 1977 for his work on the thermodynamics of systems far from equilibrium, identifies a "growing coherence" between what we know of humanity and what we know of nature. He describes "a new synthesis, a new naturalism," in which "science . . . appears to lend credibility to mystical affirmation." He speaks of "a kind of 'convergence' between the interests of theologians, who held that the world had to acknowledge God's omnipotence by its total submission to Him, and of physicists seeking a world of mathematizable processes."[8]

The new naturalism shifts our perspective from nature as static to nature as dynamic. We now view reality as "being" *and* "becoming." Rather than being opposed to each other, permanence and change "express two related aspects of reality."⁹ Matter is not inert but "active," "capable of organizing itself and producing living beings."¹⁰

Regardless of skepticism or openness, the Big Questions continue to hold center stage. Where we humans have come from and where we are going are now explored through questions about "the instability of elementary particles," "the evolving universe," or "the incorporation of irreversibility into physics," to name a few.¹¹ As quantum cosmology probes our origin, so neuroscience explores our destiny.

We find that emerging theories of complexity and self-organization link cosmic origin and human destiny.¹² Our origin, as Stuart Kauffman, a leading thinker in complexity theory, puts it, lies in "natural expressions of matter and energy coupled together in nonequilibrium systems which increase beyond various thresholds of complexity." The collective result is a living system. Although its parts "are just chemical," according to Kauffman, the beautiful order is "spontaneous, a natural expression of the stunning self-organization that abounds in very complex regulatory networks. . . . Order, vast and generative, arises naturally." The abundance of life was "bound to arise, not as an incalculably improbable accident, but *as an expected fulfillment of the natural order.*" That natural fulfillment encourages us to believe that *"we truly are at home in the universe."*¹³

Because *Homo sapiens* is *Homo religiosus,* we truly *are* "at home in the universe." In sketching sources of religion we intend to keep before us this basic humanizing brain.

SOURCES OF RELIGION

A quick survey of nonreligious theories about the sources of religion identifies three main clusters of ideas. One suggests wish fulfillment in the face of fear. Another identifies social solidarity in the presence of fragmentation. A third advances religion as providing a plausible interpretation of ambiguous reality.¹⁴

Ludwig Feuerbach (1804–1872) has been singularly significant in exploring and attacking religion in the modern era. In his view, religion came about because of deficiencies or lacks in individual human lives. To compensate for these lacks, people developed religious ideas that expressed emotional attitudes and ideas about what humanity ought to be. Feuerbach regarded statements about God as projected statements about human beings. People attributed these ideas to an imagined deity. In other words, "God as a mind 'beyond' human reason is an objectification of human intelligence stripped of all accidental imperfections."[15] Thus, "religion is the dream of the human mind."

> Man's being conscious of God is man's being conscious of himself, knowledge of God is man's knowledge of himself. By their God, you know men, and by knowing men you know their God; the two are identical. God is the manifested inward nature, the expressed self of man; religion is the solemn unveiling of man's hidden treasures, the reflection of his most intimate thoughts, the open confession of what he secretly loves.[16]

According to Feuerbach, what humanity previously regarded as God "is now recognized as something human." "God is merely the projected essence of Man."[17]

Object relations theory provides a conceptual instrument with which to explore, elaborate, and explain this anthropomorphic view of God and the humanizing brain.[18] From a psychodynamic orientation, British psychiatrist D. W. Winnicott contends that "man continues to create and recreate God as a place to put that which is good in himself, and which he might spoil if he left it in himself along with the hate and destructiveness which is also to be found therein."[19] The God-image provides an abstract generalization capable of bearing all that one can imagine that is worthwhile and cherishable. Such generalization avoids the pitfall of an idolatry that would locate all that is good in any particular human being, even Jesus as Savior,[20] or in any particular religion or culture.

The phenomena explored by object relations theorists undeniably play a role in the development of religious consciousness.[21] They are probably a necessary segment of the road toward spiritual maturity. They do not, however, account for all the twists and turns in this road. For one thing, in their emphasis on individual development, such theories take too little account of the larger world in which humans must find their place.

Anthropologist Clifford Geertz takes a more integrated view of religion. He sees religion as a synthesizing of a people's ethos and worldview, a fitting together of how they believe things are and how they believe things should be. With that understanding, he defines religion as:

> (1) a system of symbols which acts to (2) establish powerful, pervasive, and long-lasting moods and motivation in men by (3) formulating conceptions of a general order of existence and (4) clothing these conceptions with such an aura of factuality that (5) the moods and motivations seem uniquely realistic.[22]

In essence, he construes religion as purposeful. It energizes people to believe the universe to be coherent and meaningful.[23] Instead of detachment, there is commitment; instead of analysis, there is encounter.[24] Mystical encounters and practical actions intermingle.[25]

It does appear that human beings are basically *Homo religiosus*. We are symbolizing, conceptualizing, meaning-seeking animals.[26]

The drive to make sense of experience, to give it form and order, is evidently as real and "as pressing as the more familiar biological needs," Geertz adds.[27] And this being so, it seems unnecessary to continue to interpret symbolic activities—religion, art, ideology—as "nothing but" thinly disguised expressions of something other than what they seem to be: attempts to provide orientation for an organism that cannot live in a world it is unable to understand.[28]

Taking this insight a step further, such symbolizing—humanizing—capacity may in fact be as basic to the biological needs of *Homo sapiens* as "the more familiar" ones. Biogenetic structuralists refer to this genetic predisposition as "the cognitive imperative" or "the primal urge to know."[29]

Human and humanlike reality, or anthropomorphism, therefore, results from our inherent drive to find that pattern that makes the most sense of the most data. Anthropologist Stewart Guthrie states the case succinctly:

> The most important pattern in most contexts is that with the highest organization. The highest organization we know is that of human thought and action. Therefore we typically scan the world with humanlike models. Scanning the world with humanlike models, we frequently suppose we find what we are looking for where in fact it does not exist. This is most apparent when we are most aware of ambiguities (a sound in the night, a shadow on our path, an unexpected death); but such cases are not aberrant. All perception is interpretive and all interpretation follows a pattern: *we look first for what matters most.*[30]

As we have described in the previous chapter, what matters most to us humans is the human face and our relatedness with one another. An anthropocentric perspective is unavoidable. But this acknowledgment does not automatically negate the validity of what is perceived. A case can be made that reality *is* of a piece with the human brain and its perceptions. Reasons for this assertion are developed in the sections that follow.

THE UNAVOIDABLE SUBJECTIVE BRAIN

Those working in the natural sciences take pains to distinguish between what is objective and what is subjective, what is true and what might be only meaningful. Their goal, since Francis Bacon (1561–1626) in the late sixteenth and early seventeenth centuries, has been to erase every subjective feature in the pursuit of objective reality.[31] In this schema, impersonal, objective, explanatory, causal knowledge matters more than anything that is personal, subjective, experiential, meaningful.

But as Paul MacLean insists, they "cannot avoid the realization that in the final analysis, everything reduces to subjectivity and that there is no rigorous way of defining a boundary between the subjective and what is regarded as objective."[32] By the very nature of things, everything (the so-called objective world and our subjective world) must be processed by the "soft brain." Internal relations between ourselves as subjects capable of being objects of reflection and all else as objects reflect the brain-mind as intricately involved in both receiving and creating what matters to us as part of a dynamic universe. We filter everything through the lens of what matters to us.

Unavoidably, the brain humanizes what it perceives. Perception is always selective. It is influenced by what "fits" an individual's patterns of thought. All perceptions necessarily have a human bias. "Because human manifestations vary widely, and because a human presence is so important, we superimpose widely different human forms on widely different phenomena."[33]

A Holistic Orderliness

The humanizing brain reflects and expresses what we receive from the outside and what we experience from the inside. The human brain, as we are insisting, receives and interprets what matters to us as we humans together seek to find our place in this universe.[34] Its mapping of external reality goes beyond apprehension of sensory data.

The brain also calculates the relationships and interactions of objects with their surroundings. These functions, which involve computation and prediction, are carried out at both nonconscious and conscious levels. In conjunction with the frontal cortex, the nonconscious cerebellum contributes to computation and prediction.[35] The cerebellum is located at the back base of the brain, adjacent to the brain stem (see figure 1.1). Traditionally, researchers regarded the function of the cerebellum as simply the coordination of motor functions, but more recent research, on which MacLean builds, shows that its neurocircuits include processes used in planning, prediction, and implicit memory.

More specifically, the cerebellum functions "according to some inherent algorithms ... [and] 'a kind of built-in calculus.'" Algorithms "link problems, input data, and solutions."[36] It would seem that the highly developed technology that can put people on the moon, launch probes into space, or estimate how old a geological deposit might be result from the neocortex's capacity to make explicit the implicit calculus of the cerebellum.

The cerebellum, along with the primal or instinctual brain, takes account of locality, particularity, context. Think of the behavior of a physical system. It is "determined entirely by the forces and influences that arise in its immediate vicinity."[37] Similarly, through collaboration of the cerebellum with other parts of the brain, linear systems—the sequencing of step-by-step contingencies—are inseparably linked with nonlinear and local effects—all-at-once intelligibilities. Mathematical physicist Paul Davies refers to the result as "holistic orderliness," or something like "a principle of maximum diversity."[38]

At the very least—and this is not so "least"—an organizing brain-mind reflects a reality capable of being organized. In the precise language of Jewish psychotherapist and theologian Moshe Halevi Spero, we may discern "a structure-creating God, a structure-bound world, and a structure-deducing human being."[39] The biblical writers witness to that fundamental worldview by telling a story of God creating the world and all that is therein. Their intent was theological rather than scientific. They portrayed a "world [that] is orderly, purposeful, good, and dependent on God."[40]

This depiction of God and humanity in terms of neuroanatomy underscores our point about the humanizing brain. We do not need to fall into an intellectualistic Neoplatonism about humanity's presence in the created world. We do not need to fall into the anthropocentric trap of "attributing to things and events only those characteristics relevant to human needs and interests."[41] *The human brain is orderly and purposeful precisely as the universe is orderly and purposeful.*

The "maestro" of the microscopic study of the brain, Santiago Ramon y Cajal (1852–1934) linked the universe and the human brain. He claimed, "As long as the brain is a mystery, the universe, [which is] the reflection of the structure of the brain, will also be a mystery."[42]

Bracketing the central issue of "mystery"—that of the brain and that of the universe—MacLean paraphrases Ramon y Cajal's statement by saying "the universe" reflects "the structure of the human brain." In any event, the whole of experience and its interpretation certainly "is dependent on the structure and function of one's own brain."[43] What we humans know of the universe depends on what we generate in our brains—by inventing technological instruments, by assigning emotional meanings, by constructing interpretive impressions, and by drawing conclusions. "We can never hope to discover more about it [the environment] than is provided by the brain's built-in neural networks."[44]

ORGANIZED COMPLEXITY IN NONPERSONAL REALITY

It may seem that the physical realm per se offers the most promise of objectivity—that human penetration and calculations here approach an approximate absoluteness. Emotional meaning is minimal. The hope and faith of scientific research has traditionally been that the physical realm possesses a repeatable order that follows rules comprehensible to the human brain/mind. And in fact, "even though chaos is rather common," notes physicist Davies, "it is clear that on the whole the universe is far from being random. . . . It possesses a subtle kind of complexity that places it part way between simplicity on the one hand and randomness on the other."[45]

The absence of emotion or the minimal presence of emotion suggests that the cognitive processing of such "organized complexity" takes place not only below the neocortex but also below and apart from the limbic system, the locus of emotional meaning. However, the notion that absolute physical knowledge is available, while often attributed to "science," actually went out with the nineteenth century—certainly with the demise of modernity.

Quantum Theory. Today, scientific thinking cannot ignore quantum theory, including the uncertainty principle. This principle holds that the more fuzzy the momentum of an electron, the clearer is its position. Conversely, the fuzzier the position, the clearer its momentum. The upshot of such observational difficulties, according to philosopher Holmes Rolston, III, is an issue of instrumentation. That is, the quest to build "more precise measuring instruments to gain access to formerly inaccessible data . . . has become also a *mental* one." Macroscopic models fail to describe the microscopic world nonsymbolically. "What started as an empirical cloudiness is now a theoretical epistemic indeterminacy," claims Rolston.[46]

Thus, since early in the twentieth century, quantum theory has denied *on principle* that any epistemological certainty is possible at the subatomic level. "Oh well," said advocates of cause-and-effect relations, "quantum theory doesn't apply at levels higher than the subatomic." Now, chaos theory and, in particular, complexity theory are muddying these waters.

Chaos Theory. This refers to phenomena in which cause and effect do have a linear relationship but the causes are so subtle, so many, and so interrelated that it is impossible to know what they are. A familiar example is the "Chinese butterfly effect." In this example, a butterfly in Beijing flaps its wings, creating a bit of turbulence in the air. This turbulence, in turn, has other consequences, which give rise to other effects—including rain in Chicago two weeks later. If the butterfly in Beijing had not flown when it did—but all other events had been the same—the entire chain of events would not have taken place as it did. Chicago would have had sunshine instead of rain.

Complexity Theory. Of course, all other events never are the same. This fact is what complexity theory addresses. In *complex* phenomena, there are a number of decision makers or natural causes acting in parallel. They interact with one another, and then each adapts to the actions of the others. These adaptations, in turn, create more new situations. Again, everything must readapt to the changes. Furthermore, there are adaptations at various levels—for example, at the levels of molecules, cells, and organisms—and the levels also interact with one another. Continual coadaptation leads to more intricate interrelationships and the emergence of novel situations.

A complex system never reaches equilibrium; it is always in a state of flux. One of the keys here is that the parts of the system *actively adapt*; they are not simply the passive consequences of cause and effect. This power for change within the system is called *autocatalyzing*. Since new organizational structures originate within the system, the system is called *self-organizing*. The novelty that continually results is called *emergence*.

Complexity thus has several hallmarks: highly dispersed agents, acting in parallel; a rich web of interactions; and coadaptation leading to coevolution, self-organization, and the perpetual emergence of novel phenomena.[47]

We see these *complex adaptive systems*, as they are termed, at many levels of experience. The economy may be one example. Many different individuals decide to buy or sell, work at one thing or another, import or export. These decisions affect business conditions, which in turn influence high-level corporate decisions as well as individuals. The adaptations they make may lead to the emergence of new products, new corporations, or new ways of doing business—which in turn have other outcomes. All the decisions continue to be made in parallel; various levels continue to affect other levels. Novelty continues to emerge, and the system is never at rest.

We see complexity in ecosystems, computer phenomena—and activities of the human brain. In the brain, for example, various events activate *cell assemblies*. Each cell assembly has as many as 10,000 neurons distributed over a large part of the brain. They communicate with each other across their synapses; each of the neurons has as many as 10,000 synapses (see figure 1.2).[48] The signals of one neuron may thus affect many other neurons, which adapt in turn, leading to unpredictable, novel phenomena. These interactions never reach complete equilibrium; something new is always taking place. These complex systems operate at all levels of the brain. We find them in the conscious processes of the neocortex, in the emotions of the limbic system, in dreaming,[49] and in the unconscious processes that precede consciousness or coordinate muscular activity, even breathing.

Yet, there is in complex adaptive systems an element of stability. Certain rules of interaction remain the same over time. Certain elements, certain players, change little or not at all. Thus, a final hallmark of complex adaptive systems—including the brain—is that *they exist at the interface between stability and instability*. This mix of the stable and the unstable, of causality and chance, is a requirement for the emergence of the novel. Because these conditions exist in the brain-mind, it is possible for the new and undetermined to emerge.

In the ubiquity of complex, dynamic systems, one may see a model of human interaction with all levels of our world. In size, humans stand at the midpoint. We are about as many orders of magnitude larger than subatomic particles as we are smaller than the cosmos. The particle, the cell, the brain, the political-economic system, the ecosystem, the solar system, the cosmos—all roil in continual interaction with levels above and below, catalyzing self-organization at ever more complex levels.

British astronomer James Jeans, writing in 1931, had an intuitive grasp of the realities of complex adaptive systems when he argued:

> We discover that the universe shows evidence of a designing or controlling power that has something in common with our own individual minds—not, so far as we have discovered, emotion, morality, or aesthetic appreciation, but the tendency to think in the way which, for want of a better word, we describe as mathematical.[50]

"Whether one wishes to call that deeper level 'God' is a matter of taste and definition," observed physicist Paul Davies. However, he concludes, as we have already noted, that mind is

> an absolutely fundamental facet of reality. That is not to say that *we* are the purpose for which the universe exists. Far from it. . . . [Rather] we human beings are built into the scheme of things in a very basic way.[51]

We will unbundle some of these claims later. For now let us consider the fact that the human mind, for its size, is the most complex entity in the known universe. If the universe is structured as a self-organizing, complexifying system, then we may see the human brain as one of its premier expressions. Processes of interactive complexity expressed by the brain's billions of synapses play out an ever changing symphony of organized and reorganized thoughts and actions. The ongoing processes of the universe are clearly manifest in the human brain, the humanizing brain.

As astronomy has found millions of galaxies in a cosmos of unimaginable scope, the perceived place of humans has shrunk to minute proportions. We seem as specks of protoplasm—meaningless, futile bits of life lost in space. But in light of such new insights, the human brain may not be so insignificant. In fact it may be a harbinger of a novelty to come, on a time scale measured in eons. The brain may be our best exemplar of the built-in nature of the cosmos.

No particular brain-mind carries the whole of reality. No individual brain—of premier, of president, of pope, or of Jesus, Muhammad, or Buddha—can be taken as the final criterion of meaning seeking. Instead, the brain-mind of humanity as a species contains evidence of—and contributes to—the way things really are. The human brain is the locus of our reality: the initiating alpha and the culminating omega of meaning seeking.

PERSONAL REALITY AND RELATIONAL LOGIC

The brain-mind, in truth, bears the weight—the glory—of the universe. Yet *Homo religiosus*—the creature that carries knowledge of the whole—ever searches to find ways to make that knowledge explicit. The old mammalian brain and the neocortex, discussed in later chapters, combine to transform nonpersonal reality into personal reality, a human and humanlike universe. The brain develops both emotional meaning and cognitive coherence. The whole brain and the whole of reality are intimately intertwined. Grand as the universe may be, the world in which we live and the ways in which we engage that world, according to biogeneticist Lindon Eaves and theologian Philip Hefner, "demand personal language."[52]

The Ultimately Personal

We are joining the human and the universal—the part and the whole. We find precedent for that linking in the Alexandrian theologian Origen in the third century and in the mystic Bernard of Clairvaux in the twelfth century, as we have already indicated. Each expressed the idea of the creature carrying knowledge of the whole: the mystical marriage of the Logos and the soul.[53]

This metaphorical yoking evokes the wise ordering of the universe in terms of the Christological vision. The letter to the Ephesians gives us a glorious expression of that vision: "With all wisdom and insight [the God and Father of our Lord Jesus Christ] has made known to us the mystery of his will . . . to gather up all things in him, things in heaven and things on earth" (Ephesians 1:8b–10), or, we might add, the many agents interacting in the complex systems of the universe.

Philosopher of science Ian Barbour lifts up a comparable interactive view of the universe. He describes reality in terms of process: "The world is a community of interdependent beings rather than a collection of cogs in a machine."[54]

Soul, for example, connotes the core of what humanity can uniquely call its own,[55] the identity and spirituality of each individual human being. In each person, accumulated complexification contributes to an identity that may be understood as that person's unique "soul." The soul, far from being a nonmaterial entity, bears and expresses the unique stamp of each person's mind/brain, as we explore more fully in chapter 5. Thus, in some mysterious way, the universe reveals itself in humanity, and humanity seeks to understand its origin and destiny in the universe.

The Judeo-Christian scriptures wrestle with this interface between the human and the ultimate. The Old Testament views God as humanlike. God scoops up clay as a potter. God breathes breath into the clay as in cardiopulmonary resuscitation. God walks in the garden. God talks with a terrified couple. God is zealous, even jealous, over infidelity. The instances of God being humanlike are endless. The New Testament also proclaims God as human. The Word becomes flesh, incarnate. God opens the eyes of the blind, feeds the hungry, liberates the oppressed, dies on a cross, turns the world upside down.

The *Imago Dei*

There have been many interpretations of the concept *imago Dei*. To us, the notion that humans reflect the *image and likeness* of God refers neither to physical appearance nor to gender. Instead, it refers to the complex adaptive behavior by which humankind, through relationships and activities, may manifest God's liberating transformation on earth.[56] Masculine domination, with its exclusivity, privilege, and superiority,[57] has no ontological justification in the notion of humanity being created in the image of God. Thus, in biological terms there is no permanent justification for masculine domination in understanding the brain-mind of males and females.

What, then, can we say about God and humanity?

A Humanlike God

The brain "humanizes" reality. How we humans orient ourselves to what is, how we organize what we perceive, how we interpret what matters, how we cocreate new, emergent phenomena—each of these issues rests on our needs for order, relationality, meaning, understanding. Strategies for understanding order change over time. We reinvent them to accommodate new developments in scientific knowledge,[58] new economic realities, new forms of political organization. Understand we must. And because we are inevitably symbolizing, conceptualizing, meaning-seeking beings, "we need to give more attention to how people define situations and how they go about coming to terms with them," according to anthropologist Clifford Geertz.[59]

We humans use certain basic strategies for defining situations: anticipation, purpose, organization, integration. We rely on processes that are both piece-by-piece and all-at-once, both a bottom-up way of organizing experience and a top-down variety of causal relationships. At the culmination of his career, Nobel Prize–winning neuroscientist Roger Sperry advocated a view of brain activity that included both tendencies. He observed that "conscious experience appears in the causal chain of brain activity at upper (i.e., cognitive) levels of brain processing in the form of irreducible emergent properties"—in other words, top-down.[60]

Brain-cell excitation, in this view, no longer waits solely on biophysical forces but also obeys a higher command involving subjective feelings, wants, choices, intentions, moral values, and all other things of the mind.[61] These include "beliefs that concern life's purpose and meaning, beliefs about God and the human psyche, and its role in the cosmic scheme."[62] "This reciprocal, two-way control in opposing directions is not in conflict because different forms of causation are operating in the upward and downward directions."[63]

Ian Barbour likewise rejects a solely bottom-up view of causal relationship when dealing with "organisms and human beings." He insists, "we need to speak of top-down causality . . . [because] events at higher levels of organization in integrated systems impose constraints and boundary conditions on events at lower levels without violating the physical and chemical laws applicable at those levels."[64] The universe in which we live, of which we are a part and whose future we influence, is a changing, adapting, ever complexifying whole, not foreign to humanity as a species.

RELATIONAL REALITY

The modern worldview, from which many of us are just emerging, was mechanistic. It placed humanity in a bottom-up reality in which people, like molecules and cells, were controlled by deterministic forces of cause and effect. In such a setting, to be humanlike was to be alien.

Despite our generation's best efforts at impersonal rationality, however, we find ourselves to be both stable and unstable, predictable and novel, adaptive and creative. In the postmodern world, we may again feel at home. We have a place in this world, for we are like it. As "created cocreators," to use the powerful phrase of theologian Philip Hefner, we may indeed reflect the "image of God." To turn the issue around, God may be apprehended through the image of humanity.

This chapter has been advocating a view of reality mediated by the lens of the human. While such a view suggests anthropomorphism, it actually goes beyond that. It suggests that reality itself is *actually* humanlike. Put another way, the human brain-mind and the larger reality share a fundamental likeness. People can only perceive things in a humanlike way—*and* any reality that we perceive must of necessity be humanlike. Though one may argue that humans construct not only reality but God, one may go a step further and contend that such constructs are not inaccurate. The inner representations of God and reality and their outer referents are intricately related. They reflect each other. We elaborate these affinities in the following chapters.

The painter-sculptor-architect-poet Michelangelo (1475–1564) has shaped Western culture's image and interpretation of God and the Godlike as much as any other single person.[65] His work reflects traditional Hebrew-Christian theology and Neoplatonic philosophy.[66] To Michelangelo, humanity held a "supreme place in the universal scheme of things," and the artist's figures mediate between the human and divine spheres.

In the Sistine chapel ceiling fresco, Michelangelo thematized the creation of the world, the fall of humanity, and humanity's ultimate reconciliation with God. The depiction of God shifts from a patriarchal human figure in the *Creation of Eve* to a cosmic spirit discerned as "a swirling abstraction in the realm of pure being." This may have referred to the Neoplatonic goal of the union of the soul with God, with the soul portrayed as ascending into the pure light of knowledge and the freedom of infinity. As Pico della Mirandola put it, in this view humanity "withdraws into the center of his own oneness, his spirit made one with God."[67]

In Michelangelo's depiction of the Creation we see God and humanity juxtaposed in a way "unrivaled by any other artist" (see figure 2.1).[68] An earthbound Adam and an energized God, rushing through the heavens, are about to activate the divine spark—the soul, the breath of life—as the index fingers of God's right hand and Adam's left hand are almost touching. The God of creation is an intentional God.

Figure 2.1——The Creation of Adam *by Michelangelo. From Alinari/Art Resource, NY. Reprinted by permission.*

The artist depicts God as a dynamic older man, with flowing hair and a crisp beard, surrounded by celestial beings. "Adam strains not only toward his Creator but toward Eve, whom he sees, yet unborn in the shelter of the Lord's left arm."[69] Some interpreters have suggested that the figure is not Eve, but Wisdom,[70] an idea that can be linked with Logos/Sophia as a male/female personification of divine Wisdom.[71]

For almost five hundred years this imaginative view of God has influenced the way we Westerners have conceived of God. Then in October 1990 in *The Journal of the American Medical Association* physician Frank Lynn Meshberger published an interpretation of Michelangelo's Adam based on neuroanatomy. In it he brought together the energizing God and the humanizing brain. He contended that in depicting the creation of Adam the artist had "encoded a special message" based on his belief that "the 'divine part' we 'receive' from God is the 'intellect.'"

In addition to the main characters of God and Adam, Meshberger believed that there was a third "main character." This previously unrecognized "character" is the image of the human brain. Figures 2.2 and 2.4 show the human brain; figures 2.3 and 2.5 show Michelangelo's outlines of God.

A close examination of the Sistine chapel ceiling reveals that, unlike almost all the other figures depicted there, this image of God is set against a contrasting area of abstract shape. Meshberger shows that the overall impression of this background, as well as detailed portions of it, is "compatible with a brain."

Meshberger concludes that this is no accident. Because of Michelangelo's intimate knowledge of anatomy, he knew very well how a brain was constructed. Michelangelo meant to portray that "what God is giving to Adam is the intellect, and thus man is able to 'plan the best and highest' and to 'try all things received.'"[72]

It is true that much religion consists of prejudices projected into the heavens. The God we humans conceptualize sometimes supports the narcissistic wishes of our hearts and the ethnocentrism of our communities. Yet, built into our brains is the necessity for relatedness to one another and the drive for the seeking of meaning. God beyond God—beyond narcissistic and ethnocentric projection—combines transcendence and immanence, otherness and relationality, elusiveness and interaction. What matters most to our existence consists of a relationship between ourselves and all that we know of the universe of influences in which we find ourselves. We have been created by that which is not of our own doing and yet we are cocreators with that which has brought us into being.

Since we are created in the image and likeness of God, we have the ability to think and imagine and decide—yes, and the ability to distort and destroy. Yet we can get outside our own individualistic perspectives. We can look back on our involvement. We can ask questions. We can obtain evidence. We can weigh alternatives. We can anticipate consequences. We can interrupt a strict reptilian stimulus-response reaction by taking into account other values and other perspectives. The yardstick by which we measure life is within us yet beyond our capacity to capture rationalistically. The Ground of Being is always more than we can comprehend and other than we can articulate. God is always more than our idea of God.

If God were nothing more than the projection of human wishes, we would be caught in the quicksand of our own subjectivity. There would be no way of breaking out of self-centeredness. There would be no way of breaking out of ethnocentrism. If the only reality were the reality of our own creation, it would

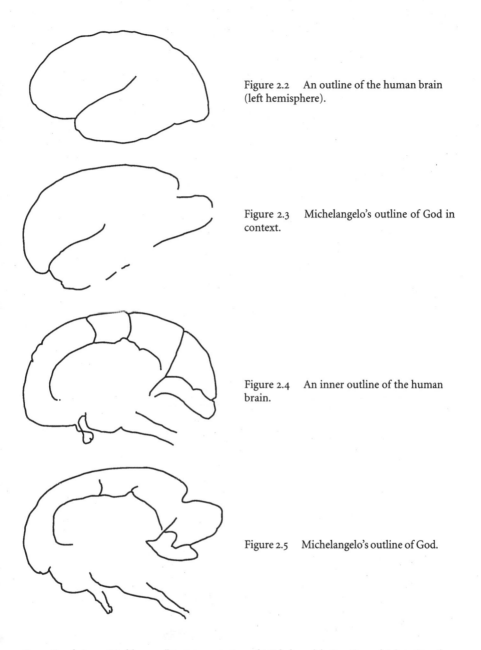

Figure 2.2   An outline of the human brain (left hemisphere).

Figure 2.3   Michelangelo's outline of God in context.

Figure 2.4   An inner outline of the human brain.

Figure 2.5   Michelangelo's outline of God.

From Frank Lynn Meshberger, "An Interpretation of Michelangelo's Creation of Adam *Based on Neuroanatomy,"* Journal of the American Medical Association, *vol. 264, no. 14 (October 1990), 10:1837–41. Copyright 1990, American Medical Association. Reprinted by permission* be impossible to discern anything other than what we wished to see. God's will would be nothing more than our own whims.

But God is more than we can imagine and other than we can conceive. God is not simply a mirror reflecting the image of any particular person or any particular culture. Because God is the truth about the whole of reality, reality eventually shows up our distortions and projections. Falseness cannot be consistently maintained or elaborated. Misperception breaks down—whether in the faulty foundation of a building or the faulty foundation of a racist and sexist society. There is a judgment, an accounting, a reckoning—however it may be said—that is inescapable. The wheels of the really real grind exceedingly slowly, but they do grind, and they grind exceedingly fine.

We as individuals may never let go of our notions about God. But the fruits of such conceits finally show them up as a distortion of the God who makes us relationally in God's own image. The human face of God is always more than and other than any particular face, but we can only imagine the humanlike quality of God through the lens of our own humanness.

In the chapters that follow we work out our understanding of possible correlations between a humanized brain and a humanizing brain, between a humanlike God and a Godlike humanity. We use MacLean's understanding of the triune brain, a brain of three minds, to organize our understanding of God as attending, relating and remembering, organizing and intending.

PART TWO

THE WORKING BRAIN AND GOD'S WAYS OF BEING GOD

THREE

THE UPPER BRAIN STEM, ATTENDING, AND AN EVER-PRESENT GOD

THE REPTILIAN BRAIN IN AROUSAL

In part 2 we turn to a systematic configuration of neuroscience and religion, using the concept of the triune brain as a suggestive analogue for understanding clues to God's ways of being God.

The human brain provides its owner with a highly complex way of dealing with both external and internal realities. What we humans believe to be true of ourselves and our world is influenced by the characteristics of our apparatus for perceiving and thinking—in other words, by our brain. But this apparatus, in turn, is suited to deal with the world as it exists. As Albert Einstein remarked, "'The eternal mystery of the world is its comprehensibility.' It is one of the great realizations of Immanuel Kant that the postulation of a real external world would be senseless without this comprehensibility.... The fact that it is comprehensible is a miracle."[1] The brain and its world seem to demonstrate a "fit."

Taking this line of argument a step further, it is true that human mental abilities affect perceptions of ourselves and the world, and also of God. *And, in fact, the nature of God may, to an imperfect extent, be indicated by the brain, which does allow us humans some perception of the world's basis.* In other words, human perceptions of the Deity may be more than anthropocentric projections, more than a self-centered, unfounded belief that there is a God, and that God is like us. It is true that characteristics often attributed to God tend to run parallel to natural perceptions by the brain. But clearly, that brain is marvelously suited to receiving and processing relevant information in other realms of knowledge. Might it also be suited to perceiving some of the real attributes of the Ground of Being that undergirds our immediate reality? In fact, do the brain's perceptions provide telling clues to the nature of the Ground of Being? We believe the answer to those questions is yes.

As we trace the faculties of various areas of the brain, it will quickly become apparent that various traditional, long-standing assertions and perceptions regarding the Deity are linked to operations of each of the regions of the brain. We discuss them layer by layer—reptilian, mammalian, and neocortical.

LEVELS OF ANALYSIS AND ANALOGICAL ATTRIBUTES

Neuroscientist Paul D. MacLean first advanced the concept of the triune brain and a mind of three minds.[2] Initially, he spoke of the visceral brain and the word brain[3] and discerned in this distinction "a clue to understanding the difference between what we 'feel' and what we 'know.'"[4] Subsequently, he identified a three-tiered structure, which he called "the triune brain" or a mind with three distinct, independent minds—the reptilian, the mammalian, and the neocortical or rational. These are radically different in structure and chemistry, yet extensively interconnected (see figure 3.1).[5] The two older minds lack the capacity to communicate in speech. We have chosen to use MacLean's notion of the triune brain—a brain of three minds—as a guide to our exploration of a meeting between religion and neuroscience.

This choice anchors our speculations in the physical world, as it exists and as it has evolved. That anchoring also allows us to reflect on the role of human thought and culture.[6] However, we are mindful of the controversy surrounding MacLean's particular view of emergent evolution.[7] For our purpose, what is significant is not so much *how* the brain emerged but *that* it emerged.

Saint Augustine intuited a similar hierarchy back in the fifth century:

> And so step by step I ascended from bodies to the soul which perceives through the body, and from there to its inward force, to which the bodily senses report external sensations, this being as high as the beasts go. From there again I ascended to the power of reasoning to which is to be attributed the power of judging the deliverances of the bodily senses. This power, which in myself I found to be mutable, raised itself to the level of its own intelligence, and led my thinking out of the ruts of habit. It withdrew itself from the contradictory swarms of imaginative fantasies, so as to discover the light by which it was flooded. . . . On this ground it can know the unchangeable, since, unless it could somehow know this, there would be no certainty in preferring it to the mutable.[8]

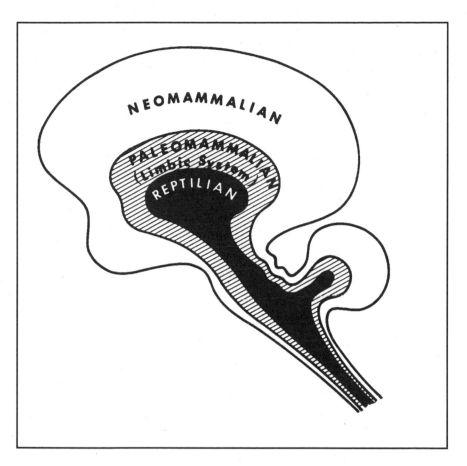

Figure 3.1——— Three basic brain patterns. In evolution, the primate forebrain expands in hierarchic fashion along the lines of three basic patterns that may be characterized as reptilian, paleomammalian, and neomammalian. *From Paul D. MacLean, "The Brain in Relation to Empathy and Medical Education,"* Journal of Nervous and Mental Diseases *144:374–82, 1967. Reprinted by permission of the author.*

While unaware of an evolutionary perspective, Augustine recognized progressively "upward" developments from sensory processes to imaginative constructions to abstract reasoning. "Somehow" people can identify cognitively what is permanent or fixed from what is impermanent or changing, according to him.[9] Rather than relying solely on experiential perceptions or a philosophical worldview such as Augustine's, with MacLean this discussion turns to empirical data to inform an understanding of humanity and God.

MacLean compared the design of the human brain with the brains of other creatures and found significant similarities, along with telling differences. We humans are part of the biological order. It is true that brains become more complex going up the evolutionary tree from reptiles to mice to primates. On the other hand, there are also surprising similarities.

Besides the brain stem, which controls such fundamental life functions as breathing, reptiles, birds, and mammals share a large group of ganglia situated just above the brain stem. In species from lizards to horses to chimpanzees to humans, this portion of the brain functions on the basis of the same characteristic neurotransmitters. Under a microscope, the tissues look about the same, and they take the same stains in tissue studies. Because these structures first appeared in reptiles, MacLean calls them the "reptilian brain" or the R-complex. He thinks of this complex as "the primal mind." We discern in these features affinities to an understanding of God as concrete presence.

Certain other brain structures are found only in mammals; these are sometimes called the "old mammalian brain" or the limbic system. MacLean refers to them as "the emotional mind." Still other structures appear primarily in primates, especially humans, and these form the neocortex, or what MacLean indicates as "the rational mind." In all the various species that the two latest levels of brain development serve, the mammalian brain and the neocortex have distinctive anatomies, take tissue stains differently, and rely mainly on their own sorts of neurotransmitters. In the following chapters we suggest affinities to the limbic system and the neocortex in understanding God as nurturing and purposeful, respectively. This chapter is concerned with the reptilian brain, the R-complex—and with what it may mean for an understanding of humanity and God.

A word of cautious qualification is needed at the outset. As MacLean has pointed out, it is important to guard against a reductionistic interpretation of the tripartite brain. Some of his critics have focused on his formulation of "three quite different mentalities," as though each brain-mind were totally independent and autonomous in its operation and control. While improved techniques of investigation have clarified the three basic formations, he intends "to guard against such interpretation" of independence by using the expression "the triune brain":

> *Triune*, a concise term, derives . . . from the Greek. If the three formations "are pictured as intermeshing and functioning together as a *triune* brain, . . . they cannot be completely autonomous, but [this] does not deny their capacity for operating somewhat independently." Moreover . . . the triune relationship im-

plies that "the 'whole' is greater than the sum of its parts, because the exchange of information among the three brain types means that each derives a greater amount of information than if it were operating alone."[10]

MacLean goes on to note that some misinterpret the idea of "triune" as "a consecutive layering of the three main neural assemblies, somewhat analogous to strata of rock."[11] Such layering is not the case, even though it would reflect emergent evolutionary development.

FUNCTIONS OF THE REPTILIAN BRAIN

How can we tell what is controlled by the reptilian brain (also called the responsive brain)? Because of its location, it has often been thought to play a role in motor functions. However, some patients have suffered the loss of large areas of this part of the brain with no noticeable motor deficit.[12] What significance, then, might this basic level of neural organization have for the humanizing brain?

Taking another approach, MacLean and other researchers have observed animals whose activities depend on this part of the brain—since they have nothing else to work with—to see what they can do. These animals fall into four main categories: snakes, lizards, turtles, and crocodilians (alligators, crocodiles, caimans, and gavials). From observing them, MacLean's team deduced the capacities now associated with the reptilian brain, specifically life support and self-protection. Table 3.1 sets out the relatively few kinds of behavior that most of the terrestrial animals hold in common.

Behaviors reflective of self-preservation come first in the list, while those connected with social and procreational activities follow.

Since most of us do not keep pet reptiles (though a not insignificant number of us do), we tend to be less familiar with their lifestyles than we are with those of, say, canaries or cats or dogs. But in fact, reptiles define for themselves a home place. They stake out and defend their territory. They not only hunt for food, they also hoard it, "squirreling" as it is sometimes called. Some of these reptilian creatures form social groups, establish social hierarchies, and even greet and groom one another. They locate and court their mates. A few kinds of reptiles attend to their young.

In addition, reptiles pay attention to their environment. To the extent their brains allow, they watch for the moving insect that may be "good" to eat or for the looming shadow of a bison that may tread them into the dust. They watch for rivals, for mates, for each other.

Table 3.1——Special Forms of Basic Behavior

Selection and preparation of homesite ⎰
Establishment of territory   ⎱   Domain
Use of home range
Showing place preferences
Trail making
Marking of territory
Patrolling territory
Ritualistic display in defense of territory,
    commonly involving the use of
    coloration and adornments
Formalized intraspecific fighting in defense
    of territory
Triumphal display in successful defense
Assumption of distinctive postures and
    coloration in signaling surrender
Use of defecation posts
Foraging
Hunting
Homing
Hoarding
Formation of social groups
Establishment of social hierarchy by
    ritualistic display and other means
Greeting
Grooming
Courtship, with displays using coloration
    and adornments
Mating
Breeding and, in isolated instances,
    attending offspring
Flocking
Migration

From Paul D. MacLean, The Triune Brain *(New York: Plenum Press, 1990a),*
100, table 65-1. Reprinted by permission of the author.

One of the striking features of reptilian behavior is its conservatism. There is reason to believe that the behaviors reptiles perform today they performed in essentially the same way before humans appeared on the planet. Their behaviors are ritualistic and "programmed," with no hint of playfulness or joy.

In order to accomplish these things, they must communicate with one another in at least a rudimentary way—and, in fact, they do, through behaviors called "displays." There are four main kinds of display: (1) signature, (2) courtship, (3) territorial challenge, and (4) submissive or assertive.[13] Displays comprise basic consistent sequences of behaviors. When other reptiles see these ritual displays, they tend to know what they mean and respond accordingly.

Signature Displays. When one lizard encounters another lizard, it behaves in a way that humans might interpret as "Hello, I'm here." That is, it nods its head several times and does some pushups (in contrast to waving its hand). It may briefly puff out a bright-colored "bubble" in the vicinity of its throat (see figure 3.2). These displays seem to play a role in helping reptiles to identify members of the same species.

Courtship Displays. These begin with a signature introduction but proceed into activities that signal one's intentions to members of the opposite sex—for example, a male may approach a female with a prancing strut. Some reptiles, however, have difficulty deciding whether a given individual is of the opposite sex (which is not too surprising, since the gender of reptiles is not always obvious to humans either). Some male reptiles take what may seem to us an experimental approach: they make advances to all comers. "If the challenged lizard fights back it is a male; if not, the only alternative is to regard it as a female lizard and make appropriate overtures."[14]

Challenge Displays. To stake out territory, establish dominance in a hierarchy, or fend off invaders or attackers, a reptile uses a challenge display. Following its "signature" self-introduction, it may engage in maneuvers to make itself appear larger—puffing up its throat or much of its body, rearing up on its hind legs or (in snakes) raising its head and anterior body. Two rivalrous lizards or snakes may carry out a protracted "dance," circling each other like two boxers or entwining their heads and necks like dual performers in a snake charmer's show. Some hiss or rattle their tail—although many reptiles are hard of hearing and do not rely much on sound. Reptiles that are not dangerous may hiss and spit like those that are, in what seems to be an instinctual attempt at deception.[15]

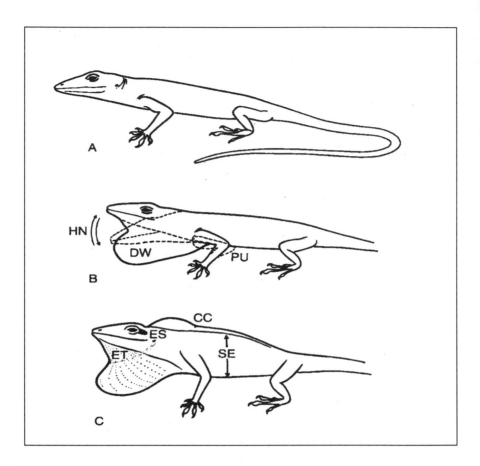

Figure 3.2———A lizard puffing out its throat. Features of the signature and challenge displays of the common green anolis lizard (*Anolis carolinensis*). (A) The usual attentive posture. (B) Diagrammatics of the signature (assertion) display. The signature display consists of three to five head nods (HN) and pushups (PU) along with an extension of the dewlap (DW). The broken lines indicate the excursion of the head and flexion of forelimbs during pushups. Note absence of static modifiers. (C) Diagnostic features of the challenge display of adult male lizards. In addition to the dynamic components of the signature display, the challenge display has several static modifiers. The first to appear are the extended throat (ET) and sagittal expansion (SE), followed by an elevation of the nuchal and dorsal crests (CC). A darkly pigmented eyespot (ES) may appear after 2 to 3 minutes. *From N. Greenberg, P. D. MacLean, and J. L. Ferguson, "Role of the Paleostriatum in Species-Typical Display Behavior of the Lizard* (Anolis carolinensis)*," Brain Research 172:229–41, 1979. Reprinted by permission of Paul D. MacLean.*

Domination and Submission. In terms of lives of reptiles saved or lost, it is less costly to maintain a hierarchy than to fight to the death. Thus, from the point of view of survival of reptiles as a species, a hierarchy is an evolutionary adaptation. And so, while some reptiles dominate in a social group, others submit. They signal submission or assent through ritualized displays—for example, by repeatedly bowing their heads or throwing up their hands as humans do in surrendering.

THE REPTILIAN BRAIN IN NONREPTILES

It takes little imagination to conclude that species other than reptiles perform reptilian behaviors. We humans commonly nod our head to acquaintances in passing, reflective of a "signature display." When male and female humans don showy clothes and strut along the street, hoping to gain recognition and/or attract members of the opposite sex, this seems very much like a "courtship display." In fact, "dressing up" for special occasions such as academic processions seems "as *natural* as the desire to eat."[16] The moves of sumo wrestlers are uncannily reminiscent of the maneuvers usually seen when two male lizards vie for territory.[17] Most mammals, including humans, select and maintain a homesite and try to keep intruders away. In common with reptiles, we humans forage and hunt for food (in the forest or the grocery store) and often hoard it. In common with reptiles we form social groups and maintain hierarchies.

Reptiles make ritualistic displays in defense of their territory and triumphal displays after a successful defense or a successful conquest. During and after every human war one can expect similar displays—parades, flyovers, TV appearances, medals. All across America, people flock to ritualistic displays every weekend in the autumn. After a good deal of rhythmic singing and shouting led by a scepter-wielding chieftain, they cheer while a line of brightly clad young males, shoulders padded, prances onto the football field, and a line of young females dances along the sidelines urging them on. After every victory in competition, the audience celebrates while a ritual dance erupts in the end zone.

It is tempting to dissociate human behaviors from those seen in reptiles and birds and lower mammals: any similarities in behavior must be purely coincidental! Or so it seems. *Human* behaviors, it is said, are learned and cultural, and they must have little or nothing to do with reptiles.

Yet MacLean appropriately asks, "If that [dissimilarity] is so, one might ask why it is that in spite of the high degree of human intelligence and culturally learned behavior, human beings continue to do all the ordinary things that animals do."[18] One reason people ignore human proclivities, he asserts, is that it is so difficult to find words to express them, the reptilian brain being speechless. "Unlike emotional feelings and thoughts, we are either oblivious to, or cannot find the words to express, mental states connected with proclivities. Even the most gifted writers flounder in this area. . . . It was as though proclivities were like an itch-without-an-itch."[19]

These display activities in humans seem to signal to others who we are and what we are about. Quite literally, the primal mind is territorial—my place, my rights, my space, my entitlements, my niche in the scheme of things. Various strategies aim to protect our "conceptual space," "personal space," "domestic space," "intellectual and research territories," and even "outer space." Our rules reiterate concern over "trespass" and "no trespass."[20]

In the mid-1960s, science writer Robert Ardrey put scientific caution aside and boldly described the "territorial imperative," in which he linked ownership and the formation of nations with our animal origins. He defined "a territory" as "an area of space, whether of water or earth or air, which an animal or group of animals defends as an exclusive preserve. The word is also used to describe the inward compulsion in animate beings to possess and defend such space. A territorial species of animals, therefore, is one in which all males, and sometimes females too, bear an inherent drive to gain and defend an exclusive property."[21]

Ardrey went on to contend that territory satisfies the basic needs for identity, security, and stimulation:

> "This place is mine; I am of this place," says the albatross, the patas monkey, the green sunfish, the Spaniard, the great horned owl, the wolf, the Venetian, the prairie dog, the three-spined stickleback, the Scotsman, the skua, the man from La Crosse, Wisconsin, the Alsatian, the little-ringed plover, the Argentine, the lungfish, the lion, the Chinook salmon, the Parisian. I am of this place which is different from and superior to all other places on earth and I partake of its identity so that I too am both different and superior, and it is something that you cannot take away from me despite all afflictions which I may suffer or where I may go or where I may die. I shall remain always and uniquely of this place.[22]

The territorial imperative has peace-maintaining implications as well as warlike implications. Historian Dorothy V. Jones has identified an emerging "code of peace" as an ethical framework to guide sovereign states in dealing with their relationships with one another. Basic to the nine principles she identifies are the integrity and respect of territoriality.[23] These principles are a guide to international behavior as well as a standard with which to judge that behavior. Rather than generating conflict, a recognition of the territorial imperative can generate cooperation, individually and collectively.

In short, these reptilian behaviors ought not be devalued. It seems clear that they would not have continued if they did not promote life. And in any case, who among us would want to give up the establishment of a home, social recognition, some safe boundaries in our neighborhood as well as our world— or football? (Don't ask.)

Certainly these kinds of behaviors are modified in humans: they are informed by memory, by long-term planning, by empathy, by conscience. Reptiles, having only a reptilian brain, are incapable of such refinements. They do what they have to do, not what they plan to do or what they deliberately value. In humans, however, signals from the reptilian brain interact with plans and analyses from the neocortex, with playful and caring signals from the old mammalian brain. As the old instructions merge with new considerations, there is something new under the sun. The new is greater than the sum of its parts. The human may thereby be called "emergent." Our reptilian brain is a responsive brain, not a reactive one.

In fact, the organizing, integrating, meaning-seeking process in humans, according to neurosurgeon Wilder Penfield, appears to be focused in the higher brain stem—the R-complex—rather than in the new mammalian brain, as one might expect.[24] Neuropsychologist Karl Lashley (1890–1958) and others[25] later saw these central processes as working to construct "the logical and orderly arrangement of thought and action." This arrangement came not by means of linking successive sensory elements but rather in an integrative mode.[26]

Such ordering begins with a process known as *orientation*: an immediate "assessment of place, person, and time" followed by an ongoing process of evaluation.[27] Initially, the orienting response is rapid, with little cognitive input. "It readies our muscles" for the survival choices of fight or flee or freeze. "Once we orient, then we begin to evaluate," aided by the emotional meaning of what is happening. These two aspects of orientation and assessment are "sequential and serial, but also simultaneous and parallel." Both depend "on the brain stem."[28]

How can the orientation process make such rapid initial evaluations? A clue is its location in the R-complex. There it draws upon the reptilian ability to attend to concrete details, to locate the self in space. These are highly useful abilities. And in humans, there is more: evidence indicates that humans assemble in this region of their brain a prototypical "set of instructions" on the basis of information transferred from the higher brain centers for purposes of "long-term storage."[29] Not all memory is in the R-complex, however; later we discuss meaningful memory in relation to the mammalian brain.

How does the transfer of stimuli from short-term input to long-term memory take place? Apparently, dreams play an important role in this process, and in the integrative process in general. The organization of materials to be remembered is a tedious process that seems to take place, night after night, during states of dreaming.[30] Repeatedly, the mind sorts through what has happened, integrates that with what has gone before, keeps what fits, and discards material that seems extraneous.[31] The process of transferring materials into the brain's "permanent files" may take as long as three years.[32] One may speculate that babies and young children need many hours of dreaming sleep because they have so much new experience to process.[33]

The dream state is known to us through experience—through *mind*—and it has a material correlate in the *brain*. The control center for dreaming is in the R-complex. We can fluctuate between vivid dreaming and vivid waking because of "a strongly centralized and highly hierarchical control system . . . at the base of the brain." This strategic location "can command the state of the upper brain (where our thoughts and feelings are represented) at the same time it controls the lower brain (which conveys sensations from our bodies and enacts our volition through muscular action). This switching system is as reliable as it is flexible."[34]

Chemically, the aminergic system controls our conscious state of waking and the cholinergic system controls our unconscious state of dreaming. These two systems are "in dynamic equilibrium," generating "a rich continuum of aminergic-cholingeric interactions and an equally rich continuum of brain-mind states."[35] A further integration meshes brain stem orientation and the memory of cognitive maps of meaning. This process takes place in the hippocampus of the old mammalian brain.[36] We say more about this in a later chapter.

The word *triune* implies this integrative quality of the human brain. As MacLean notes, "with the exchange of information among the three [brain mentalities] each derives a greater amount of information than if it were operating alone." Each mentality, including the reptilian one, has "its own special intelligence, its own subjectivity, its own sense of time and space, and its own memory, motor, and other functions."[37] To ignore the likelihood that some of the instructions of our mental equipment are carryovers from the distant past of life on the planet is to underestimate their force and their necessity.

THE REPTILIAN BRAIN AND THE *IMAGO DEI*

To look for images of God in the activities of the reptilian brain may seem a bit insulting to God. Doing so might involve, not anthropocentrism, but *reptilocentrism*, which does not seem an especially complimentary term.

Still, to the extent that these behaviors are fairly central to our everyday lives—and they are—we cannot deny them without denying our basic humanity as well. And if our humanity reflects the image of God—well, then, we cannot *not* reflect on just what those images might be.

Several examples come to mind. While they may not suggest the God of process theology or liberation theologies (feminist, third-world, political), they do reflect attributes of God advanced by many religious traditions.

The territorial imperative of the primal mind contributes to, and explains, the persistence of the intensity of what is called "my turf" mentality. We suggest that it provides a biological base for the linguistic expressions of territoriality in religion.[38] These expressions point to geographical territory such as the biblical concept of a Holy Land for the people of God.[39] They may also provide psychological and theological analogies of territory, for instance: "You shall have no other gods before/besides me" and "For your God is a devouring fire, a jealous God" (Exodus 20:3–5; Deuteronomy 4:23–24).[40]

Hierarchy is another example. "God Most High" is certainly at the top of the hierarchical heap (e.g., Psalms 7:17, 9:2, 46:4, 47:2, 57:2, 73:11, 83:18, 91:1). In any contest of wills, God the Almighty must by definition be the winner. Another image is the watchful deity. God attends to the created order. God's eye is on the sparrow, and God surely watches over us (Matthew 10:29–31, Luke 12:6–7, Matthew 6:26). Furthermore, God persists, and so does God's nature. God is seen as eternal, omnipotent, immutable.[41] God, like Jesus Christ, to use the language of the Book of Hebrews, "is the same yesterday and today and forever" (Hebrews 13:8). And the God of these traditions is, traditionally, male. The cosmic order has been used to justify and reinforce a patriarchal social structure.[42]

All these images—of the territorial, hierarchical, watchful, persistent, unchanging God—may be reflective of the activity of the R-complex. This part of the brain is associated with similar activities and tendencies in human nature. Yet in humans these behaviors take on a subtlety and complexity that no lizard can match.

Hierarchy exists, yes, but not so simply. We find Ardrey's concept of "the open instinct" particularly applicable here. The idea of open instinct combines "in varying portion . . . genetic design and relevant experience." By virtue of our human dependence on others for learning the ways of the world, we have become "the most variable of all wild species . . . [permitting] the widest latitude of adaptation to circumstances. We retain genetic resolve while obtaining the diversity of experience."[43] Human variability includes both differentiation of experience and the capacity to integrate such differentiation. Thus, human reality is moving toward ever greater self-organizing complexity.[44]

From a Judeo-Christian perspective, differentiating adaptation and order in the world must aim to be in service to the whole, to community, to every living creature, to the entire created universe. From this perspective, God invests in humanity "dominion" over the earth as stewardship, not domination (Genesis 1:28); partnership, not patriarchy.[45] The high and mighty are to be brought down from their pedestals and the lowly are to be lifted up; the hungry are to be "filled" with good things and the rich to be sent away "empty" (Luke 1:52–53). The emptying of God in "being found in human form" (Philippians 2:5–8) comes to fulfillment in our loving one another as God has loved us and in our being called "friends" (John 15:8–11, 15), equals within the community of reality. This does not imply scrambling to attain the pinnacle of creation—the top of the heap—in a closed universe predetermined by hardwired instinctual patterns in which one need attend only to oneself and one's own immediate needs. Creation and creativity, expressive of copartnership between the divine and human, are ever an "advance into novelty,"[46] "the co-creation of something genuinely new by processes immanent in the world," as theologian James Will describes it.[47] With the author of First John, we can say "we are God's children now; what we will be has not yet been revealed. What we do know is this; when he [God] is revealed, we will be like him [God], for we will see him [God] as he [God] is" (1 John 3:2).

THE REPTILIAN BRAIN AS A HUMAN PROBLEMATIC

Many of the behaviors we humans share with reptiles are hard to see as divine. They cause us trouble. Furthermore, one may even be led to speculate that the main trouble with us humans—our original sin—is that we have three brains fighting it out within one skull. And the metaphor of conflicting mentalities is not without suggestive value.

There are some "direct lines" between the mentalities, but in general, they do not communicate as well as they might. Language is available only to the rational mind, not to the primal and emotional minds. Further, their neurotransmitters tend to differ. We might say, metaphorically, they speak in different tongues so that the action we intend—with our neocortex and rational mind—may not be what we actually do—on the advice of our reptilian or our mammalian brain.

The Epistle of James is not alone in detecting "disorder . . . of every kind": "Those conflicts and disputes among you, where do they come from? Do they not come from your cravings that are at war within you?" (James 3:16, 4:1). And then there is the classic confession of conflict by Saint Paul in Romans: "I find it to be a law that when I want to do what is good, evil lies close at hand. For I delight in the law of God in my inmost self, but I see in my members another law at war with the law of my mind, making me captive to the law of sin that dwells in my members. Wretched man that I am! Who will rescue me from this body of death?" (Romans 7:21–24).

Refer again to the lists of reptilian behaviors in table 3.1. They may suggest why some cultures use the serpent as a symbol of evil[48]; the snake in the grass, which connotes treachery; or being bitten by poisonous serpents, which reflects the massive disruption caused by anxiety (Numbers 21:6). Reptilian mate seeking and sexual display omit regard for the well-being, even the identity, of the mate. Reptiles can be highly aggressive, even murderous, toward sexual rivals. They are not big on "family values" (which appear with the advent of the mammalian brain). While a few reptiles, such as female alligators, do give their hatchlings some care, most of them do not; some will even kill the off-spring if given the opportunity. These reptilian behaviors, we are painfully aware, are not restricted to reptiles but have their human counterparts, as is reported almost daily in the newspapers and on television.

Reptiles attack and sometimes kill animals that encroach on their territory. This warlike behavior tends to be ritualized (as are lynchings, military parades, and street-gang shootings of outsiders who wear the "wrong" clothing or flash the "wrong" hand signal). Guarding and patrolling territory, so characteristic of animals, finds its counterpart in the regular vigilance of police and military groups.[49]

Reptiles can be masters of deception. If the harmless hog-nosed snake is threatened, it mimics a poisonous snake; if its attacker persists, the hog-nose rolls over and imitates a dead snake that would surely not be good to eat.[50] Being deceitful can be beneficial to the reptile; deceit can be profitable to humans as well. In fact, when the young child engages in deceptive behavior we have evidence of the beginning of the development of a sense of individual identity. "Keeping a secret" reflects having a "say" over one's world. But the issue here is less that of deception and more that of maintaining one's boundaries, one's privacy, something that is "positively owned" rather than "fearfully hidden."[51]

For the human community, deceptive behavior ultimately undermines trust and hampers constructive interaction.[52] Anger flares up in the person deceived. Some religiously minded individuals, in the face of adversity, believe that God has deceived them, abandoned them, used and abused them without consideration for their integrity. And they feel violated.[53]

If reptilian conservatism could be summed up in a cliche, it might be, "We've always done it that way and we see no reason to change." In point of fact, "reptiles are slaves to routine, precedent, and ritual."[54] There are indications that the coding within the human R-complex is especially resistant to change, particularly when compared with the more dynamic neocortex.[55] People experience great emotional stress when their routines are disrupted and drastic alterations are made.[56]

Human conservatism, however, serves a stabilizing role. Routinizing saves energy. If every morning everyone had to invent a life from scratch, nothing else could be accomplished. When expectations are usually met, plans can then be made with confidence.

But life changes, and failure to adapt tends to be dysfunctional, sometimes disastrous, as the French learned with their Maginot Line mentality during World War II.[57] It is true that going beyond routines is destabilizing and requires energy. However, remaining the same yesterday, today, and forever may mean being left behind by the evolutionary parade and God's eschatological activity.

RELIGION CO-OPTS THE REPTILE

Most communities—whether tribal villages, modern cities, or organizations— have an interest in "civilizing" the tendencies of the reptilian brain—tendencies toward impersonal sexuality and aggression, behavior that runs on "automatic pilot," deception. The fundamental activities prompted by the reptilian brain are necessary to survival—but unless they are integrated with other faculties, survival will be threatened in the long run. Sexual bonding and sexual violence are not the same, obviously. To ensure the future, children must be carefully nurtured, and many arrangements and customs must be in place to support this need.

Humans have a drive to have a place called home, something of their own, and this need must be acknowledged as fundamental. We must maintain peaceable ways of settling disputes over boundaries and entitlements, as we indicated earlier in citing historian Dorothy Jones's analysis of the "code of peace."

"Insiders" and "outsiders," various cultural and ethnic groups, must find ways to get along. Ritual group behavior cannot be allowed to spin out of control, for in a noisy, anonymous group people can be dangerous. The advantageous lie is tempting, but people who intend to work together must be able to believe what they hear and see. The ubiquity of change in the human environment makes rigid behavioral responses a liability. It is essential to practice adaptability in new situations. That, if you will, is the purpose and glory of the new brain.

Individual responses can go a long way toward meeting these survival needs. The reptilian brain is not, after all, our only equipment. As the human personality grows and adapts, a person learns to integrate (1) the basic requirements encoded in the older brain, (2) the playful, nurturing behavior pioneered by the mammalian brain, and (3) the goal-seeking, history-making, symbol-using, meaning-making, analytical neocortex.

A fully formed human can think and feel, love and play, intuit and perceive. Such a person is at ease with the embodied self that needs a nest, food, a mate and/or a companion, others like oneself, and safety—and also with his or her tiny but significant place in the human community of past, present, and future. The fully realized human intuits the wholeness of the universe, seen in the divine, and finds significance by assuming her or his place within that context. Thus, after the manner of Jesus, such a person lives in both body and spirit, a fully human person who may, to a degree, be empowered by a much greater reality.

Religions have traditionally provided resources for people seeking such growth and integration (although religions have engaged in undeniably destructive activities as well). Through the centuries, wisdom accumulated in religions has provided guidance regarding sexuality, child rearing, violence, defense of turf, and deception. People have used religion to locate themselves within the flow of history, the whole human enterprise, and the planet itself; thus, many have found a sense of meaning and purpose in their lives. They have heard descriptions of their divided selves, found guidance in perplexity, comfort in loss, and expiation for the inevitable failures. "If the significance attached to such endeavors is any indication," observes social psychologist Mihaly Csikszentmihalyi, "the reduction of conflict and disorder through spiritual means appears to be very adaptive. Without them, it is likely that people would grow discouraged and confused, and that the Hobbesian 'war of all against all' would become an even more prominent feature of the social landscape than it already is."[58]

Religions establish communities that, at least officially, endorse altruism over selfishness.[59] In their buildings, they provide the group with a home territory, a place to call their own, a location in which they belong, and, most of all a locus of the holy.[60] By acknowledging the worth of each individual, they provide the equivalent of a "signature display" that says, "Look! I'm here!"

In the spirit of "using fire to fight fire," traditional religions use rituals to tame the troublesome drives of our primeval reptilian selves. (We say more in the next chapter about the power of ritual to reconcile opposites, cognitively and emotionally.) Confucius even saw ritual as "one of the manifestations of the divine order that held the stars on their courses, that made the crops grow, . . . kept order in the state . . . and helped to maintain the order of the universe."[61]

Rituals of baptism, coming of age (bar mitzvah, bas mitzvah, confirmation), betrothal and marriage, house blessings and leave takings, rituals of healing and dying, funerals and mourning (sitting shivah) mark such passages. The cycle of the church year—the Christmas affirmation of new life in the dead of winter, the solemnity of Lent and Yom Kippur, days of remembrance, the sharing of the eucharist and communion, the celebration of renewal at Easter—these rituals and others in different traditions serve to knit together communities in observance of commonalities of humanity, bringing order to the incipient chaos of experience. As anthropologist Victor Turner observed, "the ritual process [performs] noetic functions in ways peculiar to itself, as a *sui generis* [unique] mode of knowing."[62]

Other rituals mark the chaotic tendencies in human nature, and by observing them, we may "tame" them. Yom Kippur, the Jewish Day of Atonement, is only one of the rites that acknowledges human disorganization and enables a new start and growth. Listen to the Yom Kippur ritual:

> We abuse, we betray, we are cruel.
> We destroy, we embitter, we falsify.
> We gossip, we hate, we insult.
> We jeer, we kill, we lie.
> We mock, we neglect, we oppress.
> We pervert, we quarrel, we rebel.
> We steal, we transgress, we are unkind.
> We are violent, we are wicked, we [fear and hate the stranger].
> We yield to evil, we are zealots for bad causes.[63]

Yet there is hope, a chance for a new start, the opening of a future freed from the constraints of the past:

Our God and God of our fathers, forsake us not, shame us not, break not your covenant with us. . . .

Soften our hardened hearts, so that we may love and revere You, returning to You wholeheartedly. . . .

Our God and God of our fathers, forgive us, pardon us, grant us atonement. For we are Your people, and You our God.[64]

The reptilian brain is anchored in the tangible, the embodied, the concrete. Abstractions are beyond its comprehension. Rituals point to abstractions by way of the tangible—the bread shared on Shabbat Eve or at the eucharistic or communion table, the water of baptism, the Babe whose incarnation engendered Christmas. Rituals can tame the beast. Thus the attending reptile, the nurturing mammal, the abstracting primate within the human skull can focus together on truth that makes us whole.

ALL TOGETHER NOW

The *imago Dei* that is beginning to emerge is reptilocentric, mammalocentric, anthropocentric, ecocentric—all of the above and none of the above. The reptile's world is ready to hand (or to claw or to darting tongue); it is not the least bit abstract or equivocal. For the reptile, the tangible world, the concreteness of food and territory and mate and foe—the earth and the water and the air—are the *Stoff*—the basic stuff—of life.

The same could be said of humans. Without these things—*Stoff*—we would not exist. Furthermore, without the stubborn animal persistence of our reptilian heritage, we would fail to look after our basic tangible needs. We need our oldest brain, with its capacity to attend to the physical environment and our interpersonal world. Without it we would not survive. Without it we would have no place.

But, as subsequent chapters will show, our whole cerebral equipment is vital to our well-being in other ways as well. We are not simply reptilian, not simply mammalian, not simply creatures who manipulate symbols. As clearly seen in the emerging science of psychoneuroimmunology,[65] our feelings influence our thoughts, our thoughts influence our feelings, and both feelings and thoughts, in turn, influence our bodies. Our bodies interact with our feelings and thoughts, round and round like the Uroboros—the symbolic snake whose mouth devours its tail. Whatever *imago Dei* comes into focus will be concrete and abstract, intentional and contemplative, emotional and analytical, with all qualities interpenetrating.

"The sacred view," observes Jungian analyst Anthony Stevens, "possesses supreme value, for it elevates the experience of human life above the mundane practices of subsistence . . . it makes us aware that each of us . . . [is] both temporal and eternal, that although we are subject to the conditions and constraints of our daily lives we nevertheless transcend them through the nature of our humanity."[66]

The German theologian Wolfhart Pannenberg would take this observation a step further. He suggests that the multidimensionality of human nature, recognized by Stevens and MacLean (among many), mirrors a multidimensionality in the universe.

> How does one explain the fact that human mind and language are fit to grasp the reality of things as they really are? The possibility of truth in human statements would cause no great problem, if the human mind were completely passive and receptive in its perceptions. But today we know that on the contrary, the mind and brain are active in every moment of experience, starting with sense perception. How is it possible that the information we receive from the outside is not hopelessly distorted? On the basis of the biblical conception of spirit and mind, the answer would be *that the same spirit that the human mind shares is also the origin of "life"* in the beings outside ourselves, the creative origin of their particular "gestalt."[67]

The concreteness of our selves is at one with the emotion, the will, the goal seeking and analytic bent of our being. The basic structure of our brain seems to reflect a God who is at one with the concreteness of creation, yet transcends it in dimensions as vast and powerful and mysterious as the galaxies. Only our grounding in specific places enables us to explore the wider reaches of our humanity.

However, our capacity to "tune in" on the meaningfulness of reality—what MacLean would call knowledge of the subjective self or "epistemics"—"appears to have depended in large measure on the evolutionary development of the limbic system."[68] In the next two chapters we turn to the limbic system—the old paleomammalian brain and emotional mind. There is the focal region for the emotional information that guides behavior necessary for self-preservation and for the preservation of the species.

FOUR

THE LIMBIC LOBES, RELATING, AND A NURTURING GOD

THE MAMMALIAN BRAIN IN PLAY, NURTURANCE, AND MOTIVATION

The deepest sense of self or soul dwells in the cave of memory, watered by the wellsprings of emotion. In contrast, Enlightenment rationalism, signaled by René Descartes's (1596–1650) ringing cry *Cogito, ergo sum* ("I think, therefore I am"), elevated mathematical logic as self-evident and made it the sole basis for understanding the universe. Passions were viewed as "irrational intrusions" and imagination rejected as "a source of delusions."[1] Since then the soul—and the sense of the sacred—has been crucified on the cross of "objectivity." The ideal of reason is predicated on doubting.[2]

Reason has in fact conferred many benefits. But the twentieth century has taught only too well that rationality can be co-opted in the service of irrationality, control can result in out-of-control consequences, and technology can give birth to a Frankensteinian monster known as ecological disaster. Reason and calculation too often separate people from one another and from the natural setting of which all are a part. Empathy and memory, in contrast, serve to relate people to each other and to the natural world. In terms of physiology, both empathy and memory rely heavily upon the limbic system.

This chapter deals with the issues of empathy and relatedness. The next chapter continues the focus on the limbic system by dealing with memory and meaning or meaning seeking. Emotion is the motivating source of both empathy and memory. Emotion unites relatedness and meaning.

STRUCTURE AND FUNCTION OF THE MAMMALIAN BRAIN

The complex of brain structures called the limbic system caps the reptilian brain like a claw.[3] These structures form the middle zone of brain tissue. Draped over and around them like fingers in the padded mittens of winter is the folded, convoluted "gray matter" of the cerebral cortex. This in turn nestles beneath the bony surround of the skull. The cortex of the limbic convolution is found in all mammals; in other land vertebrates (such as reptiles and birds) it occurs in abbreviated form. For this reason, MacLean dubbed this system the paleomammalian brain and calls this region the limbic system, from the Latin word *limbus,* meaning "border." The term limbus refers to the structures surrounding the brain stem.[4]

The principal structures of the limbic system are shown in figure 4.1. Much of what we know of this brain, which MacLean also refers to as "the emotional mind," comes from studies of patients with epilepsy. Their seizures originated in various parts of the system, allowing both the seizures and other mental

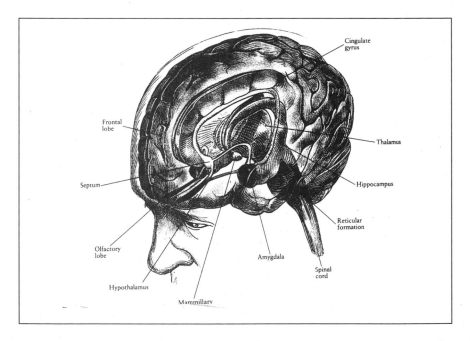

Figure 4.1——The limbic system. The major brain structures forming the limbic system in context. From this view, their locations around the border, or limbus, between the brain stem and the cerebral cortex can be appreciated. *From:* Brain, Mind, and Behavior *by Bloom and Lazerson.* © *1988 by W. H. Freeman and Company. Used with permission.*

phenomena to be studied and localized.[5] More recently, such imaging techniques as positron electron tomography (PET) scans have increased our knowledge further.[6]

The Emotional Labeling of Information

Because of their location, the limbic structures are involved in the transmission of information from one part of the brain to another. Incoming sensory information, "after travelling through pathways in the brainstem, the various processing levels in the cortex, or both, [passes] through one or more of the limbic structures. . . . Outgoing messages down from the cortex also pass through these structures."[7] Messages in, messages out—all traverse the limbic system. There the information is given an emotional "label"—this situation is pleasurable, that is unpleasant. But events may also *trigger* emotions—news of a disappointment makes a person feel sad; after a narrow escape from being hit by a bus fright mingles with relief.

Other Basic Functions: Survival, Play, Nurture

In addition, the limbic system has functions of its own, all of which are involved intimately with emotion. These functions include emotions related to eating, mating, and fighting for food or mates; play; and the care of the young. Memory, while not strictly emotional, is closely involved with emotion. That which matters to us is that which we remember most easily and most fully. We deal with memory and meaning more fully in the next chapter.

Why does emotion occupy so central a position? In Western culture, we are often taught to distrust it. However, in mammals, including humans, emotion fulfills a guidance function analogous to the taste of food. (Natural) foods that taste good tend to be good for us, and bad-tasting things are to be avoided, as they may be dangerous to eat. Similarly, pleasant emotions signal attractive experiences and unpleasant emotions steer us away from potentially damaging situations.

Besides that, emotion is a motivator and mobilizer. The good taste of food stimulates the appetite, and similarly, emotions stimulate one's "appetite" for life itself. Love for parents, fear of punishment, joy in mastery, and sadness in falling short nudge the child into adulthood and keep the adult on track through victories and responsibilities, love and loss. Emotion moves us—like the other mammals—to blaze a trail through life, finding supplies for our basic needs and for continuing the species. Fear galvanizes us into action—fleeing or fighting or freezing; anxiety signals a situation that threatens our integrity, even life itself, and must be resolved. Playfulness provides children with practice in adult behaviors and promotes bonding in adults. In humans, the infant's primal need for attachment, when met by nurture, builds an identity, even a mind.[8] And this need for attachment finds an answering echo in the need for intimacy and generativity later in life, in care for others. Through empathy, we can effectively express altruism, concern for the well-being of others apart from ourselves.

In short, emotion is cognitive, motivational, and relational, basic to survival and crucial in adaptation.[9] It depends on cortical functioning as well as subcortical processing. "Indeed, since emotional functioning is most developed in creatures like man and chimpanzees, less in dogs, and still less in chickens, it may even be that the neocortical part of the brain has been as crucial for emotional characteristics as for traditionally recognized sorts of perception, learning, and thinking."[10]

So the limbic system gives us emotions of joy and love, of anger and fear. It tots up the desirability or undesirability of experiences and potential experiences. It provides for the nurture of the young and the ability to play. Memory lives there. We need to map this territory piece by piece, or function by function. And we will consider how it molds our identity, our sense of the real, our sense of the sacred, our understanding of God.

SEX, AGGRESSION, AND APPETITE

Advertisers and mass-media moguls know what sells. What sells is what appeals to the two primary lobes of the limbic system (see figure 4.2). Located there are the emotions which propel all mammals into behaviors that perpetuate their own lives and promote the survival of the species to which they belong—to wit: feeding, breeding, and aggression to promote the accomplishment thereof. The *amygdala* is associated with activity related to preservation of the self/organism, while the *septum* is associated with activity related to continuity of the species. Both are closely linked with the olfactory apparatus.[11] Think of the amygdala as the physiological correlate of Tillich's courage to be as oneself and the septum as the physiological correlate of the courage to be part of the whole.[12]

It is true that even reptiles feed, breed, and fight—but they do so in a curiously cold-blooded way. (They are, after all, cold-blooded.) For them, there is no excitement of the chase, no panic at becoming another predator's prey, no hot-blooded coupling—just ritualized behavior. Mammals (hot-blooded as

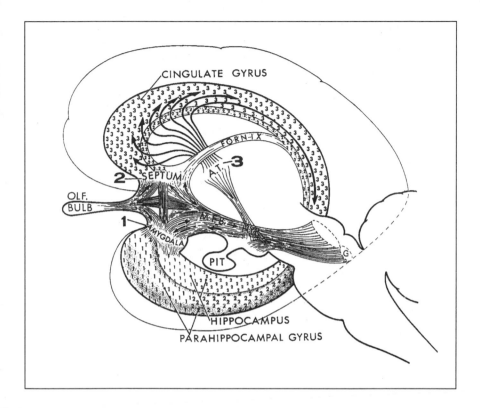

Figure 4.2——The main divisions of the limbic lobes. The nuclear groups associated with the amygdalar, septal, and thalamocingulate divisions are respectively labeled with the large numerals 1, 2, and 3, while the cortical sectors primarily associated with them are overlain with the smaller corresponding numerals. The numerals overlying the archicortical areas are somewhat smaller than those identifying the rest of the limbic cortex. Abbreviations: A.T., anterior thalamic nuclei; G, dorsal and ventral tegmental nuclei of Gudden; HYP, hypothalamus; M, mammillary bodies; M.F.B., medial forebrain bundle; PIT, pituitary; OLF, olfactory. *After Paul D. MacLean, "Brain Evolution Related to Family, Play, and the Separation Call,"* Archives of General Psychiatry, *vol. 42 (April 1985a):405–17, and* The Triune Brain in Evolution *(New York: Plenum Press, 1990a), 315. Reprinted by permission of the author.*

they literally are) have a richer set of experiences. To a greater or lesser degree, depending on their complexity of development, mammals exhibit anger in competition, emotion-laden cravings for food, and lustful drives to mate.

Upon reflection, it may come as little surprise that these feelings seem to be centered in closely related areas of the limbic system. It seems relatively easy to displace them from one to the other. How often do people eat instead of expressing anger; or comfort their loneliness or sexual frustration with a dish of ice cream? How often does sexual rejection trigger rage? These are the stories that fill the tabloids, the problems that provide grist for advice columnists and comical situations for cartoon artists.

If we were the best of all possible people, our sexuality and our affections and our competitiveness and our hunger and our ties to the past and our hopes for the future would be operating in a smoothly interacting "win-win" manner, along with logic and ethics. If we managed this, we would be truly mature and integrated personalities. All the parts of our brains—our reptilian brain, our limbic brain, our cerebral cortex—would be intricately coordinated in a magnificent personal symphony that also took full account of the needs of others and of the environment.

Instead, parts fail to mesh, and one part is expressed at the expense of the others. Frequently our slipups are trivial, inconsequential, easily dismissed. But beyond the occasional ice cream indulgence (even one that violates the Commandment Against Saturated Fat), in situations of unbridled anger, greed, or lust—a runaway, out-of-control limbic system—we are dealing with lack of growth into full maturity and with alienation from self and others.

In *Civilization and Its Discontents,* Sigmund Freud, like many other interpreters of the human situation, assumed a basic dualism of part against part, life instinct against death instinct.[13] Thus, his outlook was basically pessimistic. In characterizing the relationship between the needs of the self and the needs of society, he used Schopenhauer's famous imagery of freezing porcupines: "No one can tolerate a too intimate approach to his neighbor."

> A company of porcupines crowded themselves very close together one cold winter's day so as to profit by one another's warmth and so save themselves from being frozen to death. But soon they felt one another's quills, which induced them to separate again. And now, when the need for warmth brought them nearer together again, the second evil arose once more. So that they were driven backwards and forwards from one trouble to the other, until they discovered a mean distance at which they could most tolerably exist.[14]

This problem, he believed, was the foundation for basic pessimism about life. Every culture requires renunciation of instinctual needs in order that the society that supports our basic needs may continue.[15]

But the tension between the needs of self and society need not lead to such a pessimistic assessment of the human condition. Built in to the limbic system, at each end, is the amygdala's activity to preserve the self and the septum's activity to continue the species. And these two are intimately interconnected and integrated in all behavior. So, preservation of the self may be in the service of continuity of the species, and continuity of the species may require preservation of the self. What separates them is self-consciousness, a split between ourselves as subject and all else as object. Here is the basis for all alienating experience.

These observations about limbic disturbance lead us toward those familiar/unfamiliar concepts, sin and grace. Theologian Paul Tillich observed that

> "sin" should never be used in the plural, and that not our sins, but rather our *sin* is the great, all-pervading problem of our life. . . . It is arrogant and erroneous to divide men by calling some "sinners" and others "righteous." . . . This kind of thinking and feeling about sin is far removed from what the great religious tradition, both within and outside the Bible, has meant when it speaks of sin. . . .
>
> I should like to suggest another word to you, not as a substitute for the word "sin," but as a useful clue in the interpretation of the word "sin," "separation." Separation is an aspect of the experience of everyone. Perhaps the word "sin" has the same root as the word "asunder." In any case, *sin is separation*. To be in the state of separation. And separation is threefold: there is separation among individual lives, separation of a man from himself, and separation of all men from the Ground of Being. . . . It is the fate of every life. . . . Before sin is an act, it is a state.[16]

To those of us who are accustomed to seeing specific *acts* as sinful, such thinking seems passing strange—perhaps a convenient way to escape blame. However, such insight is meant to drive us inward, to the "imaginations of our hearts": As people think in their hearts so they are. The responsibility for growing in maturity is a far more demanding one than the responsibility for giving up various acts, salutary as certain reforms might be. For

> we are not merely separated from each other . . . we are also separated from ourselves. . . . That mixture of selfishness and self-hate permanently pursues us [and] prevents us from loving others. . . . Thus, the state of our whole life is estrangement from others and ourselves. . . . That is the experience of the separation of ourselves from others, which is to say "sin," whether or not we like to use that word.[17]

Whatever we call the problem, the two older lobes of the limbic system—amygdala and septum—do not represent our "highest and best" when they are acting alone. But it does not do to call them our "lower selves." In concert with other sources of the self and soul, their services are invaluable. Only because of them do we exhibit the ability to individuate—that is, the courage to be as ourselves—and the ability to participate—that is, the courage to be part of the whole.

NURTURING, TEACHING, AND PLAYING

The third major subdivision of the mammalian brain, the newest part in evolutionary terms, establishes behavior that is not found in reptiles in any form—namely, (1) nursing and maternal care, (2) audiovocal communication for maintaining maternal-offspring contact, and (3) play.[18] Each of these behaviors reflects a relational structuring of mammalian reality. This subdivision, sometimes called the thalamocingulate division, is shown in figure 4.2. Care of the young and play are extremely emotion-laden, of course, and both are essential for the healthy emotional development of the emerging generation.

Thus, the behaviors linked to this neomammalian brain, as MacLean calls it, are tremendously important. Tracing their consequences shows that they help shape many of the characteristics that seem to give human life its dignity and worth. In truth, when they function adaptively they constitute the core of human nature and human possibility.

Teaching the Young

For instance, mammals are distinguished from other animals by having intergenerational ties. To make these relationships work, there need to be forms of behavior that look altruistic, at least among kin. The young require care; unlike baby reptiles, they cannot hatch and run. All mammals care for their young, and in many species the investment of time and energy is considerable.[19] The parents need to have some sense, then, of what promotes the well-being of the offspring. This knowledge may be "hardwired" or learned; in carnivores and nonhuman primates, one may even detect glimmers of empathy.

The smallest mammals, like mice, grow to maturity in a few weeks and have little time to learn from a parent. But as species' intelligence increases, more and more time is invested in "education" of the young, teaching them behaviors necessary for survival.[20] This kind of teaching implies a whole new way of transmitting information, in addition to the genetic method of inheritance. Information is passed along as "memes"—learned packets of information—as well as genes.

Humans, of course, have unique modes of social communication: they can translate emotions into speech. Although "so-called social signalling has a long evolutionary history in the vertebrates,"[21] only humans have "direct voluntary control over [their] vocal cords. . . . This new pathway is clearly a prerequisite for the emergence of social communication in the speaking mode where the acquisition of learned vocal gestures is required."[22]

The practice of passing on information through teaching has given rise to the whole edifice of human culture. The discovery of early tools, for instance, suggests the sharing of food, a division of labor, and informed cooperation.[23] In fact, "human evolution is characterized in its later stages [especially the European Upper Paleolithic period] by the appearance and development of such capacities and activities as tool manufacture and use, using fire for various purposes, burial of the dead, language, art and culture, and other higher intellectual faculties including conscious self-awareness."[24]

The limbic system does not accomplish this symbolic communication alone—to transmit culture, for example, the limbic brain needs substantial help from the cortex. And a culture of great complexity requires permanent records—books, laws, traditions, customs—so that information can be passed between people who are distant from one another, in time or in space. Nonetheless, the dedication that drives the transmission of learned behaviors derives its energy from the emotions of the limbic system, including those related to play and parenting. Without relatedness to those of one's own species one fails to develop one's own potential specieshood. One remains an impoverished or deformed caricature of a human person, as is so tragically found in children who have been isolated and abused.

Playing into Community

Play has been observed in all mammals studied so far. Reptiles do not play, and what some observers have called "play" in birds is momentary. Play is prominent in the most intelligent mammals—"the primates, the Cetacea or whales and porpoises, and the terrestrial and aquatic carnivores." Playfulness and "the educative" go together.[25] Humans, however, may be the only species in which play continues into adulthood.

There may be several reasons why young animals play. First, they learn skills necessary for survival in adult life, for example, creeping up and pouncing, or climbing and leaping, or attacking and avoiding. Human children play with dolls or computers or build secret hideouts. Their "work" is to play. Play teaches basic skills of living as well as social expertise. Play may also help keep peace in the nest or family by channeling aggressive energy. In humans, play helps teach both children and adults how to "play by the rules."

Anthropologist Victor Turner and social psychologist Mihali Csikszent-mihalyi both point out the ties between creativity and play. Creative people—musicians, scientists, designers, for example—report that their creative activity often feels like "play"; "the activities are fun"; "the doing is enjoyed for its own sake."[26] In creative play people abandon the systematic, plodding, linear methods of task completion and lightly grasp thoughts from all levels of experience. Playfully, they recombine familiar elements in unfamiliar patterns they find pleasing. They may even evoke, in themselves or others, the transcendent recognition of the exactly right—the Aha! These creative processes draw on higher cerebral centers, to be sure, but they are clearly connected as well with "arousal and pleasure . . . where the limbic system is clearly engaged."[27]

Finally, play may build bonds of cohesion between animals in a pack or kids on the block or members of a golf club so that, if necessary, they may cooperate in other ways as well.[28] Such bonds are necessary for survival in many mammalian species, including humans. While some mammals are loners, many live in small groups or large herds for their entire lives. Such social organizations are beneficial to their members, even those who rank low in the "pecking order"—the established hierarchy of social privilege. Although there is competition within the clan, there are dangers outside it, and benefits to be found in banding together to mislead predators, build dams, burrow out underground tunnel systems, or attack prey. Without the mammalian herd or pack or family, the young would probably not survive.[29]

In fact, mammals as disparate as elephants and wolves and beavers and prairie dogs—and certainly most primates—cooperate in watching over and instructing the young of the "clan."[30] In many species, the young thus learn not only from their parents but from an "extended family." Human children learn from parents and playmates and baby-sitters and teachers and grandparents and neighbors. The mammalian brain codes not only for competition but even more for cooperation,[31] and cooperation is learned, to a significant extent, through play.

Nurturing for Survival

Care of the young by the mother is initially linked with the cry of infant and parent—the mammalian "separation call" or "separation cry."[32] Young mammals cry in distress when they become aware that their nurturing parent is not by their side, and sometimes they cry out in excitement when she reappears. Little kittens, absent the mother, quickly progress from squeaks to frantic calls, which rapidly subside to contented peeps when she returns to their side and they settle in for a meal. And why not? For the young mammal—whether mouse, bear cub, kitten, or human infant—the nurturing parent is the key to life itself. Without her, the baby simply dies. The parent uses the separation call as well; if a kitten is missing, the mother cat calls, searches, and listens for an answering cry.

Unlike reptiles, which lay multiple eggs and let the hatchlings take their chances, mammals have fewer young and provide them with more care. The trade-off is not merely one of quantity. A "growing sophistication in the care of the offspring" provides the young with apprenticeship in survival skills; "training periods" become lengthier as intelligence increases and survival strategies become more complicated.[33] For example,

> to become successful hunters, [young carnivores] must undergo a complicated process of learning, and this requires a prolonged period of association between parents and offspring.
>
> Of course, much of the behavior which leads to successful predation is instinctive, as anyone who has watched a month-old kitten stalking a piece of wind-blown paper will realize, but much more has to be learned by the parental precept, and this is where an extended apprenticeship is so valuable.[34]

In humans, the "apprentice period" goes on for years.

> The child, even in the most primitive societies, generally does not become truly independent of its parents until it is at least 12 years old. In . . . societies where elaborate cultural traditions have to be transmitted by a protracted process of education, this period is longer still, and the young human is generally not regarded as being fully emancipated until the age of 21.[35]

Today, for the first time in the eons of human history, most people live to be twenty-one, and more. In a great irony of progress, care for the young is becoming "too successful," and the relatively few children that humans can produce have become too many. The haunting prospect of overpopulation, impoverished resources, and anxious crowding of planet Earth suggest that another evolutionary scenario may be emerging, and a frightening one at that.

NEURONAL CONNECTIONS AND COMPLEX DEVELOPMENT

Human children have a long period of dependency, not only because they have a lot to learn, but also because their brains are unusually underdeveloped at birth. The physical process of brain development goes on for many years. For example, the corpus callosum—that band of nerves connecting the two hemispheres—does not fully mature until late childhood or the early teens.[36] Only then does a youngster become capable of abstract thought—what Jean Piaget (1896–1980) called formal operations in contrast to concrete operations. Many cultures recognize not only sexual maturity but also brain maturation through such initiatory rites as bar (bat) mitzvah[37] or confirmation[38] or believers' baptism.[39]

The "wiring" of the brain is based on cells called *neurons*, which send out axons—long fibers that carry signals to other cells—and also sprout the bushy structures, known as *dendrites,* that receive signals from other cells.[40] Some axons are "thousands of times as long as the cell bodies from which they spring, and some have to make right or left turns as they grow and find their appropriate targets."[41] Axons and dendrites meet at junctions called synapses, where signals cross from one to the other, mediated by chemicals called *neurotransmitters.* The synapses in an ordinary brain number in the billions.[42] Synaptic connections are "highly selective" and "the precision of neuronal circuitry can be accounted for only by chemical affinities between nerve terminals and their target cells," a hypothesis and discovery called chemoaffinity, which was developed by Roger Sperry prior to his breakthrough in split-brain research.[43]

Strange as it may seem, babies have many more neuronal connections in place at birth than they will have a few years later. But many of the hookups are essentially random and serve no identifiable purpose. Many of them wither away and disappear during the first couple of years of life. A good deal of research is being devoted currently to the question of why some thrive while others die. It seems that, in order to stay alive, neurons and their appendages may need to interface actively with other neurons, thereby receiving some kinds of chemical signals.[44]

Even in infancy, our brains apparently are hardwired for certain responses: many experiments have demonstrated that babies preferentially focus on the human face or even a sketch of the human face, rather than some other object, as we described in chapter 1. But many more circuits are required, and apparently they are "etched" in place through use. Which of these circuits develop, and how many of them there finally are, seems to depend to a great extent upon the stimuli the child gets—or doesn't get—from others. In other words, even for infant neuronal connections, the watchword may be "use it or lose it."

A classic study with laboratory rats is suggestive:

Mark R. Rosenzweig and his colleagues at the University of California, Berkeley, compared the brains of laboratory rats that had been raised in enriched environments with those of animals raised in standard cages. (The enriched environments contained a small community of animals, along with many toys and opportunities for exploration. [The impoverished environment was a small cage with only one other rat and a limited opportunity for exploration.]) They found many differences between the two groups of brains. . . . Animals from the enriched environment proved to have a thicker layer of gray matter than that found in deprived animals. The cells in the cortex also made more connections with other cells.[45]

Of course, psychologists and other observers have maintained for years that the first years of human life mold a personality in long-lasting ways. Current brain research seems to suggest how this process may take place. The baby's interactions with its world—with an "enriched" or "impoverished" environment, with welcoming or rejecting caretakers—may collaborate with the baby's genetic potential to tease out and link up the axons and dendrites, and so call a personality into being.

Object relations and self-psychology theorists, such as D. W. Winnicott and Heinz Kohut, have focused on similar processes in their discussions of personality development. Their theories are more psychodynamic than neurologic, but the two perspectives have interesting convergences. Kohut, for example, emphasizes that early development is enabled, first, by a process called "mirroring," and second, by association with a "self-object."[46] The process of mirroring is exemplified by the close, often joyful, "dance" of empathic interaction between mother and infant.

When the baby looks at the mother's face, "the baby . . . sees himself or herself. In other words, the world is looking at the baby, and *what she looks like is related to what she sees there.*" The mother's face mirrors the infant's aliveness, or lack thereof. In turn, that mirrors the aliveness, or lack thereof, of the world as the infant experiences it.[47]

In the light in her eyes, the baby sees confirmation of its worth, and, indeed, assurance of its very existence.

As time passes, the baby learns that gratification—which at first seemed to appear automatically, when needed—actually is supplied by the outer world. He or she reaches out toward that world to interact with it. But how to do that effectively? The best way to learn would be to observe those who already know how to do it—the caretakers. Around their personalities, the baby models its own personality. In a sense, it takes their personalities into itself. Thus, this *object* of interest, the other person, in effect becomes melded with the *self*, especially the part of the self that needs to learn about the world. Hence the term *self-object*. A good self-object becomes a framework around which an emerging personality can be built. Individuation comes later.

What happens to children who lack mirroring and positive self-objects because of an absence of empathy on the part of their caregivers? If the deprivation is extremely severe, they usually die in early childhood.[48] If they do manage to stay alive, they may hardly be recognizable as human.

> As an extreme instance, I recall with horror an 8-year-old girl who presumably had spent all of her life chained in a closet. She was about 2 feet tall and looked more like a monkey than a human being. She crouched and walked in an apelike manner. She had no capacity to speak; rather, she grunted like an animal and showed no emotions or affects that could be recognized at an interpersonal level. The only feeling observers could identify was anxiety, which occurred when she seemed to be confronting a situation that was too complex for her limited mentality, her initial reaction being confusion. This happened when someone tried to talk to her. . . . At most she seemed to be operating at a reflex level, with little mentation, but with some perceptual awareness. It would have been ludicrous to ascribe to her internalized regulatory psychic structures designed to obtain gratification and to relate to external objects beyond their caretaking potential.[49]

This account, of course, suggests that without nurture, without an empathic caregiver able to pick up and respond to the emotional needs of the other, the brain itself cannot develop, and the potential human being cannot become fully human. If this is true, then only through interaction and nurture—supplied by way of the parent's mammalian brain—can the infant brain develop the neuronal connections required to make a functioning self.[50]

A well-known series of experiments with rhesus monkeys supports this conclusion. At the University of Wisconsin Primate Laboratory, monkeys were raised in germ-free isolation so as to obtain disease-free animals for scientific experiments. It became apparent, however, that the animals' behavior was severely abnormal. "The laboratory-born monkeys sit in their cages and stare fixedly into space, circle their cages in a repetitive stereotyped manner and clasp their heads in their hands or arms and rock for long periods of time. They often develop compulsive habits, such as pinching precisely the same patch of skin on the chest between the same fingers hundreds of times a day." When caged with normal monkeys, the disturbed monkeys sat by themselves in a corner and refused to interact. No sexual behavior between male and female cagemates was ever observed, even when one partner was normal.[51]

In an effort to learn more about the origins of this behavior, the researchers, led by Harry F. Harlow and Margaret Kuenne Harlow, separated sixty-four baby monkeys from their mothers at birth and raised them in separate cages. Four had as a surrogate mother "a welded wire cylindrical form with the nipple of the feeding body protruding from its 'breast' and with a wooden head surmounting it." The other babies had "cozier surrogate mothers covered by terry cloth." In adulthood, the monkeys who had had terry cloth "mothers" remained emotionally attached to them, but none behaved normally, sexually or otherwise. Four females did become pregnant but refused to care for their babies.[52] Even though nourishment and contact comfort were provided,

> the surrogate cannot cradle the baby or communicate monkey sounds and gestures. It cannot punish for misbehavior or attempt to break the infant's bodily attachment before it becomes a fixation. The entire group of animals . . . must be written off as potential breeding-stock. Apparently their earlier social deprivation permanently impairs their ability to form effective relations with other monkeys.[53]

In nonhuman primates, a lack of parental care has disastrous consequences for personality formation. Recent research indicates that the problem lies in an actual deficit in midbrain development, caused by a lack of empathic interaction and physical stimulation.[54] The necessity of physical and emotional relatedness becomes even greater in humans than in other mammals.

NURTURING RELATEDNESS

Developmental psychiatrist Daniel N. Stern places this nurturing relatedness in a critical developmental sequence. During the first two months of life the newborn is mainly preoccupied with regulating and maintaining the basic physiological needs of sleep and hunger. After six months the infant begins to become fascinated with manipulating external objects. Between these two periods, roughly from two to six months, lies what Stern regards as "perhaps the most exclusively social period of life": "the social smile is in place, vocalizations directed at others have come in, mutual gaze is sought more avidly, predesigned preferences for the human face and voice are operating fully, and the infant undergoes that biobehavioral transformation resulting in a highly social partner." Only as physiological and affective equilibrium are established does the infant become "relatively more engaged with things than with people."[55]

On the infant's part, the relationship is at first one of dependency; the infant's vulnerable neediness is expressed in the cry of separation. Initially, the infant has no sense of the caregiver's needs and has only the most rudimentary sense of the caregiver's frame of mind. What the baby sees in the mother's face tells the baby who *he* or *she* is—precious, delightful, burdensome, or disgusting—not who the *mother* is.

A good caregiver, in contrast, does possess empathy—the ability to discern many of the needs and motivations of the baby (although what caregiver has not been baffled by the cries of an infant who is *not* wet, hungry, or startled!). The neocortex and especially the frontal lobes play a critical role in the development of empathy. (Significantly, goal setting and long-term planning for oneself and others are also associated with this part of the brain.) But human relatedness, based in the mammalian brain, is the wellspring of empathy. From an empathic caregiver, a baby learns the rudiments of empathy. When the caregiver smiles, the infant smiles too, in an intricate "dance" of interaction that melds the young human into the human community.

By the age of seven to nine months, human relatedness begins to move from purely emotional empathy to a more cognitively intersubjective process.[56] Together the caregiver and the care-eliciter deliberately seek to share experiences. Together they play patty-cake and manipulate toys.

Even without reliance upon language there are three mental states basic to an interpersonal reality: "sharing joint attention [through the gesture of pointing and following another's line of vision], sharing intentions [through gestures, postures, actions, and vocalizations prior to language], and sharing affective states [through looking towards mother to assess her affective appraisal and identify the match or mismatch with the child's own affective state]."[57]

Years ago, the British-American mathematician-philosopher Alfred North Whitehead crystallized empirical data such as Stern's. Whitehead insisted that "the basis of experience is emotional. . . . The basic fact is the rise of an affective tone originating from things whose relevance is given."[58] We spend much of our life's energy dealing with objects—cars and clothing, baseball gloves and baking pans. But the real significance of these objects to us is relational—they play a role in our relationships with other humans. As Whitehead observed, every object has "a 'relational essence.'"[59]

A THEOLOGICAL CORRELATE TO THE EMOTIONAL MIND

We have been contending that the structuring of reality as we know it reflects the reality of God. Here we are pointing to a God whose universality derives from the relationality manifest throughout the universe.[60] In particular, here we have been focusing on the relationality basic to the human brain. The limbic system, as the seat of emotions, supports this relationality. But as we have seen, without the interplay between child and caretaker, none of the brain seems to develop properly. Cognitive understanding, manipulation of objects, even bodily development—none proceeds properly without interaction with empathic others. Relatedness is a fundamental theme in all human experience. In neuroscience as well as other domains of science, reality increasingly is seen as radically interrelated, a product of continual, reciprocal interaction, among subatomic particles, molecules, cells, organisms—and so on to the cosmos.

These findings support a religious understanding that emphasizes what Whitehead identifies as "a profound sense of world-relatedness and world-loyalty."[61] In the same vein, philosopher Charles Hartshorne argues: "Human nature is the supreme instance of nature in general, as known to us (apart from the 'nature' of God himself), and . . . human nature is social through and through. . . . Now, further, not simply man, but all life whatsoever, has social structure. All organisms on the multicellular level are associations of cells. . . . Cells themselves are associations of similar molecules and atoms. It becomes a question of how broadly one wishes to use terms where one says that the social begins, if indeed it ever begins, in the ascending scale of emergence. And the higher one goes in the scale the more obviously do the social aspects assume a primary role."[62]

From here Hartshorne goes on to suggest that "the social structure is the ultimate structure of all existence." He found this most fully expressed in Whitehead's "supreme conception . . . [that existence is] a society of actual occasions, related one to another by the sympathetic bond of 'feeling of feeling.'" Furthermore, Hartshorne held "that deity is the supreme case of the social principle."[63]

His argument for a social view of God is related to the belief that

God orders the universe . . . by taking into his own life all the currents of feeling in existence. He is the most irresistible of influences precisely because he is himself the most open to influence. In the depths of their hearts all creatures (even those able to "rebel" against him) defer to God because they sense him as the one who alone is adequately moved by what moves them. He alone not only knows but feels (the only adequate knowledge, where feeling is concerned) how they feel.[64]

In a sense, then, the essence of the Deity, to Hartshorne, is reflected in the nurturant parent who helps to call our consciousness into being and, by interacting with our genetic endowment, helps to shape our self. However, only God is fully empathic. Only God is truly moved by what moves us.

Yet, this God is an *interactor*, not an "unmoved mover." This God, like the good caregiver, allows the individuality of humans to emerge freely:

[God] finds his own joy in sharing their lives, lived according to their free decisions, not fully anticipated by any detailed plan of his own. Yet the extent to which they can be permitted to work out their own plan depends on the extent to which they can echo or imitate on their own level the divine sensitiveness to the needs and precious freedom of all.[65]

Hartshorne, like others cited in this book, sees a "great drive toward a synthesis of freedom and order."[66] Order itself supports freedom. Our human bodies behave in orderly ways, by and large, so that we may have freedom to act.

As German theologian Karl Schmitz-Moormann points out,[67] a cancer cell multiplies "freely," unrestrained by the normal metabolic order. But it may eventually undermine the existence of its host, and hence of itself. Thus, we need a framework of orderly processes in the world if freedom is to thrive. But freedom and order always exist in tension. God provides order, but *invites* freedom.

Whitehead regarded the intuition that "the divine element in the world is to be conceived as a persuasive agency and not as a coercive agency" as "one of the greatest intellectual discoveries in the history of religion."[68] In parallel fashion, says he, the worth of individual persons depends, not upon their ability to coerce, but upon their ability to persuade and to be open to persuasion. Civilization itself, he insisted, maintains its social order "by its own inherent persuasiveness as embodying the nobler alternative" of the better over the worse.[69] In our own tradition, Christianity's example is one of transformation through complete, vulnerable interaction with the world.

The Mother, the Child, and the bare manger: the lowly man, homeless and self-forgetful, with his message of peace, love, and sympathy: the suffering, the agony, the tender words of life ebbed, the final despair: and the whole with the authority of supreme victory.[70]

The world and God are thus in continual process of interaction, and true interaction—in contrast with coercion—leads to bilateral change. God is affected by this world and affects the world.[71] Hartshorne believes that by "molding himself ... God molds us, by presenting at each moment a partly new ideal or order of preference which our unself-conscious awareness takes as object, and thus renders influential upon our entire activity." By changing God's self God brings about changes in us. We take our signals for this inspiring of us with novel situations "by seeing, that is, feeling, what God as of this moment" longs for.[72]

By holding together the empathic relatedness of the mammalian brain and emotional mind with the theological conviction of the ultimate reality and persuasive power of God, one is carrying out the task of theology as conceived of by Whitehead. That task is "to show how the World is founded on something beyond mere transient fact, and how it issues in something beyond the perishing of occasions."[73] God shares in the world's suffering as "the supreme instance of knowing, accepting, and transforming in love the suffering which arises in the world."

This, for Whitehead, is an affirmation of "the divine sensitivity." Without it, he could "make no sense of the being of God." For God is "the great companion, the fellow-sufferer, who understands."[74] God, in effect, is structured into the empathic processes of the limbic system and these processes, in turn, reflect the nature of ultimate reality.

The failure of human life comes with a shift from persuasion to coercion, from sensitivity to force. Wherever people have enjoyed power over others, including men over women, the result has been "fatal to the subtleties of life."[75] Resort to force and its resulting antagonism "bars cooperation. ... The Gospel of Force is incompatible with a social life."[76]

CONCLUSION

The old mammalian brain and emotional mind form a bridge between the reptilian instinctual brain or primal mind and the neocortical, rational mind. In a sense, then, the emotional mind holds together the powers of nature and the forces of culture. This emotional dimension embraces both our human relationships with each other and our cognitive construction of what matters to us. But, if our adaptation rests on emotional relatedness, it is guided by our meaning seeking.

Having explored empathic relatedness as a correlate of God as nurturer we turn in the next chapter to meaningful memory as another facet of the God who cares.

FIVE

THE LIMBIC SYSTEM, REMEMBERING, AND A MEANING-MAKING GOD

THE MAMMALIAN BRAIN IN MEMORY AND SELF-RELATEDNESS

E motion, sometimes demeaned as uncontrollable, is cognitive, motivational, and relational. As already noted, emotion is basic to survival and crucial in adaptation.[1] It depends on cortical functioning as well as subcortical processing. "Indeed, since emotional functioning is most developed in creatures like man and chimpanzees, less in dogs, and still less in chickens, it may even be that the neocortical part of the brain has been as crucial for emotional characteristics as for traditionally recognized sorts of perception, learning, and thinking."[2] Whereas empathy and relatedness express one facet of emotion, memory and meaning reveal another facet. Cognitive constructions of life are outward expressions of basic emotional reality.

This chapter explores more fully the meaning-seeking activity of the limbic system. This activity is anchored in memory, particularly autobiographical memory, and engages efforts, particularly through ritual, to reconcile cognitive discrepancies and dualisms.

MEMORY

In addition to the basic mammalian functions of survival, play, and nurture, emotion helps to determine what memory retains, particularly what is known as working (episodic) memory, which deals with the immediate past, or autobiographical memory, which provides a life story.[3] In general, researchers also distinguish between conscious memory, which is recoverable, and unconscious memory, which is implicit—for example, motor skills.[4] A strong emotional experience carves a deep track in memory's cave. Emotion-generated memory, thereby, results in unique, individually adaptive patterns.

In 1953 surgeons operated on a twenty-nine-year-old man with the initials H.M. in a final attempt to relieve the effects of severe epileptic seizures.[5] The procedure involved cutting some of the connecting neural pathways between the frontal lobes and the old mammalian brain, more particularly the amygdala and almost all of the hippocampus. Although the amygdala "plays as large a part in memory as the hippocampus,"[6] without the hippocampus, newly processed information is not "stored in an enduring and useful form."[7] The hippocampus serves both to consolidate *and* to construct memory.[8]

H.M.'s seizures stopped; so too did his memory. He continues to remember remote events, those up to three years before the operation. But his memories of events during the three years prior to the operation appear vague and unreliable. Since the operation, he remembers nothing. Even though he can learn new tasks—procedural memory—"he cannot remember new events."[9]

Other patients suffering from the disorder of amnesia show the same pattern. Cognitive functions such as attention, perception, and general intellectual ability are not affected. There is seldom a "discernible impairment of higher function except an inability to accomplish new learning and a loss of memory for some events that occurred prior to the onset of the disorder. Remote memory for distant events can also remain normal. In addition, the ability to reproduce information immediately after its presentation can remain normal, provided that the amount of information presented does not exceed immediate memory capacity."[10]

Meaning and the making of meaning depend intimately upon memory. "The term memory, and the still broader term neural plasticity, encompass an enormous variety of phenomena. Survival of species is obviously advantaged not only by the capacity for genetic variability but also by the capacity for adaptive accommodation to environmental change. This latter, nongenetic mode of change is ubiquitous in biological systems and arguably deserves the label memory when it can be shown to operate by integrating environmental information across time,"[11] but memory is not a single phenomenon or a single process.

Memory and Soul

It has been observed that the great hall of memory is the place where the soul or the self resides.[12] As Saint Augustine wrote:

Great is the power of memory, an awe-inspiring mystery, my God, a power of profound and infinite multiplicity! And this is mind, and this is I myself. What then, am I, my God? What is my nature? It is characterized by diversity, by life of many forms, utterly immeasurable. See the broad plains and caves and caverns of my memory. The varieties there cannot be counted, and are, beyond any reckoning, full of innumerable things. Some are there through images, as in the case of all physical objects, some by immediate presence like intellectual skills, some by indefinable notions or recorded impressions, as in the case of the mind's emotions, which the memory retains even when the mind is not experiencing them, although whatever is in the memory is in the mind. I run through all these things. I fly here and there, and penetrate their working as far as I can. But I never reach the end. So great is the power of memory, so great is the force of life in a human being whose life is mortal.[13]

The power of memory is the power of life itself, and the cave of memory is the lair of soul and the dwelling place of meaning.

Augustine described an intuitive awareness of the union of body and soul by saying that "the soul . . . is the life of the body."[14] In other words, soul has the power to affect and change bodily substance. It is simultaneously present in the whole body as well as in each of its parts.[15] While he thought of soul as lacking measurable dimensions, he believed it was located within the body.[16]

Augustine's understanding of soul is similar to what is being learned about memory. Memory, understanding, and willing come to mind apart from information from the outside. By the very act of understanding the experience of knowing, the mind knows itself. It is impossible to doubt that one lives, remembers, understands, wills, thinks, knows, and judges, he claimed. The mind's beholding itself is inherent in its very nature.[17]

For Augustine, the soul has been endowed with the ability "to be aware of intervals of time, and to measure them."[18] Therefore it must be both within time, in a chronological sense, and beyond time, in a gathering together of future and past into a present full of meaning. To have such a sense of time is simultaneously to stand above it and to shape it.

Human beings are made to seek a center of meaning and power inside themselves, that is, within yet beyond consciousness.[19] In light of current knowledge the idea of "beyond consciousness" seems linked to the rhythmicity of older brain activity.

Within consciousness, meaning involves memory. In the vast palaces of memory, to continue Augustine's imagery, people confront themselves with themselves: when, where, and what we have done and under what feeling and with what meaning.[20] Augustine believed the image of God resided not in the capacity for abstract thought[21] but rather in the capacity for self-knowledge and introspection. When people lack memory—as in amnesia or in not taking time to remember—then they have lost their soul. And in losing their soul they lose contact with the sacred, the depth of meaning itself.

Memory and Identity

In a real sense, those who lose their memory lose themselves, their soul, their uniqueness. Without a history there is no identity. With no record of loved persons or familiar places, the heart has no home. Whatever happens then is a random event, signifying nothing beyond its momentary impact on bodily comfort or emotional well-being. Without a memory there not only is no past, but there is also no future, or none that can be held in the conscious mind.[22]

Memory involves incorporating highly organized and emotionally significant information into a sense of the continuity of reality.[23] Based on experiments with rats comparing and contrasting different odors and reinforcement schedules, as well as generalizing from known to unfamiliar circumstances, researcher Howard Eichenbaum and his associates conclude that the hippocampus is critical to relational representations and is involved in organizing memories and supporting their flexible use in novel situations.[24]

What is novel and uncertain gets our attention. Thus—with the amygdala serving the "gatekeeping function" of "selective attention" between our senses and our emotions[25]—the brain selects information, sorts it, filters it, takes it in according to whether it is interesting and pleasurable or dangerous and painful, to be approached or to be avoided. But unless the hippocampus computes that information it cannot be "stored in an enduring and useful form."[26]

Kinds of Memory

Memory is divided into two types:[27] declarative memory, which includes "what can be declared or brought to mind as a proposition or an image," and procedural memory, which includes various skills such as catching a ball, playing the piano, and other activities "improved by experience." These two types differ in the kind of information stored, how that information is used, and which neural systems are involved. Declarative memory is more cognitive and capable of one-trial learning, whereas procedural memory is more automatic and adapted to learning in small increments over time.[28]

Declarative memory involves both a short-term and a long-term stage.[29] In addition it is subdivided into episodic or working memory and semantic or reference memory.[30] Working memory involves the specific personal context, while reference memory ignores the context in that it emphasizes information that applies to many similar instances.

Meaning seeking involves working memory. This memory refers exclusively to "acts of remembering that are specifically autobiographical" and ordinarily permit "a sense of personal connection" to what we are part of.[31] Our view of what has gone on is more constructed than photographic. This is an inside process that organizes and interprets outside information.[32] Here is found memory for past events, events that are "specific and personally experienced."[33] By storing and retrieving the cumulated events of a lifetime, a person develops an individual history, a unique self-repeating style, and stories that contribute to the emergence of models of self-world interactions. Here are the continuities—yes, the essence and soul—of who you and I experience ourselves to be. Without working memory people lack soul. They become soul-less, although not valueless. Experience with a loved one suffering from Alzheimer's disease conveys the poignancy of such a condition.

"What" a person remembers may not be accurate historically. Instead, it will be "narrative truth,"[34] truth that accurately reflects "some overall characteristic of the situation."[35] Knowledge of oneself appears to be a "by-product" of ordinary everyday memories. These recollections provide life themes and a sense of self.[36] A sense of coherence[37] and cohesiveness[38] is the result of knowing one's own life stories. Other people have access to these memories only to the degree they share one's own experience of the world. Events that may seem isolated to them make sense for oneself "only because [these events] fit into a broader framework of self-knowledge."[39] But our process of knitting it together will, to a greater or lesser extent, be influenced by the larger historical context in which our particular life story has taken place. Our understanding of ourselves is affected by society's understanding of itself.

Without working memory nothing is personally meaningful. Without that which is personally meaningful no one can have a unique identity. Without connecting present and past there is no sense of continuity. Without a sense of continuity we humans lack a sense of self.[40] In truth we lose our soul—that basic structuring of our unique essence in a supporting context.

Working memory and its consolidation[41] appear to constitute the core or essence of a functioning human being. Memory consolidation takes place "during memory retrieval as well as memory storage; that is, consolidation takes place when output is required in the same way as when input was established."[42] Without the capacity for long-term memory one exists in the hell of an eternal present, a present without a future because it is a present without a recoverable meaning-making past.[43]

Memory, Soul-Making, and Biorhythms

The physiological correlates of meaningful memory as the core of our experienced self seem to be found in the three mind states of waking, sleeping, and dreaming—the biorhythms that govern the state of consciousness.

In 1957 researchers William Dement and Nathaniel Kleitman reported a 90- to 120-minute rhythm, continuing around the clock, which they called the "basic rest-activity cycle" (the BRAC hypothesis).[44] During the day's ultradian cycle there is an alternation between a 90- to 100-minute period of optimal attention and activity and a 20- to 30-minute period of withdrawal and rest. This withdrawal from active engagement in the outside world seems necessary for assimilation of what one has been doing and resiliency to reengage. Psychobiological researcher Ernest Rossi focuses on "the 20-minute break" as crucial for reducing stress, maximizing performance, and improving health and emotional well-being.[45]

A nighttime circadian rhythm of deep sleep and dream sleep parallels this waking rhythm.[46] People alternate between about 90 minutes of mostly nondreaming sleep (non-REM)[47] and 20 to 30 minutes of rapid-eye-movement sleep (REM).[48] Normally, people cycle through non-REM and REM stages about five times a night.[49] Evidence suggests that "delta [very slow brain waves] sleep is related to somatic recovery, while REM sleep has something to do with the recovery of higher mental functions. Blood flow measures support such a view. During delta sleep blood flow is directed mainly to the muscles [which are at rest], while cerebral arteries are constricted [with little activity, if any]. During REM sleep cerebral blood flow increases [with activity comparable to being awake], while blood flow to the large skeletal muscles is constricted [so there is little or no bodily movement]."[50]

Thus, deep sleep is followed by REM sleep, a meaning-making process in which the body is inhibited while the brain is active. It is hypothesized that this activation process is a synthesizing activity. Our human brain processes information basic both to "how" we are as a physical organism and to "who" we are as an intact mammal. The function of the dreaming state is not so much resting as reorganizing the meaning of what has been going on. J. Allan Hobson, professor of psychiatry at Harvard Medical School and director of the Laboratory of Neurophysiology of the Massachusetts Mental Health Center, has called this REM state "a *meaning-added process.*"[51]

By "meaning-added," Hobson refers to residue from our being awake together with persistent concerns cumulated over time (whether we are conscious of them or not). Residue from the day and concerns over time are transformed into enhanced information, that is, information weighted in the direction of what matters emotionally in our survival as psychophysical mammals. Who we are now, who we have been, and what will happen—these images of ourselves and our model of self-world interaction—converge. These form a narrative with persistent themes of our unique way of being in the world.[52]

REM sleep has been found in all mammals, appearing first *in utero*.[53] It is thought to prepare "the young organism to handle the enormous quantities of stimulation to which it is exposed during the early stages of growth."[54] The meaning of information depends on the accumulation and consolidation of input from the outer world and input generated by the inner world. In humans, lack of sleep, especially REM sleep, tends to result in disturbed behavior:[55] people become irritable, disoriented, anxious, uncertain. Extreme sleep deprivation can even make people forget who they are.

Apparently, REM-like mentation bridges the biological brain and the psychological mind. That combination of brain-mind activation and motor inhibition (in REM) couples sensory perception with emotional states "to establish memories and associations" that subsequently influence actions.[56] Under normal conditions life appears regulated by a typical pattern of acting and resting, with something like a REM-reorganizing process part of the cycle, both day and night.[57] Ashbrook calls this cycle *mini-Sabbath* because in it people gather up and reorganize their own mosaic of meaning.[58]

From a biblical-theological viewpoint, the phenomenon of Sabbath is the means of making meaning.[59] The two myths of Creation in Genesis provide a picture of the God-world interaction and the generating of emergent meaning. Genesis 1 sketches the glory of the natural world in all its goodness, and was written during the trauma of the Babylonian captivity. Genesis 2, in compensation for the arrogant unaccountability of the supposedly divinely ordained monarchy of its time, portrays the ambiguity of the sociohistorical order in all its anxiousness.[60]

Coming as it does, between the first group of commandments, which focuses on our relationship with God, and the last group, which deals with our relations to our neighbor, the commandment to remember the Sabbath day connects heaven and earth. In Exodus the commandment is linked with creation (Exodus 29:11), while in Deuteronomy it demonstrates Israel's being free to rest because it has been redeemed from bondage (Deuteronomy 5:12–15). The Sabbath reflects a periodic recognition of our natural, God-given context, that "superior system of reality" to which people must "adapt . . . or else cease to be," to use the language of theologian Ralph Wendell Burhoe.[61]

The Genesis account of the Sabbath seems strikingly similar in psychic meaning to the three states of waking, dreaming, and deep sleeping: the rapid-eye-movement process connects with the passage "God saw everything that he had made"; a sense of fulfillment that comes with the full dream experience reflects the passage that states "and indeed, it was very good"; the reference to God finishing "the work that he had done" furthers that sense of a reorganizing of the day's experience to bring about a sense of fulfillment; and God blessing the seventh day and hallowing it by resting "from all that he had done in creation" reflects a single-minded constancy that accompanies REM sleep (Genesis 1:31–2:3).

Here is the eternal cycle of creation and Sabbath, which is reflected in the rhythmic cycle of brain-mind states: work, rest, reorganization, integration. The coordinating center for these brain-mind states lies in the upper regions of the reptilian brain, with its instinctual mind; the reorganizing integration comes in the mammalian brain, with its emotional meaning-making mind. We humans have the old brain-mind in common with other vertebrates. It connects us with nature itself and, in faith, with God. The results of consciousness, which means cultural-historical activity, are taken in by the neocortex, the new brain. We humans are ever making sense of our senses by synthesizing and interpreting what they mean to us. In short, memory is adaptive to an ever changing scene. For life to be meaningful, people need to be able to remember. Without memory they are without meaning.

The making of meaning requires purposeful behavior, and purposive behavior is the result of a working memory. Consolidation "proceeds for a long time,"[62] more specifically "a period of 1–3" years.[63] To be retained, memories must be dreamed, and dreaming involves intense emotional appraisal over time.[64] Perhaps that is the neurobiological basis for the typical experience that it takes about three years to assimilate major changes in life—be they death, divorce, moves, failure, or success.

Imagining a future requires remembering a past. As one researcher says, "memory development is about the future, not the past."[65] Without a past there is no future, no sense of purpose, no awareness of anything as personally significant. It is only in retrospect, in remembrance, that one discovers and creates a universe full of meaning. A pattern of events comes as one sifts and sorts what happens, taking in that which matters to well-being and letting go of that which does not matter.[66]

Memory, therefore, is "a dynamic process." It changes over time. Consolidation involves reorganizing and assimilating pre-existing memories. And it is this synthesizing process that is affected by the ability to store in memory what goes on in daily life.[67]

The core of the biblical witness revolves around memory. "Remember" is the recurrent theme, from the Sabbath commandment (Exodus 20:8), to the escape from Egypt, to Jesus' "Do this in remembrance of me" (Luke 22:19; 1 Corinthians 11:24), to the Book of Revelation's injunction to have one's name "found [remembered] . . . in the book of life" (20:15). Imagining a future requires remembering a past; remembering a past creates a future.

We speculate that the limbic process of memory and meaning making may be the most identifiable, though not exclusive, locus of the core structure of self-world interaction. To use the philosophical language of Tillich, it is here, in the older brain, that "the infinite and finite interpenetrate."[68] It is here, in the older brain, that we humans become "at one with our own essence." It is here, in the older brain, that we take outer and inner stimuli, organizing and modifying them for optimal adaptation. This is an active process, one that includes the peripheral nervous system and subsymbolic processes as initiators and integrators of cortical and symbolic activity.

MEANING

The last chapter made an explicit connection between empathic relatedness and a relational view of God. This chapter proposes that memory and the making of memory comprise the process of soul making. Lack of memory or loss of memory undermines a sense of self and a capacity for a purposeful future, an openness to novelty and creativity, and to God's leading activity. The dimension of the sacred, the dimension of depth, is lost.

Transitional Objects, Transitional Space, and a Nurturing God[69]

Memory and empathic relatedness work together to provide the foundation upon which meaning seeking builds. The groundwork is laid—or left unlaid—in early childhood. As we saw in the previous chapter, the infant's sense of identity and worth takes root in the delight, acceptance, and responsiveness of caregivers. Neglect can kill the spirit and even the body. But imperfect care can actually help humans learn to deal with an imperfect world.

Fortunately, catastrophic neglect by caregivers is relatively rare, though much more prevalent than society has been wont to acknowledge. No one, however, gets the best of all possible caregiving. Caregivers have their own needs and responsibilities. They make mistakes, even falling far short of what British psychiatrist D. W. Winnicott called "good enough" parenting. Thus, every infant must face the absence and inadequacy of the caregiver and deal with the trauma of possible abandonment on the one hand or of invasive abuse on the other.

Most infants devise ways to comfort themselves. In fact, the ability or lack of ability to comfort oneself and/or to receive comfort from others is a diagnostic indicator of serious concern.[70] Winnicott identified the strategy of using what he called "transitional objects."[71] A transitional object may be as simple as a favorite blanket or a tape-recorded lullaby that substitutes for the mother in her absence.

Adults, too, need and use transitional objects. People continue to encounter disappointments. Others do not always do as they would like. Needs for connection and safety are frequently frustrated in a world not always organized around individual needs. As a means to deal with these problems, people construct a way of thinking that Winnicott called "transitional space," "an intermediate area of *experiencing* to which inner reality and external life both contribute . . . a resting place . . . in the perpetual human task of keeping inner and outer reality separate yet interrelated."[72] The transitional activities may be as simple as watching television, or as complex as composing a symphony. We all fill the uncomfortableness of the absent (m)other with relational objects and activities that hold us.

In short, the cry for connection becomes the cry of creation, the creation of a world of meaningful activity and symbolic significance. This creativity, founded on the infant's disillusionment, "is retained in the intense experiencing that belongs to the arts and to religion and to imaginative living, and to creative scientific work."[73] Emotional connection and symbolic comprehension are intertwined.

In a penultimate sense, creativity in all its forms—from architecture to painting to sculpting to cooking to weaving to parenting—represents such activity. In an ultimate sense, religion in all its forms—from Western trajectories of belief to Eastern trajectories of wisdom to African trajectories of the communal—reveals this meaning-making core of human experience.

Growth through the Life Cycle

Intellectual and emotional growth may thus continue throughout life. And recent research indicates that this growth may in fact be correlated with modifications in the organization of the brain. It is true that the number of neurons remains relatively stable after the age of two unless disease intervenes, in which case the number may decrease. However, the number and design of axons and dendrites attached to each neuron is *not* fixed, and it is the design of axons and dendrites that determines the actual abilities of the brain. Even though the number of neurons does not increase, the *weight* of the brain continues to grow for the first two decades of life. "Cell bodies undoubtedly expand in size, and dendrites both in length and number, to partially explain this weight gain."[74]

It appears likely that the potential for rearrangement of the dendrites—development of new connections and atrophy of old ones—continues for decades more. Consider that "a single neuron may be involved in thousands of synaptic connections. Meanwhile, it is estimated that there are over 15 billion neurons in the brain. Considering the number of connections possible for a single neuron, the number of possibilities for intercommunication among the 15 billion is truly awesome."[75]

Can the aging brain add connections or modify its neural networks? Much research is under way in regard to such questions. Brain researcher Marian C. Diamond, for example, repeated Rosenzweig's experiment, cited in the last chapter, regarding the effects of an enriched environment on the brains of rats—but this time, aged rats, not young ones, were the experimental subjects. In the old rats, like the young ones, an interesting life full of new experiences led to neurological elaboration. Her striking conclusion is that

> if properly maintained, supported and stimulated, the cortical nerve cell possesses a unique potential for adaptation at any age. The results . . . caution us against entering into inactive life styles that reduce the sensory stimuli reaching our brains, and they provide hope, if we continue to stimulate our brains, for healthy mental activity throughout a lifetime.[76]

In other words, people continue to deal with new situations throughout life, and may do so in creative ways that draw on their brain's continued plasticity. Intensely emotional experiences—traumatic stress, for example, but also psychotherapy and some kinds of religious experiences—may significantly modify personality. One may theorize that the personality changes are related to actual modifications in the limbic system, in response to the intense emotional stimuli. Even highly vulnerable children give evidence of "the self-righting tendencies within them that produce normal development under all but the most persistently adverse circumstances."[77]

Limits and Human Imagination

In the language of self psychology, one might say that such modifications are accomplished within transitional space. For, of course, transitional space is not just for babies. In a world that truly threatens danger at every turn—job loss, crop failure, physical or verbal violence, dread disease—humans old and young may feel as much at risk as the infant whose mother is nowhere to be seen. Humans inevitably face death—the ultimate separation—and they know that they face it.

Transitional activities, then, are not constructed solely because of the memory of childhood dangers, real or imagined. They are motivated, as well, by the inherent and unceasing risk found in even the most carefully regulated life. They are triggered by the unpredictable nature of experience, good or bad—including what theologian David Tracy has called the "'boundary' situations of guilt, anxiety, sickness, and the recognition of death as one's own destiny," and also by "'ecstatic experiences'—[peak experiences of] intense joy, love, reassurance, creation."[78] Transitional activities are nurtured by our human urge to grow, to become "more of a person," to make sense of our experience.

We humans are confronted, from infancy onward, with the limitations of our world to meet our needs for security and certainty. We are motivated, from infancy onward, by a memory full of life experiences and a transcending capacity to create objects-ideas-relationships-structures that not only hold us in the absence of the other but empower us to seek out and create enriching experiences.[79]

Transitional Space and the Religious Dimension

Creativity may produce specific solutions to specific problems, but broader outlooks and perspectives may also be fruits of maturity. These may often be described as "religious," defined broadly or narrowly.

Religious experience—except for the most rigidly prescribed rituals, the strictest ethics, or the most logical theology—takes place in transitional space. It often echoes the child's earliest transitional activities devised for comfort in a puzzling world. God the Father, or the Mother, or the Lover, or the Friend[80] could be seen as a substitute for the parent who turned out the lights and left us in the dark. God could be sensed in the friendly others who once made our world seem safe.

The fading of ego boundaries in the transcendence of mystical experience recalls the infant's feeling of merger with the parent. Modeling oneself after a saint or a hero or heroine of the faith has parallels to the child's modeling of the self-object, using the other to make up for what one lacks in oneself. The warmth of religious devotion, the strength derived from religious trust, confidence in what is to come—all are ways of establishing a "safe and secure" relationship, not simply with a parent, but with a world, a cosmos.

As the great old gospel hymn has it:

What have I to dread, what have I to fear, Leaning on the everlasting arms.
I have blessed peace with my Lord so near, Leaning on the everlasting arms.
Leaning, leaning, Safe and secure from all alarms;
Leaning, leaning, Leaning on the everlasting arms.

A God who is Father-Mother-Lover-Friend is an icon of a universe where humans do indeed belong. In a cosmos that seems both threatening and human-like, religion can provide an anchor to windward.

Such arguments may seem to demonstrate that religion is merely comforting illusion—or might one entertain the belief that humans *truly* are at home in the universe? To repeat theologian Philip Hefner's question, we might ask, "Can nature truly be our friend?"[81] This would mean that

> *the reality system of nature in which we live is itself an ambience in which we truly belong, an ambience that has brought us into being and that enables us to fulfill the purposes for which we were brought into being. The central reality that undergirds all of concrete experience and to which we continually seek to adapt is disposed toward us in ways that we can interpret as graciousness and beneficent support.* Nature conceived in these terms would qualify as friend to us.[82]

Certainly such a belief does not suggest that the hazards of life do not exist. As theologian Langdon Gilkey so poignantly asks, "How can nature be conceived of within the divine life, as a medium of love, as friend, when it finally destroys life, often with the infliction of great pain?"[83] "Such a theological interpretation," Hefner continues, "must face head on the excruciatingly difficult task of explaining how vulnerability and selection are to be brought *within* our understanding of nature's love and friendship rather than leaving them as external to theological understandings."

As we humans live in transitional spaces, our vulnerabilities are both outside in the world and nature and inside in the psyche and soul. In the daily task of addressing these vulnerabilities, we return to an insight of Tillich. For him, the "transitional space" is real, and it includes the real experience of a mysterious—but "grace-ful"—presence.

> Grace strikes us when we are in great pain and restlessness. It strikes us when we walk through the dark valley of a meaningless and empty life . . . when our disgust for our own being, our indifference, our weakness, our hostility, and our

lack of direction and composure have become intolerable to us. . . . Sometimes at that moment a wave of light breaks into our darkness, and it is as though a voice were saying, "You are accepted. *You are accepted*, accepted by that which is greater than you, and the name of which you do not know. Do not ask for the name now; perhaps you will find it later. . . . *Simply accept the fact that you are accepted!*" If that happens we experience grace. After such an experience we may not be better than before, and we may not believe more than before. But everything is transformed.[84]

The ambiguities of life will not go away. But religious understanding, attained in the transitional space, absorbed in a deep sense by the activity of the limbic system, can enable men and women to conduct their lives with meaning and dignity, that is, in the context of a gracious reality.

Ritual and the Transformation of Limits

Religious understanding must also involve analytic cognitive processes that most clearly mark human evolution.[85] These processes are apparent in all abstract thought and problem solving, and they are mainly located in the cerebral cortex, which we will discuss in the following chapters. In real life, abstract thought, emotion, and the messages of the reptilian brain are of course intermingled, and nowhere is this more the case than in religious understandings.

The religious dimension of transitional space may be expressed most fully in the myths about what matters most and the rituals that enable people to participate in that meaning-seeking activity. Anthropological psychiatrist Eugene d'Aquili describes the way that myth addresses life's ambiguities—as analyzed by the cognitive brain—and addresses ultimate concerns felt by the limbic system. Myth, for him, performs "*two distinct but related functions*. First, a myth presents a problem of ultimate concern to a society. This problem is always presented in antinomous form in the surface structure, that is, in terms of juxtaposed opposites such as life-death, good-evil, and heaven-hell. Second, once the existential problem is presented in the myth, it is solved by some resolution or unification of the seemingly irreconcilable opposites which constitute the problem . . . usually achieved by expressing the myth in the form of ceremonial ritual."[86] As we have seen, ritual brings in the reptilian brain as well.

Rhythmic repetition synchronizes affective, perceptual, cognitive, and motor processes within individuals—and among individuals participating in group rituals. People are "marching to the beat of the *same* drummer," to revise a saying of Thoreau. A level of arousal is generated "which is both pleasurable and reasonably uniform among the individuals so that necessary group action is facilitated."[87]

One result is that "*the cognitive assimilation of logically irreconcilable polar opposites presented in the myth structure*—such as god and human in a solar hero or a Christ figure—*represents a shift of predominating influence from the [left or] major hemisphere [and its observational analysis] to a predominating influence of the [right or] minor hemisphere* [with its participatory synthesis. This process] *allows the antinomies to be perceived as a cognitive unity*."[88] There is a cognitive *and* an affective shift from pieces and parts to a pattern and whole. Relatedness transforms and replaces fragmentation.

Biogeneticist Barbara Lex proposes an integrated-explanatory model of this ritual resolution of dualisms.[89] She marshals evidence to suggest that the duality of left brain–right brain activity is paralleled by the duality of autonomic sympathetic-parasympathetic activity. She does this by drawing upon W. R. Hess's model of an energy-expanding system and an energy-conserving system within the central nervous system, which operate in a complementary fashion.[90]

This model extends the sympathetic-parasympathetic peripheral nervous system to the central nervous system.[91] The relationship between the septum and the amygdala is like a claw (see figures 4.1 and 4.2). The septum, at the front end of the limbic arch and where the fingernails would be, facilitates accommodative activity; the amygdala, at the tail end of the arch, which would be the end of the thumb in the claw, facilitates assertive activity. The sympathetic processes of arousal project from the amygdala to the left hemisphere. The parasympathetic processes of relaxation project from the septum to the right hemisphere.

> The parasympathetic nervous system governs relaxation and the blurring of boundaries—that is, limits—even as the central nervous system maintains a homeostatic stability. Basic vegetative and equilibrium functions reduce the heart rate and blood pressure and increase estrogens and androgens. This system, thus, contributes to inactivity, "cooling down," and trance-like conditions.
>
> The sympathetic nervous system triggers tension and the enhancing of excitement—such as ecstasy—even as the central nervous system expands energy arousing responses. Arousal not only includes fight-flight responses but also raises heart rate and blood pressure and increases epinephrine and other stimulants. This system, thereby, contributes to "heightened activity and emotional responsiveness, suggesting . . . 'warming up' and 'getting high.'"[92]

When either system is hyperstimulated—resulting in either intense arousal or extreme decrease in arousal—there comes a "spillover" into the opposite system which, in turn, is then stimulated, resulting in the rhythmic activity of ritual, or in the quieting of meditation. People experience "positive, ineffable affect,"[93] a transcending and transforming sense of oneness that overcomes conceptual contrast and contradiction.

Transcendence and Human Destiny

In reflecting on his experience of himself, Augustine voiced the dilemma of people trying to understand human destiny in terms of consciousness alone: "I do not myself grasp all that I am. Thus the mind is too narrow to contain itself. But where can that part be which it does not contain?"[94]

The cognitive revolution is returning "mind" to an embodied place in people's understanding of themselves and how they function. No longer can we humans view ourselves—nor even other mammals—as passive objects, mechanical organisms, machines to be manipulated with no attention to the experiential and expressive reality that is expressed in and through the physical. People are discovering the crucial role the limbic system plays in that integrity. There is a bodily base in all that we feel and imagine—and about which we reason.[95] This includes our soul, our sense of destiny, our awareness of the sacred.

The cognitive revolution gives "human" meaning to the mind's biological origin, integrating nature and nurture, instinct and experience. As brain, the concept of mind gives *human* meaning to the evolutionary matrix out of which both itself and culture have emerged. Similarly, as brain, the concept of mind gives *human* meaning to the universe in which it finds itself. Thus, the human brain embodies the *human* meaning of divine purpose.

By understanding the older and newer brains as an integrating mind-and-heart-and-soul, one can approach the cognitive dimension of life as an emergent phenomenon of a basically expressive ordering in and through nature.[96] Mind comes out of nature and does not function apart from nature. Mind shapes the way people construe the physical world even as the physical world shapes mind. Mind creates human destiny even as our destiny comes in and through our mind. Through every cell of the body we all integrate our cultural contexts and our genetic inheritances into the living realities that we are.

At the loose interface between physical data and vivid personal experience— that nonphysical yet imaginable space that science interpreter Gordon Rattray Taylor defines as mind—there are clues to the human meaning of being in a physical universe.[97] Those clues consist of "such fancy trimmings as a sense of identity, a sense of humour or a sense of deity."[98] These trimmings reflect core features of the human brain: our identity as persons; our capacity for perspective through humor; and the nature of the contextual universe in which we locate ourselves, or what in religious language people call God.

Brain research is promoting an approach to reality more in terms of a subsymbolic paradigm than simply and simplistically a conscious symbolic paradigm. The approach gives greater weight to natural processes in meaning seeking than simply conceptual formulation.[99] With Thomas Aquinas one can say that God is the name by which to identify "the origin and goal of this inbuilt orientation" of ordering itself:[100] one is "directed to God as to an end that surpasses the grasp of [human] reason. . . . But the end must first be known by [those of us] who are to direct [our] thoughts and actions to the end" of perfected ordering.[101]

These natural processes operate at every level of brain organization, and by so doing they are identified as massively parallel and widely distributed in both what is represented and how it is organized.[102] These processes combine memory and novel associations of memories. This mind-ful brain makes humanity different from the analytic, rational left hemisphere and also from the integrative, holistic right hemisphere. People construct a world in terms of all of their experience—perceptual, rational, emotional, and subsymbolic. Human destiny includes and requires biological-genetic input and limbic integration of the emotional meanings of experience.

The concepts of mind and soul, expressing as they do the human destiny of uniquely human brains, direct attention to the organized regularities of the reptilian-mammalian levels, and equally toward the emergent aspects of human purposes. The roots of the mythic Tree of Life (Genesis 2:9a) go down into the genes—humanity's old brain heritage. Its branches—the neocortex of the mythic Tree of Knowledge (Genesis 2:9b)—stretch out into the ecosystem in which we all participate. Through all this processing God works, empowering our purposes, our values, our convictions, our commitments. Just as mind discloses the human significance of the brain, so mind points to what we understand as the intentionality of God.

The prophet Jeremiah expressed this inner link between God's purposes and humanity's understanding when he had Yahweh God say: "I will put my law within them, and I will write it on their hearts" (Jeremiah 31:33). In biblical psychology, the heart is the equivalent of what people today mean by personality, the seat of psychic life including emotions, intellect, volition, the moral life, *and* the point of contact with God.[103] In technical terms, theology and ontology are dependent on epistemology, and epistemology depends on the functioning of the brain. What people know (epistemology) is related to what is to be known (ontology) and how that matters (theology). What we can know about the nature of God, the nature of humanity, the nature of the universe, the nature of human destiny depends on how people know and how they process what they know.

When life is understood this way, transcendence of the human condition requires attention, not only to the new brain, with its prominence and domination, but to the old brain as well. Destiny lies in the recovery of relatedness to the whole of creation. Only as the symbolic paradigm arises from *and returns to* the subsymbolic, parallel, distributed paradigm of what is going on in the contextual universe, only thus do we human beings become the human creatures that we are and are meant to be. We are related to the universe at all levels of our being.

Despite the supposed conflict between the selfish genes of biological nature and the prosocial motivation of the human capacity for empathy and symbolization, evidence points increasingly toward a destiny in which humans are to be "in harmony with the universe."[104] Neurophysiologist Paul MacLean speculates about our place in the cosmos: "Human beings . . . are the only creatures known to shed tears with crying. Is it possible that the misting of the eyes so commonly experienced upon observing an altruistic act is in any way owing to a reciprocal innervation of mechanisms for parental rescue and for crying represented in the cingulate gyrus [of the limbic system]?"

MacLean goes on to point out that "human beings and their antecedents are the only creatures known to have used fire." Then he advances his own conviction about human destiny in the form of a question: "In the course of millions of years did there arise some connection between smoke and tears and activities surrounding fire, including ceremonies involved in disposing of departed loved ones?"[105]

EMPATHY, TEARS, AND TRANSCENDENCE

Tears and transcendence link us humans to an evolutionary adaptation that reveals both its origin and its destiny. Human beings are not simply here, physically, like the alligators or the fruit flies. Rather, we are here on earth, in this universe, in a way that calls forth our caring for one another—in death as well as in life.

This empathic caring marks the most striking change in evolutionary adaptation. Brain and family evolved together.[106] Empathic caring came with the long period of dependency necessary to get children to functioning adulthood.

With these unceasing demands and the rewards often unseen, early human-oids must have gone through radical old brain–new brain transformation to ensure survival of the species along with differentiation of the self. Smiles and soothing sounds between parent and offspring reinforced attachment behavior necessary for physical survival and emotional security on the one hand and activated exploratory activity in response to novelty on the other.[107]

The consequence was twofold: First, the child came to be regarded as part of oneself within the family. Second, the appearance of religion promoted a perception of the other[108]—non-kin, stranger, and even enemy—as neighbor to be loved as one loves oneself (Leviticus 19:18; Matthew 5:43, 19:19, 22:39; Mark 12:31; Luke 10:27; Romans 13:9; Galatians 5:14; James 2:8). Process thought points to this caring when it claims that "sympathy, 'feeling of feeling,' is an ultimate principle, applicable to deity and every other singular activity."[109]

Research psychologist George Wolf picks up that emphasis on altruistic empathy. He describes visiting a laboratory "in which the activities of individual neurons were being monitored by transducing [transforming and translating] the neural impulses to pulses of sound." In the midst of the "popping" sounds of the neural impulses, he heard what he describes as "a soft moan." The researcher told him that "it was the sound of a dying cell—a high frequency discharge as the cell's life ebbed away." Wolf claims that his "empathic interpretation" of that event could be taken as "an empirical-hypothesis," yet he himself believes that "the moan was an expression of a feeling that all sentient creatures share—it was a feeling of perishing."[110]

Perhaps in the end humans represent moral order in the mind because in the end we see so much order in nature: parts relating to other parts, each to another to make a whole. This idea of order is so stupendous that people develop symbols to describe it, symbols that continue for us—as they must have for our ancestors in the farthest reaches of time when they first formed words—to express and articulate the inexplicable. Thus, myth and ritual resolutions make sense of life.

A cell's soft moan as its life ebbs away, a mammal's cry in recognition of separation from nurturing care, human tears in the presence of death, religious testimony to a gracious God, theological expressions of transcendent purposes, values, and beliefs—each of these bridges the simply physical and the surely spiritual. In the language of evolutionary psychiatry, MacLean says what we are groping to say in the language of religion and theology: "Perhaps we can trace to this situation [of the separation call] the evolutionary roots of unity of the family, unity of the clan, unity of the larger societies, as well as the human philosophic yearning for an abstract kind of unity."[111]

That abstract philosophic unity is turning out to be a concrete unity—a oneness with the whole created order through every level of organization, from dust to breath to belief to dust—brain is being and being is brain. Or in the poetic words of Emily Dickinson: "The Brain is just the weight of God." The brain bears the glory of divine destiny. As we humans come to understand ourselves and our place in the world, we are understanding the relatedness of everything that is.

SIX

THE NEOCORTEX, ORGANIZING, AND A VERSATILE GOD

THE RIGHT AND LEFT BRAIN AND THE SEARCH FOR UNDERSTANDING

The human brain is the most complex, organizing, integrating, differentiating organ in the known universe. Nothing compares with its elegant structure and functioning, or even with its dysfunctions and deficiencies. In this book, we have been developing the assertion that the evolutionary emergence of the brain reflects—implicitly—the nature of the universe in which human beings find themselves. *The brain is as it is because the universe is as it is.* Call this conviction anthropomorphism, if you will. Nevertheless, humanity's cultural conditioning builds upon and enhances its foundational genetic heritage. The combination contributes to an understanding of the meaningful mystery of *what really matters.*

ORIENTING ISSUES

Brain Variability

From the outside the head is one. The term "the head," however, is misleading. The definite article implies a standard entity. More accurately, we ought to speak of "heads," for no two brains are alike. Extreme variations are found at both gross and microscopic levels. The twenty-three chromosomes of each human gamete alone generate some seventy million million variations. Differences in the relation between anatomical structures and biopsychological processes are infinite. However, recent technology in three-dimensional, interac-

tive computer graphics has identified localized areas where certain mental activities take place. These studies shed light on genetic design and the specific
history of experiences that interact to produce a uniquely individuated brain.[1]
Experience shapes each brain differently.

From inside the skull, the brain appears to be two, or double. The large
cerebral cortex is made up of halves, which is the basis for reference to "the
dual brain."[2] Analogous to the earth's hemispheres,[3] these halves are known as
"hemispheres." They are also analogues of the two main characteristics of God
in that the step-by-step analytic process of the interpreting (left, or major)
hemisphere can be discerned in God's redeeming power of straightening life
up, and the all-at-once, holistic process of the integrating (right, or minor)
hemisphere can be seen in the radiant goodness throughout all of God's creation.[4] Together, the two halves make a whole.

Freed from the skull, the brain is not particularly impressive (see figure 1.1).
It is the size of a cantaloupe and weighs about three and a half pounds. The
two hemispheres rest on the brain stem. Like a central switchboard the brain
stem coordinates incoming and outgoing messages. The lower stem, or hind
brain, deals primarily with motor movement, that is, outgoing messages. The
higher stem, or midbrain, is responsible primarily for sensory activity, that is,
incoming messages.[5] In chapter 3 we characterized that area as the responsive
brain, that which orients human beings to the environment so that they attend to what matters to them and their survival. In a somewhat simplified way
we can say that sensory input is "available" and motor output is "purposeful."

The stem seems to be capped by the corpus callosum, the fiber tract connecting the two hemispheres. Between the hemispheres and the brain stem lies
the paleomammalian brain, the clawlike structure that we have discussed in
the two previous chapters. Specifically, the limbic lobe occupies the medial
(inner) part of the hemispheres surrounding the brain stem.

Both these two older structures seem to play important roles in regulating
behavior that we humans share with other vertebrates. The limbic system provides the emotional "engine" that motivates our attachments and desires. That
is why it was characterized as the emotional brain and linked to God as nurturer
and the creator of what is meaningful. The reptilian brain systematically propels us toward behaviors that help preserve and perpetuate the species. These
behaviors include acquiring and defending a home territory, gathering food,
and finding a mate. These lower structures interact with the right and left hemispheres in a variety of ways. The result is a whole brain needed for all complex
activity.

Interdependent Feedback

In every generalization we make about how the brain works, the reader must take feedback into account. Feedback makes the brain and its workings incredibly complex.[6] What is known, despite its breadth and depth, continues to be imprecise. The brain's "transactional glory," as neuroscientist Robert B. Livingston put it, combines both stable features and novelty, both specific processes and nonspecific processes.[7] No description can capture what he calls "the majesty and transcendent beauty of sensory processing, perception, and behavior."[8] As neuroscientist Steven Rose claims, "*how* the modules [of the brain] are integrated so that each of us gets an apparently seamless conscious experience . . . is still *the* great question for everyone working at the interface of mind and brain."[9]

Such caution applies to this book's use of MacLean's concept of the triune brain. The distinction between sensory input and motor output oversimplifies brain activity. The two systems are intertwined functionally. One can only accurately speak of a system as "more sensory than motor" or "more motor than sensory."[10] The processes of alerting/attending and relating/remembering are not as sequential as they sound. Some information can bypass the frontal cortex completely even as it can bypass the primary motor cortex. The problem of explaining the integrating of perception persists.[11]

At the initial contact-recognition point between stimulus and reception and before actual activation of the receptor, the central nervous system is already anticipating and selecting input.[12] A central organization of data *exists prior to* even the simplest input. It may be that neural pathways laid down in the earliest period of life affect our "decisions" about what to notice and what to ignore. In any case, the information that comes in combines coding by the peripheral nervous system—a realistic *perception,* if you will—*and* integrating by the central nervous system—an imaginative or experiential *construction,* if you will. Data in the primary zones, consequently, are abstractions and not mere replications. Distortion, based on an emphasis of some features and a neglect of other features, affects the message and its meaning!

In general, the two older strata of the brain—the reptilian and mammalian regions—provide ways into the brain. At the same time the data are integrated and further classified. The latest stratum—the neocortex—synthesizes information in conscious ways. Because these zones recall or interpret the significance of information, they are known as "interpretive areas"[13] or, in older terminology, the association cortex. They convert input from the sensory systems into identifiable schemes capable of symbolic analysis. One may think of the separate streams of smelling, sensing, seeing, and hearing converging to form a mighty river of meaning seeking and meaning making. A "neutral" environment is thereby transformed into a "human" world.

Active Convergence

As implied, this convergence is an active, not a passive process. Neuroscientist V. B. Mountcastle investigated these "neural command functions for selective attention."[14] In an elegant study of a monkey's detection of change in light, he showed these cells to be insensitive to all sensory stimuli. Put more strongly, the interpretive cortex showed complete independence of auditory, visual, and somatic cueing input. This cortex assessed information from the outer world in terms of some indiscernible inner center. That autonomous center generates "directives for actions, commands that are general or holistic in nature and unconcerned with the details of execution." Because of this autonomy, Mountcastle called these centers "command neurons."

What is rudimentary in monkeys reaches its higher form in humans. The appearance of language produces new integrative regions. Each of us looks out on the world from a unique inner universe. Our own interpretive scheme integrates the continuous input, enabling us to orient ourselves and move around with intentionality. Somehow—through a "loosely linked" operation, as Mountcastle described it—an independent command center, sensitive to inner drives, governs what each of us does "within that intensely personal space."

The interpretive areas suggest the presence of something like what is known as "will," intentionality, the cognitive integration that transcends the summation of environmental input. It is the top-down dimension of higher-level causality described by Sperry,[15] which will be examined more fully in the next chapter in understanding the cognitive brain as a correlate of understanding God as purposeful.

In early development, these functional zones come "on line" sequentially. The simpler areas are the first to become active; the more interactive areas are the last to function fully.[16] Those that combine input from many sources depend on contact with the environment in order to code and store stimuli.

A consequence of such processing is that the brain lives in a reality of its own construction. Through its perceptual systems it builds up "maps" of the way the world is. These maps are limited "images" of the territory, never the actual territory itself. Since we each live in worlds of our own making, we never rid ourselves of "perceptual commitments." These commitments are the result of genetic endowment, past experience, anticipation, and individually determined purposes. There is "no lens-free system of viewing the world."[17]

THE DUAL BRAIN

We have already alluded to the dual brain, to the right and left hemispheres and their particular contribution to the mind and its working, in chapter 1. We now return to these capacities, exploring them and their implications for understanding God's ways of being God.

Unequal Halves

Animal brains are basically symmetrical.[18] Each half is virtually the same and functions in the same way. While our human brain looks symmetrical to a casual observer, it is actually asymmetrical. Each half—in both subtle and broad ways[19]—is different enough to make a major difference in what people know and how they know it.[20] Since the mid-nineteenth century, scientists have suspected that the two sides play different roles in all sensory, perceptual, and motor activities.[21]

Neuroscientists Norman Geschwind and Walter Levitsky examined 100 brains to disprove the mirrorlike sameness of the hemispheres.[22] Strikingly, as shown in figure 6.1, the left auditory plane was larger in about 64 percent of the cases, the right was larger in about 10 percent of the cases, and the planes were equal in about 26 percent of the cases. Researchers report similar differences in the brains of thirty-one-week-old fetuses as well as in newborns.[23] Every culture and every historical period has shown a consistent right-hand preference, indicative of hemisphere contrast.[24] A preference for the right side appeared in nature long before its appearance in *Homo sapiens*.[25] However, only in humans does preference for the right side approach about 90 percent of the total population. In other animal species there tends to be a fifty-fifty split, half preferring the right side and half the left even though particular animals show a paw preference.

Why emphasize unequal halves?

The left half is associated with the ability to understand speech and mathematical calculations. The right half specializes in spatial relations and the perception of distance. From such asymmetry come verbal and mathematical "languages," with all the technological and cultural accumulation resulting from that symbolic capacity.[26] Brain asymmetry also provides the human abil-

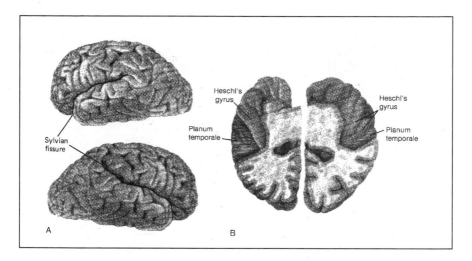

Figure 6.1——Anatomical differences between the hemispheres visible in the temporal lobes. In (A), the Sylvian fissure on the left (top) has a gentler slope than the fissure on the right. In (B), a knife has been moved along the Sylvian fissure of each hemisphere and through the brain, cutting away the top portion. The planum temporale (darkened area) is larger on the left than on the right. (B after Geschwind 1972). *From* Fundamentals of Human Neuropsychology. © *1985 by W. H. Freeman and Company. Used with permission.*

ity to synthesize and to think holistically. Almost every issue of the brain and its mind, of consciousness and cosmos, surrounds the evidence of unequal halves.

UNCOMMITTED CORTEX

To understand our "human" world—that is, language, tools, and symbolic behavior—one must look at the development of the cerebral cortex. What is distinctive about each hemisphere? The answer is crucial.

We are born with more undeveloped brain than other animals. Neurosurgeon Wilder Penfield called this "uncommitted cortex" (see figure 6.2).[27] This undeveloped brain has fewer cells with built-in instinctual patterns. This makes our brain highly flexible. Any number of cells can engage in somatic, sensory, olfactory, visual, auditory, motor, *and* cognitive activity.[28] The more complex the task, the more cells potentially can carry on if needed. This flexibility is known as "organic plasticity."

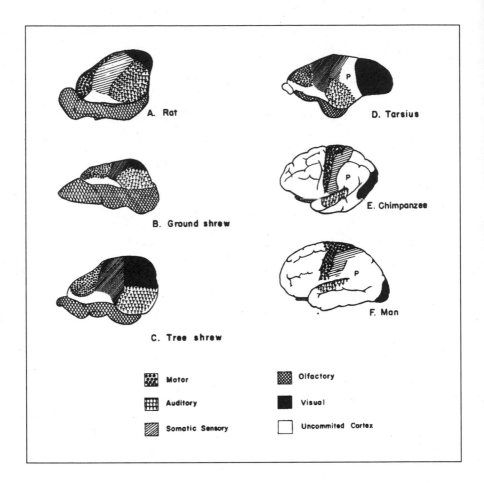

Figure 6.2——Uncommitted cortex. Functional diagrams of the cerebral cortex of some mammals. The blank areas suggest the approximate extent of gray matter that is not committed to motor or sensory function at birth. In humans, for example, the auditory sensory-cortex has really been crowded off the external surface of the brain into the fissure of Sylvus. For this figure, Penfield was indebted to Stanley Cobb. *From Wilder Penfield,* The Mystery of Mind. *Copyright © 1975 by Princeton University Press. Reprinted by permission of Princeton University Press.*

The brain uses its plasticity to fulfill its priorities. If a child is born without a left hemisphere, or if a young child's left hemisphere is damaged in some way, the uncommitted cells in the right hemisphere take up the task of language and sequential processing.[29] In other words, propositional needs—the capacity to symbolize—make first claim on cortical specialization. Priority goes to symbolic expressive activity.[30] Here may be seen a tangible expression of the prologue of Saint John's Gospel and the first chapter of Genesis: in the beginning is Word, an ordering process of reality!

After Word appears, other activities follow. In particular, those contribute to "habitual" patterns of integrating experience and forming intentions; most uncommitted cortex lies in the regulatory and integrative areas, which are central to these functions. With experience over time, the uncommitted becomes committed.

Since the entire cortex is involved, the difference between the two halves is called, in technical terms, hemispherc lateralization. Instead of duplicating what each other does, the two halves divide the work.[31] In a simplified generalization, one can say that the left hemisphere leads in step-by-step processing; the right in all-at-once processing.[32] But, while each side of the cortex takes the lead in different functions, neither exercises those functions alone. Each carries secondary and supportive capacities. And, as we have seen, if one hemisphere is impaired, the other compensates for the deficiency, particularly if the impairment occurs early in life. Although the two hemispheres differ significantly in functions, "there appears to be no structure or chemical constituent that is present in one hemisphere but not in the other."[33] The brain and its mind form a uniquely flexible instrument.

COLLABORATION AND THE CORPUS CALLOSUM

Information passes back and forth between the two halves via the corpus callosum. We have already sketched something of the function of the callosum in chapter 1 in the experience of the split-brain patient named Paul seeing the chicken claw and snow scene. Here we say more about its importance.

Before the 1960s scientists tended to regard the corpus callosum as of little importance to brain activity. Even the great brain researcher Karl Lashley thought it served as little more than a structure to keep the two hemispheres from sagging.[34] However, in 1961 a medical team cut the corpus callosum of a forty-eight-year-old veteran who suffered from terrible epileptic seizures.[35] Epilepsy results from "electrical thunderstorms" of brain waves that sweep across this great neural pathway.[36] Theory suggested that cutting the fibers would stop the spread of the waves.

No one thought there would be side effects: patients would simply be free from seizures. That was not the first such operation.[37] However, that 1961 operation marks the occasion when scientists finally recognized the deficits that resulted from separating the two hemispheres. The patient's seizures stopped; his well-being improved; but researchers began to note subtle changes in his behavior.

For instance: he favored the right side of his body; the left side showed little spontaneity. While denying that he saw a light in his left visual field, he could still point to it (remember split-brain patient Paul). Though unable to describe an object in his left hand, he could still match it with a similar object selected from an array of objects. He could spell words like "cup" or "love" with his left hand even though he could not say the word he had spelled. Intriguingly, when his left hemisphere was doing something "wrong," the right hemisphere protested with a frown or a gesture. It was as though the right hemisphere were monitoring the behavior of the left hemisphere.

Clearly, each side functioned differently. Researchers called this split-brain phenomenon "the syndrome of hemisphere disconnection."[38] The syndrome refers to a doubling of consciousness: two visual systems; two sensory systems; two memory systems; two independent streams of consciousness. Even as there are two mentalities at the subcortical levels of the R-complex and the limbic system, so there are two mentalities at the cortical level of consciousness in the two hemispheres. Suddenly, the behavioral inadequacies of split-brain patients were obvious.[39] These people suffered from marked deficits in short-term memory, problems in orientation, and fatigue from mental concentration. Most striking of all, even though the right hemisphere could not speak, *it could perform.* The silent hemisphere had a mind of its own!

As infants grow, each hemisphere lets go of doing "everything" in order to take charge of particular processing.[40] Division of labor replaces duplication of effort. The brains of other mammals are characterized primarily by duplication of effort. Both sides perform the same functions. Neither side specializes in "doing its own thing." Only in the human brain does the left specialize in the analytical and the right in the holistic. Only in the human brain is cross-talk necessary to keep one half from interfering with what the other half is doing.

Even so, neither hemisphere carries the whole of consciousness. Each side plays its part. As psychologist Donald E. Broadbent pointed out, "The two hemispheres must be seen . . . as performing different parts of an integrated performance, rather than completely separate and parallel functions."[41] The corpus callosum orchestrates the input of each half. This results in collaboration between the two sides of the brain and in the experience of a single and unified consciousness.[42]

> The right hemisphere cannot say what it knows, yet because
> of it we know much more than we can say.
>   The left hemisphere can only say what it conceives, so because of it we talk
> about much less than we experience.

After years of taking the brain apart, analyzing and conceptualizing the pieces as separate processing systems, researchers are putting "the brain back together again." The unified processing emerges from "a variety of processing sub-systems."[43] "Hemispheric asymmetries are rarely . . . the all-or-none type." There is "virtually no evidence for [the] strong distinction between 'left-brained' and 'right-brained' people." However, "there is some indication that some individuals do, in fact, differ on their relative performance on tasks that are known to be associated with left- versus right-hemisphere injury. There is also evidence of individual variations in characteristic arousal asymmetry and in an individual's propensity to use a mode of processing associated with one hemisphere or the other when given a choice."[44]

In discussing "the duality of the brain," the great English neurologist J. Hughlings Jackson (1835–1911) referred to the tendency for speech to go to the left half and vision to the right half.[45] He used the term "leading." The left took the "lead" in activity related to language; the right took the "lead" in activity related to vision. Because the left is the area for speech, scientists have called it the "major" or "dominant" hemisphere. Because the right was little understood, scientists regarded it as "minor" or "nondominant."[46]

In 1861, physician Paul Broca provided the first scientific evidence for the localization of language in the left hemisphere. Under his influence, "asymmetry not only became a distinguishing mark of humanity in general, but a means of distinguishing the 'better' vintage lineages of humankind from the standard."[47] Scientists affirmed the left side as "human" and intelligible and the right as speechless and "animalistic." They went further and associated the emotional, the organic/nutritional, psychopathological madness, and female inferiority with the right hemisphere[48] Such thinking reinforced the tradition of classifying divine and human activities as "dual"—the good right hand and the bad left hand.[49] By contrast, Jackson's term "leading" avoids the value judgments implied in words like "major" or "dominant."

Uncommitted cortex in both hemispheres is capable of taking on the function of "leading," whether linguistic and step-by-step or perceptual and all-at-once. A bias toward one kind of organizing does not preclude the development of other organizing—if the situation requires it[50]—especially in those under ten years of age. Not only do the halves contribute to each other via the corpus callosum, but they also carry secondary capacities that develop when the other side does not work. The brain exhibits great overlap of functions, which is the basis of its versatility.

We need to say more about the distinguishable aspects of the two hemispheres and the two ways of organizing experience.

HEMISPHERE DIFFERENCES

Distinctions between the way the left brain works and the right brain works have already been mentioned. Here these organizing predispositions are described more fully.

Left Hemisphere

The left half of the cerebral cortex controls the right half of the body; just as importantly, it handles input and output analytically,[51] item-by-item and step-by-step. Language-related factors significantly contribute to this strategy.[52] Experiences are "named" and thereby "interpreted."[53] Verbal labels distinguish, for instance, a pair of scissors from a pair of glasses.[54] The story of Adam naming the animals in the Garden dramatizes this power of language (Genesis 2:19). People further keep a fix on reality by counting and numbering, which are also left-brain activities.

However, mental processing also goes on apart from verbal and numerical activity. For instance, when neurosurgeon Wilder Penfield temporarily blocked the speech area in a patient by electrically stimulating the cortex, the patient reported a continuing perception of the reality underlying the verbal.[55] When shown a picture of a butterfly, he knew it but could not name it. Later he remarked, "I couldn't *get* that word 'butterfly,' so I tried to *get* the word 'moth'!" Here, apparently, is a stream of consciousness that watches and directs behavior even though the individual cannot tell about it at the time. Verbal labeling involves an ability to conceptualize abstractly. Clearly there is thought apart from language.[56]

Verbs, plurals, vowels, and speech qualifiers dominate linguistic activity.[57] These grammatical features add precision to what is thought as well as to what is said or written. "To know a verb is to know a generalization." Whereas the noun *apple* means an apple, "the verb *pour* can be used in hundreds of contexts."[58] The left brain identifies all linguistic material—such as digits, consonants, and words—more rapidly than the right brain. In contrast, the right brain transfers all incoming linguistic data to the left to process.

Even though chimpanzees give evidence of tool use, sophisticated technology requires verbal and numerical "language." Despite its oversimplification, there is truth in Tillich's assertion that language and technology go together.[59] Distinctions enable a person to manipulate both objects and ideas. We accentuate differences and minimize similarities, so as to clarify thinking. As novelty recedes, a stabilized order results. Perhaps the rewards of clarity and stability contribute to many religions' emphasis upon doing what is "clearly right."

The left brain is superior to the right in recording simple sequences.[60] It refines more precisely than the right information about what the hands touch. And complex activity requires knowledge about *what* and *where* an object is.

The left brain, as noted several times, comes at the world as an observer.[61] It stands apart from the data and thus creates a seemingly objective point of view. People call such objectivity "perspective." The ability to name and speak intentionally contributes to a sense of reality as a *conscious* fact.[62]

Recognizing the familiar provides a sense of "having been there." Without that memory, which creates a sense of history, nothing would stay put. Everything would be strange, foreign, unfamiliar, all the time. It is the organizing activity of the left hemisphere that creates that sense of inner stability.[63] Each thing has a name; every object has a place; nothing remains random.

This analytic process of step-by-step gives humans freedom from the rule of immediate stimuli.[64] They can step back, take a long view, find basic principles, and thereby figure out sequences of ideas and actions. At its most abstract level, analysis is thinking about thinking. People can imagine infinite possibilities. Even more, they can theorize, that is, develop rational procedures that depend on assumptions, limitations, hypotheses, and experiments. In the rational scientific mode they can state implications and applications with precision. In the religious experiential mode they can build upon abiding principles.

Evidence has shown that the left hemisphere specializes by directing attention, selecting reactions, designing behavior, and imagining alternatives. When the left hemisphere is impaired, mental activity disintegrates in such a way that associations break down, sequences crumble, and random reactions appear. Unable to point deliberately, a patient gestures haphazardly. In other words, the left brain facilitates the ability to be oriented, to focus on an object or task, and to act purposefully.

Thus, the cognitive style of the left brain is *deliberate*.[65] It is particularly skilled in generating the rapidly changing motor movements crucial for the mastery of the vocal tract during speech and of the hands during manual activity.[66] By responding in an orderly fashion, it can concentrate on what it regards as correct or appropriate.[67] Its ideas have created *and* preserved an orderly world.

The Right Hemisphere

What can be said of the way the right hemisphere works is less certain. Because a stroke affecting the right side of the body often leads to loss of speech, brain researchers initially thought of the left brain as the major or dominant half of the cortex. Only language mattered. People needed their left half because it spoke. It gave logic, boundaries, sequences.

Looking back across a century and a half, one can see the illogic of the "logic" that labels one hemisphere "major" and the other "minor." It seems reasonable to assume that an asymmetrical brain would have special features in each half. However, prior to the split-brain operations, few people thought so. The right half was "inferior" because it lacked the ability to speak.[68]

Nineteenth-century British neurologist J. Hughlings Jackson thought differently. He located voluntary speech "chiefly" in the left front region, as did Paul Broca. He said "chiefly" because he did "not believe in abrupt geographical localizations." He went on to propose the back part of the right hemisphere as "the chief seat of the revival of images." The right half's "emotional language" of images paralleled, for him, the left half's "expressive language" of speech. He was "convinced" that "the greater part of our intellectual operations is carried on in images-in-eye-derived . . . processes."[69] That was a startling claim: the right half was not only *not* minor; it was "major."

The right hemisphere processes input relationally and simultaneously, that is, all-at-once and by leaps of imagination. Multisensory combinations contribute to the strategy. Visceral and emotional experiences lie behind and underneath verbal expression. Sensing, seeing, and hearing are direct; there is no mediation by language. Eyes, ears, hands, nose, tongue, skin, joints, muscles combine to let people know where they are. These pieces of data form mosaic patterns.[70]

The right hemisphere responds rapidly to what it experiences from the inside.[71] It produces a sense of immersion in a pulsating environment. Time rushes or drags; space expands or contracts. Little remains fixed. Impressions are immediate; expressions are heightened; emotional richness is greater; passion is more intense.

The whole impression is more than the sum of the separate senses.[72] Boundaries blur; differences recede; commonalities emerge. Perceptual wholes generate a stereophonic and kaleidoscope mix of ever fresh impressions. The recognition of images is impressionistic.

Environmental immediacy involves spatial skill. The right hemisphere specializes in such skill.[73] This includes kinetic imagery such as discriminations about direction (up/down, left/right, in/out) and identifying objects from different angles. Investigations of visual-spatial skills have tested recall and detection of shapes, mental rotation, other geometrical and mathematical skills, and a sense of direction. Direction-skills tests include mazes depending on touch, pattern walking, map reading, left-right discriminations, aiming and tracking, and geographical knowledge.[74] Auditory skills also include spatial features, including the ability to track the position of the source of a sound. Musical compositions have spatial-like structure (high and low notes, note against note, melody against melody).[75]

Evidence such as this suggests that the right hemisphere is a concrete synthesizer.[76] It sees, senses, and hears more than the left hemisphere. Usually, it takes the lead in integrating the broad features of situations.[77]

Apparently, many scientific discoveries are initially apprehended in right-brain fashion. A familiar example is the discovery of the chemical structure of the benzene ring, which came to Friedrich August Kekulé in a dream of a Uroboros—a snake with its tail in its mouth. The great English physicist Paul Dirac, one of the founders of quantum physics, described his own discoveries as arriving spontaneously, as gifts he had done nothing to deserve. Their form was holistic and quasi pictorial. Only later did he "translate" them into the sequential language of mathematics.[78]

In fact, in many creative lines of endeavor, the right and left hemispheres may collaborate to envision the whole and then translate the holistic insight into logical language. Conversely, prior logical learning is often a necessary precondition to the arrival of the holistic vision.

Collaboration

In characterizing the ways the two hemispheres work, the line between solid evidence and suggestive speculation is fuzzy. Psychologist Sally P. Springer and neurologist Georg Deutsch have provided a comprehensive survey and evaluation of current research on hemispheric differences,[79] as have neuropsychologists Joseph B. Hellige[80] and Robert J. Davidson and Richard Hugdahl,[81] among others.

From the wide range of characteristics ascribed to each hemisphere Springer and Deutsch derived five primary groups (table 6.1). These groupings form "a kind of hierarchy," with each including and going beyond the characteristics listed above it.[82] Experimental evidence is strongest for those features at the top of the list, that is, verbal functioning for the left half and nonverbal, visuo-spatial functioning for the right half. This distinction was the earliest to arise from split-brain research, though the processing styles of sequential and simultaneous, while lacking universal acceptance, have emerged as close to the actual data.

Table 6.1——Characteristics Ascribed to Each Hemisphere

Left Hemisphere	*Right Hemisphere*
Verbal	Nonverbal, visuo-spatial
Sequential, temporal, digital	Simultaneous, spatial, analogical
Logical, analytical	Gestalt, synthetic
Rational	Intuitive
Western thought	Eastern thought

Based on Springer and Deutsch [1981] 1989.

THE NEOCORTEX AND THE MEANING-SEEKING BRAIN

These empirical data from the neurosciences have strong implications for an understanding of religion as a meaning-seeking and meaning-making activity.[83]

In his popular book *The Psychology of Consciousness*, Robert E. Ornstein identified and synthesized the theory of creative brain activity originating in the right hemisphere and rational brain activity in the left.[84] He depicted heavy reliance on ordinary left-brain consciousness as a major obstacle to effective living. Behind Ornstein lay the pioneering Nobel Prize–winning work of Roger W. Sperry and associates,[85] which has already been mentioned.

Psychologist Julian Jaynes's *The Origin of Consciousness in the Breakdown of the Bicameral Mind* fueled the interest.[86] He located the origin of consciousness in catastrophic events of three thousand years ago that forced humanity "to *learn* consciousness." He characterized the physiology and activity of the brain's right and left hemispheres in an earlier time as radically different from that of most of *Homo sapiens* today. In that ancient era (as today), stress caused language to shift from the intentional expression of the left half to the intuitive expression of the right half. People believed the resulting utterances from the "other side"—the right hemisphere—to be the voice of the gods. But in time, this breakdown of a two-chambered worldview, Jaynes argued, became

Table 6.2——Two Modes of Consciousness: A Tentative Dichotomy

Who Proposed It?

Many sources	Day	Night
Blackburn	Intellectual	Sensuous
Oppenheimer	Time, History	Eternity, Timelessness
Polanyi	Explicit	Tacit
Levy, Sperry	Analytic	Gestalt
Bogen	Propositional	Appositional
Lee	Linear	Nonlinear
Luria	Sequential	Simultaneous
Semmes	Focal	Diffuse
I Ching	The Creative: heaven masculine, yang	The Receptive: earth feminine, yin
Many sources	Verbal	Spatial
Many sources	Intellectual	Intuitive
Vedanta	Buddhi	Manas
Lang	Causation	Synchronicity
Bacon	Argument	Experience

From Robert E. Ornstein, *The Psychology of Consciousness* (New York: Harcourt Brace Jovanovich, 1977), 37. Reprinted by permission of Academic Press Inc. and the author.

the basis of the problem-solving awareness of the modern mind. He proposed that the contemporary experiences of hypnotism, schizophrenia, and poetic and religious frenzy represent a throwback of consciousness to this earlier form of bicamerality.

Evidence from split-brain research generated speculative generalizations among scientists such as Eccles, Gazzaniga, Penfield, and Sperry about the nature of human functioning. Much of the motivation seemed focused on the debilitating consequences of an Enlightenment rationalism and overvaluation of materialism in contrast to an emergent humanism and valuing of the spiritual.[87] Such speculation ignited interpretive imagination.

Ornstein himself set forth "a tentative dichotomy" of two modes of consciousness representing the polarities of intellect and intuition (table 6.2).[88] He contrasted day and night, sequential and simultaneous, argument and experience. Ashbrook added to these with further suggested contrasts.[89]

Table 6.3————Cognitive Contrasts with Suggested Hemisphere Activity

LEFT HEMISPHERE	RIGHT HEMISPHERE*

Demonstrated Contrasts

expression	perception of patterns
linguistic	kinesthetic
propositional	visual
discrete process	diffuse process
logical	synthetic
verbal	visuospatial

Suggested Contrasts

In philosophy:

knowing by argument	knowing by experience
explicit knowledge	tacit knowledge
technical reason	ecstatic reason
regularities	variations
time	eternity
discursive symbolism	presentational symbolism

In personality theory:

agency (achievement)	communion (relatedness)
secondary process	primary process
power	love
demonstrative theories	dialectical theories
digital communication	analogic communication

In mythology:

sun	moon
light	dark
good	evil
heaven	hell
yang	yin

European thinkers:

seek differences among particulars	seek order, similarity, and unity

Identified emphases:

abstract from	attend to
objective	subjective

In split reality:**

healthy	neurotic
actualized	alienated
abstract	concrete
free	bound
salvation	sin
sacred	profane
life	death

* Right hemisphere attributes can be identified with less confidence than left hemisphere attributes.
** These designations under left and right hemisphere are reversible depending upon the value orientation of the person or group. They are listed here from the perspective of a left brain bias.

From James B. Ashbrook, *The Human Mind and the Mind of God*. Lanham, Md.: University Press of America, 1984, 8–9. Used by permission.

He included Tillich's distinction between technical reason and ecstatic reason and psychologist David Bakan's distinction between agency (achievement) and communion (relatedness) (table 6.3). Jungian psychologist Anthony Stevens synthesized Carl Jung's theory of archetypes with bimodal consciousness.[90] Wholeness consists of "the union of opposites," balancing left and right.

As should be apparent by now, the analogical-metaphorical approach of this book provides what Springer and Deutsch refer to as "a convenient way of viewing complex situations," whether or not it has an actual neuropsychological basis.[91] The approach maintains the value of a systematic exploration that matches "a neuroanatomical reality" with the varieties of human and divine functioning.

Most recent research has qualified the analytic/holistic distinction and other dichotomies. The transfer of information from one hemisphere to the other is the key. Implicit or unconscious information seems accessible to the opposite hemisphere, while explicit or conscious information is not. Synchronization permits the experience of unified consciousness and reaction to be input on an implicit level, even though some inputs are underprocessed, that is, not consciously perceived. Even in intact brains integrating aspects of behavior are "relegated to subcortical pathways."[92] However inexact the dichotomies, they have been "quite helpful in guiding research on lateralization of function."[93]

Just as more attention was directed initially to the left hemisphere and the analytic and less to the right hemisphere and the holistic, so now attention is beginning to be directed to symmetrical, bilateral, and interhemisphere integration.[94] The evidence is mixed;[95] however, Ashbrook[96] and MacLean[97] among a number of researchers,[98] have argued for a sex differentiation between males and females in specialized and generalized information processing patterns. Furthermore, the interaction between the two halves of the brain "can take many different forms."[99] One hemisphere may take the lead over the other, which reflects bimodal consciousness; in other instances, interaction and integration between the hemispheres reflect a more balanced consciousness. Thus people organize and use information in various ways. It is becoming clear that these reflect various ways that people can be religious.

RIGHT AND LEFT BRAIN AND WAYS OF BEING RELIGIOUS

Earlier chapters have presented religious responses that may be related to the upper brain stem and the limbic system. The neocortex, with its cognitive integration, suggests other facets of how humans may be religious.

Although left and right brain do not operate through a simple division of duties, their characteristic operating systems present a heuristic.

The organizing activity of the left hemisphere creates a sense of inner stability. It assigns names and numbers, designs sequences, and concentrates on what seems correct and appropriate. It helps to solve problems that require logical analysis. It creates and preserves an orderly world.

Likewise, religious beliefs often serve to reassure individuals that their world is basically orderly and understandable. Such beliefs provide the assurance that "God's in his Heaven, and all's right with the world," as Robert Browning put it. They also instruct people about how to behave in order to keep their lives in harmony with that ordered world.

Although some religious groups emphasize the ecstatic, many others wish very much for religious practices to be carried out "decently and in order," as Saint Paul instructed (1 Corinthians 14:40). Their central activity tends to be the proclamation of the Word, as described by philosopher Paul Ricoeur[100] and theologian David Tracy.[101] For many branches of the Judeo-Christian and Muslim faiths, in fact, the Word—Holy Writ—is seen as key, the authority above all other earthly authorities. Many people, especially in the Western world, have learned to rely upon the left brain, and it is only natural to emphasize it in religious observances as well.

But the right brain also has its role to play. Through its good offices, we humans can sense that we are interlinked with the rest of the world in an inti-

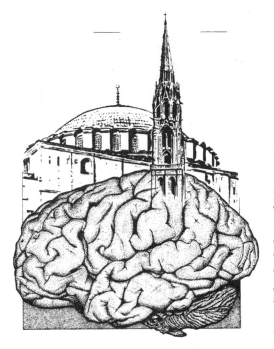

Figure 6.3——The dome and the spire. The dome of St. Sophia in Istanbul (Constantinople) rising out of a hidden right hemisphere and the spire of Chartres Cathedral in France, rising out of a visible left hemisphere. *From James B. Ashbrook,* The Human Mind and the Mind of God *(Lanham, Md.: University Press of America, 1984). Illustration by Keith McBarron.*

mate way. Our common religious activities underline our brotherhood and sisterhood, as we share the sacramental meals, the sacred observances and rituals. Our deep religious experiences teach us, in thoughts beyond words, that we are in harmony with the universe. In glimpses beyond the daily and the safe, we humans may experience a different, freeing dimension—some call it the dimension of grace. In solitary mystical experiences, and in shared religious ecstasy, we sometimes go beyond the measured, useful proclamation of the Word, celebrating our awareness of the infinite. We experience what Ricoeur and Tracy call the phenomenology of manifestation.

Ashbrook used these two types of religious experience as the basis for elaborating cognitive styles and patterns of believing.[102] The one dome of Byzantium's basilica of Holy Wisdom and the two towers of the medieval cathedral at Chartres represent central ecclesiastical tendencies and cultural convergences, archetypal images, if you will (figure 6.3).

There is a spirelike directed intentionality in religious conviction—suggesting the left brain—and a domelike imaginativeness of religious depth—suggesting the right brain. Ashbrook[103] has added a third expression of religious orientation, namely, an integrative centeredness reflective of a more balanced expression of consciousness.

LEFT AND RIGHT BRAIN AND IMAGES OF GOD

If left and right brain present further images of God, what can one say about such a deity? Those who have probed the secrets of the universe most deeply are often the most in awe of its designer. It is true that some have echoed physicist Stephen W. Hawking's defiant question, "What place, then, for a creator?"[104] But many others have been convinced, on a deep level, that they are "tracking" a Deity who is most amazingly subtle, but whose reasonableness is, quite literally, awesome.[105] To the great German mathematician Karl Gauss, for instance, "God does arithmetic."[106] For, as Gauss and many others have found, mathematical calculations made for purely theoretical reasons have had a disconcerting way of perfectly describing physical phenomena identified in later experiments.

It seems clear that a left brain that can begin to grasp the work of a creator of such surpassing reasonableness must, indeed, reflect one of the images of God.

Yet, any image of God must include more than reason, more than logic. It must reflect a God who encompasses all of reality, who comprehends it whole. The great mystics have apprehended a God "in whom we live and move and have our being," as Saint Paul put it, echoing the Greek mystical poet Epimenides.[107] This is a God who is, in fact, the very Ground of Being itself, the source of all, as Paul Tillich referred to that reality. Our human right brain, which comprehends all together, may, in a feeble sort of way, provide an image of this encompassing God who is manifested in the whole of reality.

Surely God cannot be limited to one or another way of being God. We have seen that the functioning of each hemisphere requires the work of the whole head. Truly, a God of the entire universe must have all the attributes discussed here, and more. Such a God must attend to the physical reality of the creation. And such a God provides, through this creation, love and nurturance of its creatures. As the author of the traditional Swedish hymn "Children of the Heavenly Father" perceived, "God his own doth tend and nourish."

The conclusion is that God the mother/father/lover/Ground of Being has cunningly designed the world, and supports its interactions and its inhabitants by perceiving and penetrating it whole.

SUMMARY

This chapter has sketched some major features of the neocortex. These features include the cortical areas of left and right hemispheres, with the crucial

connecting tract of the corpus callosum. These hemispheres support two conscious ways of organizing information—analytic sequential, and holistic contextual. While these two types of cognition are not confined to the right or left
hemisphere of the cerebral cortex, there are indications that the left hemisphere takes the lead in analytic, sequential thinking, while the right hemisphere supports the ability to understand situations holistically and all-at-once.

These ways of organizing information may be expressed in various forms
of religious thought and practice—for example, in left-brain-based understandings of how to live, which help to keep the world "in order"; and in right-
brain-based deep religious intuitions of our oneness with the universe.

These "images of God" modeled in the activities of the brain may provide
further insight into the nature of the Ultimate Reality of the universe. The
Ground of Being is both ultimately rational and ultimately relational.[108]

This discussion has yet to describe the integrating/intending process that
takes place in the frontal regions. This process involves collaboration, not only
with the features of the neocortex just discussed, but also with the old mammalian brain—the emotional mind—and the reptilian brain—the primal mind.
There are "large connecting pathways between the reptilian-type and
paleomammalian type brain" that MacLean suggests "provide the avenues to
the basis of personality."[109] These areas, as well as other regions of the neocortex, are heavily linked to the paleomammalian-frontal region, and these connections may constitute the neurological locus of human intentionality.

As this book has been suggesting, the human brain, with its many features
all contributing to its organized complexity, may provide the best reflection to
date of the deep nature of the cosmos. And the nature of that universe, in turn,
is a source of clues to the nature of the God who is its foundation.

SEVEN

THE FRONTAL LOBES, INTENDING, AND A PURPOSEFUL GOD

THE HUMAN FOREBRAIN IN EMPATHY, GOALS, AND PRIORITIZING

The preceding chapters have shown that the evolving brain equips people to deal well—but not perfectly—with many kinds of life circumstances. In fact, the structures and functions of the brain seem to track the eons of evolution that gave rise to it. Some parts are like those of many other animals with backbones. Other parts we humans share in common with other mammals, especially primates. The various parts are interactive. Functions cannot be strictly localized, but generally speaking, the different areas are programmed to attend to the world, to feel bodily sensations, to fight or flee or freeze, to find a mate, to care for the young, to play, to feel a range of emotions, to think holistically and sequentially, and to empathize, imagine, and make decisions about the future.

The brain has evolved to enable humans to survive and prosper in the world as it exists. It seems fairly clear that knowledge of the brain can provide indications—not perfect understanding—of the conditions under which the brain developed. Through the long eons of evolution, brain abilities that led to successful interaction with the world are those that tended to be reproduced. Think of the resulting human brain as a sort of *Let's Go Guide to the World*—not a perfect indicator, but tested and useful. Conversely, the brain is part of the universe, and generalizations about the universe apply to the brain as well. Both, for example, consist of chemical elements; both are subject to electromagnetic and gravitational forces. In short, the human brain and the universe share basic features.

This book goes a step further and asserts that God's ways of being God may be discerned from those features. Just as the brain gives us humans an innate ability to deal with gravity and to interact in great detail with the physical phenomena of light and sound, so the brain's various processes are indicators of the underlying, deep nature of the reality that gave rise to us humans.

In this penultimate chapter we focus on the intentional processes of the conscious brain as they converge in the frontal region. We use our understanding to make sense of God as purposeful.

THE FRONTAL LOBES

Emotionality

On September 13, 1848, an explosion on the Rutland & Burlington Railroad permanently disrupted the productive and positive life of twenty-five-year-old construction foreman Phineas P. Gage.[1] A metal rod three feet seven inches long, weighing thirteen and a quarter pounds, and one and a quarter inches in diameter shot through his skull as a result of exploding dynamite. It destroyed his left frontal lobe while leaving him alive and rational. The accident, however, transformed this dependable and likable person into a restless, obnoxious, and impulsive caricature of his former self. "Gage was no longer Gage."

Gage's dramatic survival obscured sustained reflection on his neurological deficits. What turned into a sideshow for P. T. Barnum must be regarded in retrospect as one of the significant events in coming to understand the brain as a sensible and purposive organ. Chapters 4 and 5 have described the contribution of the old mammalian brain to our being the human beings that we are and what they may indicate about God being the way God is God. Chapter 6 discussed the participation of the right and left neocortex in our abilities to perceive our environment as a whole and to analyze and order it. We suggested that our world and its Ground of Being also are both holistic and orderly. It remains now to connect these older and newer sectors of the brain with a characteristically human sector, the frontal lobe. The integration of limbic sites and higher cortical regions creates, as historian of science Anne Harrington puts it, "the synthetic world of affectively-toned cognition and cognitively-mediated affect."[2] Emotion and reason intermingle in human meaning seeking.

Recently, neurologist Antonio R. Damasio, among others, has highlighted the connection between frontal lobe damage and "impaired social conduct."[3]

He concludes, "The unintentional message in Gage's case was that observing social convention, behaving ethically, and making decisions advantageous to one's survival and progress require knowledge of rules and strategies *and* the integrity of specific brain systems."[4] The connection of frontal lobe damage with impaired social conduct has become clearer with research developments in recent years. Only now is there some understanding of what Damasio calls "the strange bedfellows—impaired reasoning/decision making and impaired emotion/feeling."[5]

A defining feature of the human brain is the complexity of the frontal lobes. These are located directly behind the forehead (see figure 1.1). They are considerably larger and more powerful than the frontal area of even our nearest primate relatives.

More than the rest of the neocortex, the frontal lobes receive direct input from other parts of the brain. As the Gage tragedy illustrates, they are closely linked with the limbic system, which we humans share with other mammals. The limbic system generates emotional signals. Emotions are indispensable guides to action. We humans tend to interact with those we love and avoid those with whom we feel sad or anxious, for example. Excitement fuels our ability to grasp an opportunity. Feelings of regret lead individuals to analyze their mistakes so that they can avoid repeating them. And emotions are linked with memory, where much of one's identity lies.

In addition, the frontal lobes have valuable input from the body itself. They know when the stomach churns, the muscles tense, and sweat chills the palms of the hands. They know, too, when the body enjoys a sense of well-being, relaxation, and trust. The body and its autonomic system, its fight-or-flight-or-freeze responses of tension and its positive sensations of relaxation, signal crucial perceptions in situations where people must make rapid evaluations. In a crunch, "gut feelings" give instant guidance about what to do.[6]

Evaluation and Integration

All of this cross-communication makes the frontal lobes a critical locale for evaluating the nature of the data of the brain. A person needs to know, for example, whether these data are generated internally or externally. Are they current data or remembered events? In a first-time analysis of brain images generated by PET scans of actively hallucinating schizophrenics, results showed prefrontal lobe failure in checking internal "images against sensory information and memory." This failure led to a confusion between "internally generated voices . . . [and], for instance, the voice of God or a CIA transmitter."[7]

Having gathered and evaluated so much information, the frontal area works to integrate it. Neuroscientist Terrence Deacon has shown that the most important contribution of the frontal lobes may well be their ability to organize the various kinds of input conceptually: to put perceptions and ideas into some order, to make generalizations and form concepts, to map out priorities, and to strategize action plans.[8]

Deacon theorizes that the unique contribution of the frontal lobes lies in the way they *represent* the world to our subjective experience. The subjective experience of other animals probably tends to what he calls the "indexical" and "iconic"—one might say that what they see is what they get, a one-to-one correspondence. But we humans order and *classify* our experience into types and categories. The categories we use influence how we experience our world. In other words, our experience is both "bottom-up"—starting with the stimuli—and "top-down"—starting with the categories. In short, we human beings *humanize* our experience.

This world of symbolic reference is "the world in which we discover other minds, because the ground of symbolic reference is fundamentally social and interindividual," Deacon continues.[9] "We are able to take another's perspective in this virtual world, and know something of the consequences of our actions on them. We experience a sort of empathy available to no other creature, a virtual empathy, with representations of emotions that can be simultaneously experienced overlaid with our own emotions, and which can have substantial impact on them."

This ability to empathize also burdens humanity with a moral responsibility incumbent on no other animal. We humans

> take responsibility and authorship for our actions with the aid of symbolization, because only through symbolic reference are we able to be at the same time above and within our own mental processes. We possess a form of agency which is unavailable to other species. . . . The "I" that I identify with is often pitted against the "I" that emerges from my biology moment by moment, emerging from neither social nor biological causes, but from the self-organizing dynamic of an internal symbolic dialogue.[10]

The frontal lobes are intimately involved in the pursuit of long-term goals. To do so requires people to prioritize, to plan, to strategize. People plant crops for harvest six months hence; save their money to take a trip; plan their social lives weeks in advance. People work for years to build businesses or to become authorities in some field of endeavor, and they write legal documents (called "wills") that provide for complicated disposition of their possessions after death.

People whose frontal lobes have been damaged may still pursue simple desires and seek out the pleasure of the moment. Both nonhumans and humans exercise will at this level. Persons with frontal lobe damage can evaluate situations perfectly well. They can speak well and calculate. They can even do a respectable job of predicting the consequences of various courses of action.

But what they cannot do is to conduct their own lives in a normal way, as Gage illustrated. They make plans but do not carry through. They appear to be irresponsible. They make mistakes, then repeat them. They do not seem to learn from experience. They have little empathy, and others often find them inconsiderate and annoying. Some of them eventually alienate almost everyone in their lives. Obviously, their damaged frontal lobes are not doing their jobs.

FEATURES OF THE FRONTAL LOBES

How do the frontal lobes help people conduct their lives? Although the answer is still a matter of controversy, it is clear that this part of the brain has abundant connections with nearly every other modality of the cortex, and it appears that it organizes this input through forms of symbolic reference. Certainly, the symbol system of language is almost ubiquitous in humans, and people use other symbolic strategies as well—for example, consciousness of the passage of time, imaginative preconstructions of the future, a sense of cause and effect, and empathic understanding of the effects of actions on others. All these considerations may be organized within a larger understanding of the meaning and intentionality of an individual's life.

Attention

The frontal region, as the locus of planning, imagining, and deciding, regulates attention.[11] More input comes together here than anywhere else, and more output is carried away from here than anywhere else. The motor and frontal areas combine what comes in with what is intended. These areas mature late,[12] with sharp increases in capacity coming around three and a half to four years of age and again between seven and eight years. Everyone acquainted with young children is awed by the sudden surge of cognitive capability at these periods. Also these areas deteriorate first. While dependent on the rest of the brain, the front part makes two basic contributions to brain activity: It focuses attention, and it enables people to function effectively.

Intending What We Attend To

With attention goes intention, the ability to plan, to set goals, and to follow through. To make such plans people need several kinds of capacities.

Time Consciousness. To begin with, we humans know that past, present, and future do exist, and that human life is finite. In other words, people have a sense of time—of limits and endings and of death itself. People need to remember a past in order to imagine a future.

Scenario Building. One way to think about possibilities for the future is to call up various scenarios and evaluate them. Once an appealing scenario emerges, it can stay in memory for future reference; the results are sometimes called "memories of the future."[13] These scenarios are then evoked to check out decisions: Is this action likely to promote the hoped-for results?

Cause and Effect. Answering such a question requires another capacity: the ability to judge cause and effect. We humans are probably hardwired to search for causal connections.[14] The tendency is so well established that we all tend to invent putative causal connections if none can actually be identified. (This is how superstitions arise: if the appearance of a black cat is followed by bad luck, then perhaps the cat is the cause and the bad luck is the effect.)

Empathy. The effects of some actions depend on purely physical processes. (For example, an object that is dropped will fall, propelled by gravity.) But in most cases, the responses of others are important in what transpires.

Thus, if we humans are to prosper, we need to build alliances. To do this, we need to promote others' well-being as well as our own. Sometimes our goals transcend our personal well-being. Given our consciousness of time and of death, we may be concerned for our descendants. If they are to prosper, we need to promote the well-being of our families and defend them against enemies. That is the positive core of patriotism. In addition, religions advocate doing good even to those who cannot do good in return. Such "trans-kin altruism" is necessary for the good of society.

To make any of these endeavors succeed, people must try to predict the effect of their efforts. In other words, they must forecast how others will respond. This requires insight into others' feelings and motivations. There is a need for *empathy*.

A Framework of Meaning. It is all well and good to make effective plans and carry them through with empathy, but people can be stymied by an inability to decide what plans to make. How do people make such choices? Here again, the frontal lobes are involved.

Neuropsychiatrist Richard Restak has observed that the frontal area, especially, enables us humans "to work out philosophical, religious, and ethical systems—all those activities that differentiate us from the other creatures on earth."[15] If personalities are to have coherence, then we need to set our various goals within a framework of meaning. Without one, we cannot be persons of integrity, for "integrity" implies oneness, integration, and organization within a cohesive framework of value and an understanding of the world.

Even though there is no single "grand junction" of the neural circuitry, the frontal lobes do play a unique role in the processes of being human. They bring together emotional responses and "gut feelings," symbolic logic and sensory data. They evaluate the nature of experience. They enable a person to plan and keep on track toward the future. And they help to devise the philosophical, religious, and ethical systems that provide a framework for choices. If there is indeed a neural substrate for free will, it may well depend on the frontal lobes.

PROCESS, HUMAN IDENTITY, AND SPIRITUALITY

These processes associated with the frontal lobes provide a fertile heuristic in the search for understanding what it means for human beings to be human and for God to be God. It is true that capacities for speech and numerical calculation, which depend importantly on other parts of the brain, are characteristically human and essential to a full life. Without these abilities, people could neither think nor talk about the universe in which they are embedded. Emotion and nurturance are also essential to humanity. An intimate interconnectedness with one another and, as one grows in spirit, to all who came before and come after, are central to one's well-being and to one's very identity.

The frontal lobes provide a sense of past and future; evaluation of cause and effect; empathic knowledge of the responses of others; goal setting; and an attempt to fit these into an overarching frame of meaning. *These are all processes.* They are not "hard knowledge," like a vocabulary in a foreign language or mastery of Maxwell's equations. They are not memories of things past. They are not emotions. They are not drives. They are processes!

A parallel observation can be made regarding spirituality. For spirituality—which makes us most human—is at base a process. Spirituality implies centering, and to the extent that we humans remain "centered," we do it by staying in *process*, "on track," focusing on our goals. One intends what one attends to.

Spirituality also relates to change. Staying in process leads to change, inevitably, and thus to shifting inner states of body and mind. People may modify their sense of self, but in losing themselves, they also find themselves. Only through continually letting go of what they have been and moving on to what they will be can they become part of the flow that is life eternal.

Thus, this examination of spirit will focus on dynamic process—the dimension that, upon reflection, has emerged as most central to spirituality.

PROCESS AND HOLISM

This book rests on the premise that the nature of humans and the nature of the world are intimately intertwined. It is significant here that both the physical world and the human brain can be seen as an interplay of matter and energy.

The brain operates as one's *neurons* engage in interactive *processes*. The neurons can be categorized as matter; the processes as energy, although of course the processes utilize chemical neurotransmitters, and the neurons require energy for their metabolism. The distinction breaks down even further because the neurons themselves are subject to change as some become more richly branched and others lose connectivity. Furthermore, the entire system is in a continual state of flux as certain neural networks "rev up" and become active while others lapse into inactivity.

Similarly, the distinction between matter and energy, once a cornerstone of physical science, has rather thoroughly broken down. As Einstein's well-tested special theory of relativity has shown us, and the physics of quantum mechanics have demonstrated, matter may be transformed into energy, energy becomes matter, and for some purposes the two may be seen as one and the same. Matter and process are inseparably intertwined.

The world, and we humans ourselves, are ever interactive with everything else. *Everything is at core interactive.* We humans shape the world—animate and inanimate—and are shaped by it. As the Jesuit paleontologist-philosopher Pierre Teilhard de Chardin (1881–1955) observed:

Each element of the cosmos is positively woven from all the others: . . .

It is impossible to cut into this network, to isolate a portion without it becoming frayed and unravelled at all its edges.

All around us, as far as the eye can see, the universe holds together, and only one way of considering it is really possible, that is, to take it as a whole, in one piece.[16]

Many branches of the physical sciences seem to be reaching toward parallel conclusions. It is suggestive to note that all the world's energy can be traced to three fundamental forces, which physicists classify as the strong force, the electroweak force, and the gravitational force.[17] These forces hold the stars in their courses, hold atoms and molecules together (yet also cause their radioactive decay), give rise to visible light and other electromagnetic radiation, and support the very processes of the brain. Since Einstein's general theory of relativity gained acceptance earlier in this century, physicists have believed that space itself is a function of time—and not only the vast space of the universe, but the little spaces in which people live their lives. *Pacé* Democritus, *bravo* Heraclitus: The universe is not eternal and unchanging; it is forever *and by nature* in flux.

THE DIRECTIONALITY OF PROCESS

Now processes, as Julian Huxley pointed out, "must be defined by their direction, their inherent possibilities (including, of course, also their limitations), and their deducible future trends."[18]

Does the process of the universe have directionality? There is evidence that the universe does indeed have a built-in tendency. That tendency is toward the emergence of *complexification*—a term used here in a special sense to be discussed below. If the Big Bang theory is correct, shortly after this cosmic event, the universe began its evolution. It developed from a virtually featureless expanse to the formation of the first generation of stars, to a second generation of stars that supported planets, to an Earth that differentiated into the seas and dry land, to the simplest forms of life, in the waters and on the land, and on to a creature capable of naming the rest (Genesis 2:19). The emergence of life was a watershed. The record indicates that when life emerged, it appeared "complex and whole."[19]

In his magnum opus *The Phenomenon of Man*, Teilhard addressed this issue. He assumed that the world is tending toward complexification and holism.[20] He observed:

First the molecules of carbon compounds with their thousands of atoms symmetrically grouped; next the cell which, within a very small volume, contains thousands of molecules linked in a complicated system; then the metazoa in which the cell is no more than an almost infinitesimal element; and later the manifold attempts made sporadically by the metazoa to enter into symbiosis and raise themselves to a higher biological condition, [culminating finally in the thinking creatures that are humans. We see here] the principal axis of evolution: *ever more complexity and thus ever more consciousness.*[21]

Systems theorist Stuart Kauffman speaks of "order arising naturally from the laws of physics and chemistry. Order emerging spontaneously from molecular chaos and manifesting itself as a system that grows"—he found the idea "indescribably beautiful."[22]

Systems that give rise to such order are technically known as complexifying systems, and the phenomenon is known as complexity. The word *complexity* is used here in this sense. It does not mean merely "complicated." Rather, it means that parts of the system are organized. A box of unsorted cancelled checks, for example, may be complicated. Once the checks have been filed by category and subcategory, they have been put into a *complex system.*[23] The new science of complexity is discovering that our universe, our reality, has a built-in tendency to *complexify itself*, to spontaneously form complex systems. In other words, it contains *self-organizing* systems. Computer scientist John Holland sees "each of these systems [as] a network of many 'agents' acting in parallel."[24]

Atoms "search" for a minimum energy state by forming chemical bonds with each other, thereby organizing themselves into structures known as molecules. Molecules, in turn, form compounds. With the advent of life, a new element enters the picture: *adaptation.* Through feedback loops, organisms adapt to their environment by changing their location, or their food-gathering strategies, for example.[25] If a strategy works, they will probably do more of it. Organisms are continuously adapting to one another, and in the process they organize themselves into an exquisitely tuned ecosystem. In every case, groups of agents seeking mutual accommodation and self-consistency somehow manage to transcend themselves.

The agents may be on the micro level—a protein, for example—or the macro level—a corporation or a whole nation. Regardless, "each finds itself in an environment produced by its interactions with other agents in the system," and each adapts to the new condition. Positive feedback reinforces successful efforts. As this process proceeds, systems become increasingly interconnected and complex.[26]

With increasing intensity in a multicultural, "shrinking" world, interactive process is a reality. People have no choice but continually to interact with new conditions created by all the other decision makers and contingent forces around them. By their choices they, in turn, create conditions that are new. Success is not guaranteed. People may prosper or falter, and it is important to remember that these outcomes do not indicate human worth. Luck, choice, or victimization may all play a role. But interaction is unavoidable. We humans respond as complex adaptive systems.

Interaction is also necessary for the development of the brain, for it is literally the most complex of adaptive systems. Only through interactions with loving caretakers and with other stimuli can the human brain reach its potential. In early life, the very architecture of the brain depends on such interactions. In adulthood, they are necessary to the fulfillment of individuals-in-community.

LOVE AND COMPLEXIFICATION

The discussion has now returned to the development of the human brain. The brain can reach its potential only through loving interactions. Complexification and love now appear as two different but related processes. Since there have been countless attempts to define love (each falling short of a complete description), the reader needs some idea of what is meant by it here.

When we humans love those dear to us, we desire their spiritual growth. Their success gives us as much pleasure as our own; their pain causes us pain. In a sense, they become part of us, even though we clearly are separate. Through the years, our concerns may extend not only to our most dearly beloved, but to many others. This does not mean that we confuse ourselves with them; it is essential that we remain ourselves and that they remain themselves. The courage to be as ourselves intertwines with the courage to be with others. Yet as we identify the welfare of others with our own welfare, this process also leads to an enlargement and complexification of our inner self. As theologians John Cobb and David Griffin write:

> Creative transformation is involved in all human responsive love. To love another person in this way is to allow that person's feelings to affect oneself. But those feelings, as different from one's own, cannot be simply added to them. Ordinarily, in order to protect ourselves, we largely shut out the feelings of others from any rich contribution to our experience. Occasionally we are overwhelmed by alien feelings in such a way as to lose our own integrity. But it is also possible ... to enter into a novel mode of being in which both operate with their own integrity in a larger whole that is enriched by their contrasts.[27]

Such interactions support us as complex adaptive beings. These interactions are not limited to the present, as complex as that may be. They extend back into the past and forward into the future. All of us are indebted to a forgotten lineage of those who loved and worked and thought and dreamed—those who learned how to use fire, to domesticate animals and plants, to preserve food and weave cloth. We humans are indebted to those who developed written language and law, who labored to build the edifices of knowledge and culture that now support us. We also are indebted to those closer to us who personally loved and educated us.

Through processes not yet foreseen, the personal and communal lives of those living today will affect the lives of future humans. These lives will also affect the planet itself. Everything depends, of course, not only on one's own individual decisions. Everything also depends on the decisions of many others, in a continual dynamic ecological process.

Such a process of development will almost surely involve some pain. Growth—of an individual or of a society—requires effort and risk. These are not necessarily to be equated with evil. The enterprise is larger than any of us. Indeed, humanity itself is part of a great cosmic journey in which the "whole creation groans in labor pains." As Saint Paul dramatized it:

> For the creation was subjected to futility . . . in hope that the creation itself will be set free from its bondage to decay and will obtain the freedom of the glory of the children of God. We know that the whole creation has been groaning in labor pains until now; and not only the creation, but we ourselves, who have the first fruits of the Spirit, groan inwardly while we wait for adoption. (Romans 8:20–23)

These words signify for us a powerful insight regarding the world's trajectory. Its impetus is from bondage to freedom, from chaos to complexification. The journey is not complete, and its outcome is not assured. Humanity can still turn the hope of "glorious freedom" back into "bondage to decay." As long as human beings are alive, they balance on the cusp between the two. For as we have seen, humanity lives within a nested series of complex adaptive systems.

On the scale of individual lives, of course, a good bit of what we see around us results from chance events and individual decisions. Not all of them promote order and complexity. On the level of individuals or even large groups, suffering is too often a reality. Survival does not signal virtue; bad fortune is not a hallmark of unworthiness. Only on the largest possible scale can we humans clearly see this cosmic movement toward complexification as the trailing edge of God's activity in the universe.

SEEKING A DIRECTION

As we humans use our frontal lobes to seek goals in our personal journeys, we remain aware that we are players on a very large stage indeed. We can foresee the progress of the drama only dimly.

Making decisions and setting goals are always done under conditions of uncertainty. Perhaps—and this heuristic interpretation comes from our intuition and from the testimony of companions on the journey—perhaps one can perceive that one is "on track" when one encounters what might be called "nodes of complexification." These can be single experiences, which Swiss psychoanalyst Carl Jung called synchronicity. They may be more complicated sequences of events akin to what some traditions see as Providence at work—situations where all things do indeed seem to be working together for good for those who are called according to God's purposes (cf. Romans 8:28), even though some things are not good in themselves. Theologian Gordon Kaufman speaks of "cosmic serendipitous creativity," which "expresses itself through trajectories of various sorts that work themselves out over longer and shorter stretches of time."[28]

People vary in their ability to perceive such situations in these ways. The sensitivity increases as one attends to life's processes. It is necessary to act on incomplete information and thus to proceed on faith. One must act under conditions of uncertainty. This is not the same as indulging in a reckless leap from the "pinnacle of the temple" (as Jesus was tempted to do), taunting God to send an angel to bear us up (see Luke 4:9–12). Rather, the goal is to take a step that is in harmony with the universe. When one takes such actions, one necessarily risks the old for the sake of the new, and for the unfolding story whose conclusion extends beyond our ken.

All parts of the brain contribute to this kind of living. People must recognize their drives, their perceptions, their memories. They must own their loves, their fears, their bodily signals. Such decisions require that they attend to and intend the direction of their lives.

What criteria should be used in choosing a direction for life?

The conclusion of this line of thought is that trajectories should be aimed toward the maximization of interactive love, of complexification, based on careful examination of the realities of the world and taking the broadest possible view. This criterion derives from what we now know about the brain and the natural world of which it is a part. It recognizes that "we have here no abiding city;" that we humans live in a journey, not a place; in process, not in stasis.

This recognition is congruent with the traditional understanding of *faith*—"the assurance of things hoped for, the conviction of things not seen" (Hebrews 11:1)—a forward-looking orientation. Some sort of faith is what informs the choice of trajectory. When the early Christians referred to themselves as "People of the Way," they were no doubt referring to this reality. The traditional concept of faith (which may seem irrelevant to many) takes on new life when correlated with the concept of life orientation or trajectory.

Espousing beliefs and tracing a corresponding path through time by setting goals, with guidance from "gut feelings," emotions and logic, empathic understanding and the ability to prioritize—all of these are *processes*. The prefrontal brain—in concert with the rest of the brain and body—orchestrates that which most makes us human.

RELIGION AND PROCESS

When trajectory is correlated with faith, the religious dimension of life comes into focus. Religions represent what psychologist Donald Campbell called the "well-winnowed wisdom" of a culture.[29] While specific guidelines may become outdated, the gestalt of a religion intricately informs the culture within which it relates. Religions include belief in an ultimate or holy dimension of reality, often in a concept of God.

In general, the perception of this God expresses what is seen as the meaning of the universe. Even within the same culture, some see the universe as eternal and changeless; others see it as dynamic, calling for experiment and creativity. Some experience it as fraught with danger, demanding of sacrifice and warfare. Others experience it as supporting life and growth. For some, the universe appears harsh, impersonal, and meaningless; for others, friendly, personal, meaningful. The way each of us sees the universe is probably the way we characterize God as well. As Martin Luther put it, the way people perceive God is the way they have God.

What does this variety in religious imagery mean for this book's heuristic of the person as *imago Dei*, and for its assertion that the nature of God is expressed in the universe and in its most complex emergent entity, the human brain?

AN INTERACTIVE, SELF-ORGANIZING UNIVERSE

We authors must remind ourselves and you of our own propensities to "read" our own worldview into the theology we essay. With that caveat, we venture suggestions about a God who expresses the uniqueness of the universe that we have been discerning here. Ours is an empirical natural theology, inevitably informed by our own Judeo-Christian tradition.

Throughout the book that supports this chapter, the point has been made that the evolving brain equips humanity to deal with its environment. The structures and functions of the brain seem to track the eons of evolution that gave rise to it.

Complexification has been lifted up as one important tendency in the universe in general and in living things in particular. At the same time, forces of death and dissolution are ever present. We authors have expressed our value judgment that complexification is desirable. We favor life trajectories that aim toward maximizing interactive love and complexification. That is, we favor change if it supports complexification and adaptation.

Dynamic Interaction

This chapter has correlated complexification and love. Early in life, loving interaction with others is necessary for the normal development of the complex human brain. And through the years, loving interactions and intense care for the well-being of others necessarily result in an enlarging of one's own spiritual dimensions and the complexification of the inner being. Conversely, loving work in the world weaves part of the complex tapestry of family and society. Love and complexification are reciprocal.

Dynamic interaction is also inherent in the relation of world and brain. Although there seems to be a "fit" between the two, it now seems clear that any interaction can work only if it is dynamic, since both world and brain change continually. The interactive process is the reality in a universe where there are no fixed points. Humanity has no choice but to interact continually with new conditions created by all the other decision makers and contingent forces around it. By their choices human beings, in turn, create conditions that are new. As computer scientist John Holland observed, "it's essentially meaningless to talk about a complex adaptive system being in equilibrium; the system can never get there. It is always unfolding, always in transition. In fact, if the system ever does reach equilibrium, it isn't just stable. It's dead."[30]

There is in the body and in other living systems a tendency toward equilibrium. This is known as homeostasis. But no system arrives at some ideal condition and stays there. It is always in flux, approximating the ideal but never reaching it. The edge of chaos, as described in chapter 2, is the locale where complexity develops. Only where there is a balance between the predictable and the unpredictable do systems transcend themselves, self-organizing into ever more complex systems.

In the world's process of complexification, one threshold in particular has been critical. That is the advent of living things. An organism modifies itself through an active feedback loop of adaptation to the environment. This is known as learning.

This book would be painting an incomplete picture of the world—and the fate of humanity's brain—if it did not also acknowledge that the world does indeed tend, not only toward organization and complexification, but also toward disorganization and disintegration. The second law of thermodynamics says that everything in the universe, seen as a total, closed system, ultimately tends to an undifferentiated state of entropy. On a cosmic scale, over eons of time, the universe may become a boundless, featureless expanse. However, living things—and planet Earth itself—are not closed systems, and they are not subject to inexorable entropy alone. *Life* itself is the force that can counteract the forces of entropy. This process is sometimes called *negentropy* (a term invented by physicist Erwin Schrödinger). To describe "a life-related counterflow to entropy's inevitable drift downstream," neurobiologist William Calvin coined the phrase "the river that flows upstream."[31] This book is not intended to trace the interactions of these two megaforces (and in fact, scientific study of this problem has only begun). But we acknowledge that both entropy and negentropy exist.

The Forces of Life versus the Forces of Destruction

It is possible to interpret the central tenets of religions in terms of these two megaforces. The struggle between the forces of life and the forces of death is a continuing preoccupation of the Judeo-Christian tradition. The assertion that life forces will eventually triumph is a central tenet of this tradition. The assurance that "the Lord will . . . satisfy your needs in parched places, and make your bones strong; and you shall be like a watered garden, like a spring of water, whose waters never fail" (Isaiah 58:11) is one of many biblical assertions that the forces of life will ultimately triumph over those of dissolution.

In the meantime, we humans tend toward complexification. Therefore, we necessarily teeter on the edge between stasis and turbulence. Complete order and stability characterize only nonliving systems. In total order, there can be no life, and in life, there cannot be total order. But without some dependable order, nothing lasting can be built. We humans must live in the borderland between the two. Our very life depends upon restless, interactive process.

A PURPOSEFUL GOD

Now comes the question, What sort of God might express the integrity of such a universe? God is unknowable in an ultimate sense. By definition, the originator of a universe cannot be fully comprehended by a mere denizen of that universe. However, we authors suggest that some of God's traits may be indicated by the evidence we do have—both from "the book of nature" and from the testimony of historical religious traditions. The evidence could have been interpreted differently, but this is how it seems to us.

We propose that the God of this universe is *complexifying, interactive, dynamic,* and *loving,* and that the combination of these characteristics indicates a God who is *purposeful.*

Complexifying

The fact that the development of the brain—and of the known universe—tends to complexification indicates an ultimate reality oriented to a process of increasing complexity. This universe—while once "without form and void"—is now marked by aggregations of galaxies, stars, planets, and systemic processes. Dynamical life forms have given rise to a human brain more complex than any other structure in the known universe.

It is true that complexification also gives way to disorganization. Individuals die and whole species become extinct. Many of these events result from random accidents, ranging from comet collisions to the depredations of malignant bacteria. Some are caused by human evil. But death itself is not necessarily an evil. The emergence of increasingly complex life forms often requires the disappearance of the older forms.[32] Individuals die and others take their place.

On a much smaller scale, individual spiritual growth requires the pain of giving up outworn modalities of thought and action. This is not to say that there is no evil in the world. The forces of hurt and harm, disorder and dissolution, bedevil all our lives. Some of these evils are brought about by deliberate human decisions. Even so, we authors cleave to the faith that the forces of life ultimately are stronger. We believe in a God who sides with life and complexification.

Interactive

Complexification cannot take place without interaction, among persons and among physical forces. From top to bottom, the physical forces and living things interact. The human brain reaches maturity through interaction, a process in which all the actors may be affected and modified. Is it possible to conceive of a God who is also interactive? Believing in an eternal, unchanging God, people have found the notion of an interacting, changing God hard to fathom.

Today, understandings of cause and effect are changing. Notions of causal chains are giving way to the insight that most phenomena are multidetermined and interactive. Both "top-down" and "bottom-up" forces influence their patterning. Neuroscientist Roger Sperry observed the following:

> When parts come together as a new whole, this whole exhibits features—emergent properties—that can't be predicted as a rule from the parts, and cannot be explained entirely in terms of the parts. In this context, consciousness and other subjective qualities, such as ideas, feelings, values, and emotions that we associate with "mind," [can] be thought of as emergent properties of the physical brain. They [can] also be understood . . . as having an actual functional role in brain processing.[33]

> These [properties of mind] transcend and control the events of brain physiology . . . at the same time that they are determined by them. This reciprocal, two-way control in opposing directions is not in conflict because different forms of causation are operating in the upward and downward directions.[34]

> Time will show that the new approach, emphasizing emergent "macro" control, is equally valid in all the physical sciences, and that the behavioral and cognitive disciplines are leading the way to a more valid framework for all science.[35]

Acknowledging this new scientific heuristic, one may go on to assert that God may also participate interactively in creation. When causation in the universe was seen as unidirectional, people postulated a God who was omnipotent—the Big Boss running the show. But if the nature of causation in the universe, from top to bottom, is *basically* interactive, then one can envision God as interactive. Such a God does not "pull strings" but participates in a reality subject to multiple causations. Such a God deals with us humans as "created co-creators." In this view, the very nature of the created reality is process, and God acts within this process *interactively*.

In such a world each of us must search out the Way on an ongoing basis, from week to week and year to year, as events unfold. God delineates and advocates this Way at a level that we humans cannot discern. But we authors agree with biochemist Arthur Peacocke's suggestion that God may "communicate to humanity in the world in and through events or patterns of events."[36]

Dynamic

We have maintained that humans are basically defined by their trajectory. A person's trajectory is not a predetermined, step-by-step trek toward some fore-ordained goal. Rather, it is a directionality set by a basic "faith" orientation—whether that viewpoint be "it's a jungle out there" or "love your neighbor as yourself" or (perhaps for most of us) some blend of these views and values. Human directionality responds as well to the individuality of each person's own genetic endowment and social niche and to the exigencies of existence. *The resulting process* ("The Way") *delineates for each what people know as soul.*

Earlier, we discussed soul in terms of memory. A person's remembered past is, in fact, an integral part of the process. As Shakespeare observed, "What is past is prologue,"[37] and the process continues throughout life. Without remembrance of things past, there can be no future.

Similarly, we also understand God in terms of process. The writer of the first chapter of Genesis depicted the early planet Earth as "formless and void"— a picture not radically different from the lifeless globe described by paleogeologists. But the "Spirit of God swept over the face of the waters" (see Genesis 1:1–2). Out of that "movement" came our gorgeous blue globe, through a *process* of complexification. This process continued through eons of geologic evolution. When life appeared, it emerged whole, not piecemeal, and has remained so.[38]

A great document of the Christian Church, the Nicene Creed, describes the Holy Spirit as *proceeding* from the Father [and the Son]. The English words *proceed* and *process* derive from the same Latin verb, *procedo.* The Spirit is thus defined through its process. Most of what can be known about God is knowable through process—whether seen as the process of Creation, with its resulting universe, or that of progressive disclosure through history.

Loving

We authors have suggested that the process of God is interactive, not coercive, *by its very nature.* We are not talking about a loving God who, though omnipotent, "abstains" from pushing people around for the sake of their freedom. Instead, we are talking about God whose relation to human beings is *basically* interactive, and thus nourishes the soul, as a mother nourishes the psyche of her infant. We are talking about a personal, respectful relationship of *I and Thou*.[39] People attend to God, who participates in the suffering of the world.[40]

How such a God interacts with humanity, in physical terms, remains a mystery. Trajectory, spirit, soul—these are not physical. They guide physical events and are affected by them. If God is Spirit, God interacts with the physical world as a force or tendency or trajectory or attraction. Perhaps, as physicist and theologian John Polkinghorne suggests,[41] the interaction is in the nature of information input. For now, that will have to do.

Purposeful

A God who promotes trajectories may be said to have purpose. If God has purposes for this Earth and its creatures, what might they be?

One thing that seems evident is that God promotes complexification. It seems significant that complexification occurs at the boundary between order and disorder. To Polkinghorne, "a world of intertwined order and novelty is just that which might be expected as the creation of a God both faithful and loving, who will endow God's world with the twin gifts of reliability and freedom."[42]

If it is true that love fosters the loved one's spiritual growth, then this patterning may be seen as the most loving one can imagine. Contrary to our human wishes, it does not shield humanity from pain. It does not prevent human beings from making unfortunate choices. And it does not smother their growth to maturity. Instead, it puts them in a world where they assume responsibility as created co-creators of what lies ahead. It reflects a purposeful, loving God.

The first letter of John sums up what we have been trying to say: "God is love, and those who abide in love abide in God, and God abides in them. . . . There is no fear in love, but perfect love casts out fear. . . . We love because he first loved us" (1 John 4:16b–19).

CONCLUSION

This chapter has described how the most uniquely human parts of the brain— the frontal lobes—are closely involved in directing the processes of living— setting goals, prioritizing, and carrying through—emphasizing interaction and empathic knowing. These processes are the defining qualities of soul, and they are clues to the way God is God.

God is complexifying, interactive, dynamic, loving, purposeful. We humans participate in a universe that is dynamic, interactive, self-organizing, complexifying, never at rest. And we human beings are like that too.

These traits support an orientation of love. Love for others leads to one's own complexification. Complexification and love are reciprocal. God hands humanity responsibility as created co-creators of what lies ahead.

Faith—"The Way"—guides our human trajectory of becoming!

— EIGHT —

CONCLUSION

THE MIND-PRODUCING BRAIN,
SIN AND EVIL,
AND GOD AS ALL-IN-ALL

So much remains to be explored, yet such exploration reaches out beyond the identifiable horizon. Meaning emerges even as mystery persists. Here it remains to revisit the task and to project the process.

Neuroscientist Antonio Damasio writes of the "mind-producing brain."[1] We have characterized this evolutionary phenomenon as the *humanizing* brain. There are limitless possibilities in what life is meant to be and there are limitless possibilities in what we humans are meant to be. The humanizing brain is flexible, plastic, capable of surprising reaches of thought and action even as it is grounded in biophysiological processes.

THE COSMOS AS MATRIX

This book has maintained that we humans are an intricate part of the cosmos that birthed us. Our bodies consist of the same chemical elements that compose the rest of the world; we respond to gravity and electromagnetic forces. We are *like* this matter-and-energy cosmos. Yet our world has also traversed an unimaginable process of *complexification,* beginning before we came on the scene and presently continuing into the future, with our participation.

We remind the reader that we use the term *complexification* in the specialized way employed by the emerging sciences of complexity. The term denotes a process of *self-organization* that seems to characterize the components of the universe, and of our particular world, at many levels. This self-organization is guided by adaptation to changing circumstances, in a mutual interactive process involving many elements. One result is the establishment of multiple nodes where interaction takes place—whether in the architecture of individual cells, or the development of nervous systems—or, on the macro level, in the organization of economic or political systems. *For its size, in its structure and in its process, the human brain is far and away the most complex entity known in the universe.*

Complex systems are characterized as much by their process as by their form. Two features of their process are of special note: (1) These systems are in continual interaction with multiple features of their environment, which are in turn adapting to them, so that systemic stasis is never reached. Nor are they characterized by internal stasis, for new processes give rise to new internal forms. (2) They are poised on the brink between order and chaos; they combine order and predictability on the one hand with flexibility and experimentation on the other. The notion that scientific models deal with strict predictability and causality is still widespread. However, those working on the forefront of science (many of whom we have cited) no longer believe that! They now see many fundamental natural processes as interactive, contingent, and inherently unpredictable. These features characterize all living systems, and nowhere are they more true than in the human brain.

We have also defined the mind in terms of both process and structure. Its process *is* dependent on its structures—those it shares with reptiles and with other mammals, as well as its more highly developed neocortex and the uniquely human enlargement of the frontal lobes. At the same time, the brain's structure in turn is modified by its process, as we have seen. In other words, the brain's activity affects its chemistry and its connectivity; inactivity tends to decrease its connectivity.

Furthermore, the brain is radically dependent on interaction with its ever changing environment. Before birth, the brain's development is affected by the intrauterine environment. During infancy and early childhood, normal brain development depends on interaction with loving caretakers and on stimulating experiences as well as anatomy and basic nutrition. Throughout life, even into old age, our mental activities and interactions can lead to the proliferation of axon-dendrite connections. The living brain is never static. It is always subject to ebb and flow, always seeking a balance but never settling on any one balance.

The great British neurophysiologist Sir Charles S. Sherrington noted that when the same cortical point was stimulated in various chimpanzees, gorillas, and orangutans, the results were not uniform. He also found variations from time to time in the same animal. The noted Canadian neurosurgeon Wilder Penfield took comfort in Sherrington's findings. If such variation was rampant among animals, then he could be less distressed with "the vagaries of response" that he found in the human cortex.[2] *Thus, although some writers have identified the brain's volatile processes as "mind" and its structure as "brain," it now appears clear that no such strict dichotomy can be claimed.*

It is true that one can attribute definite contributions to the biological substrate. Different behaviors are linked with various modular mechanisms, "each keyed to the peculiar logic and laws of one domain. Thus, people are flexible partly because their minds contain so many different modules, each with provisions to learn in its own way."[3] Consciousness can concentrate first on one module, then on another, then integrate. The limits of the brain's abilities also set boundaries. Without such a universal biological base for human behavior, dictators would have a ball. Anything and everything would become grist for the tyrant's mill. As linguist Steven Pinker declares, "A blank slate is a dictator's dream."[4]

CONSCIOUSNESS AND INTEGRATION

But what defines these modules as an "I"? What promotes the integration of a personality? Neuroscientists have not identified any "grand junction" of the brain, nor any location that appears to be the seat of consciousness or the "I."[5] As the foregoing chapters have shown, consciousness appears to be a process, not a place. Several primal drives apparently help to shape it. Three that seem especially important are the primal need to relate, the primal urge to know, and the primal search for meaning.

The primal need to relate—based on the separation cry found in all mammals—characterizes our species. We humans need one another far beyond infancy, and for more than infantile reasons. As evolutionary psychologist Paul Gilbert observed, drawing on the work of neuroscientist Paul MacLean, "cooperation evolved from the benefits bestowed to species who became capable of joint, coordinated action to secure a goal. Co-operation is therefore an evolved capability for the modification of individualistic competitiveness."[6] Evolutionary biologists would say that the biosocial goals of care-eliciting, caregiving, cooperating, and power seeking are means of actualizing inclusive fitness; in other words, all of the participants in the process enhance their prospects of passing along their genes to the next generation. And in terms of human emotional and contextual needs—the relating nature of life, and the binding power of nurturing care—empathy, compassion, and companionship seem to be our "ticket" to fulfillment.

The primal urge to know calls forth exploration and curiosity. Attending, investigating—and also logic and reflection—are essential if people are to navigate in the environment where they live. As neuroscientist Terrence Deacon has observed, our thought processes are driven by "the underlying combinatorial requirements for symbolic representation in general and the pragmatic performance demands of using spoken symbols to communicate in real time and to effectively organize, regulate, and manipulate social relationships."[7]

It is important to remember that the brain "humanizes" all that it learns. Each person organizes knowledge both according to characteristically human ways of knowing and according to the categories of a particular culture as well as the themes of a unique personality. Men and women operate individually, but in a context of shared experiences and shared expectations.[8]

The primal search for meaning arises from the need to make sense of the ambiguous environment in which people find themselves. Neurophysiologist Rodney Holmes, looking at the record of archaeology, theorizes that hominids since the Neanderthals have been *Homo religiosus*—creatures in search of meaning and significance. Currently, the evidence of the neurosciences "is leading us, not away from, but toward asking about the kinds of meanings humans make."[9] For many, the "cry for meaning"[10] becomes a "cry for God."[11] We are not bound simply to our senses. Humanity's connections are cosmic.

As we humans look for meaning in the cosmos, we perceive ambiguous evidence. We are "at home in the universe,"[12] yet basically vulnerable—in our bodies, in our psyches, in our social organization, and in the future of our kind and even of the earth itself. We cooperate and seek our own best interest—yet we also behave in ways harmful to others and to ourselves. What are we to make of this?

SIN AND EVIL

The notion that the universe has a built-in tendency toward self-organization might prompt an uncritical observer to conclude that progress is inevitable, that "every day in every way it's getting better and better." Or at least, one might conclude that the universe was okay until humans came on the scene. Or perhaps that humans, too, will inevitably progress, if we look at the big picture.

In fact, it is important to remember that the cosmos includes checks on "progress." Not everything that happens leads to organization and complexification. The very historical development of planet Earth has included many contingent events whose consequences have been ambiguous at best. The record bespeaks comet collisions and volcanic eruptions, droughts and floods. Some may have hastened the demise of entire civilizations; others may have opened a niche for new cultural developments.

Second, assuming that there is indeed a built-in tendency to self-organization and complexification, let us not forget the second law of thermodynamics. This law, almost universally accepted among scientists, predicts that in a *closed system,* all organization will eventually subside and disintegrate into a sort of uniform cosmic mush. This process is known as *increase of entropy.*

The key to the concept is the term "closed system"—meaning either an area completely sealed off from all outside influence, or else a system that includes the whole universe over all time. However, over stretches of time, long compared with a human lifetime, a *sub*system can be open. A subsystem such as an organism, an organization, even a planet can dance to the tune of self-organization—*negentropy,* as it is sometimes called—over exceedingly great time periods. Entropy and negentropy are cosmically opposing forces, and their interaction is still not well understood.

So, while complexification is a reality, all is not guaranteed to progress, on a cosmic scale. Furthermore, there was plenty of pain in the world before humans appeared on the scene. There may be cooperation and nurturance among nonhuman animals, but they also eat each other (as humans have been noted to do as well). And all of life—not just humanity—is vulnerable to suffering caused by natural catastrophes, such as fire, drought, and comet collisions.

Now what of humans? Did sin and evil arrive in the world along with *Homo sapiens?* Is that the underlying message of the story of the Fall? The answer, of course, depends on one's definitions of sin and evil. Needless to say, these are immense topics beyond the intent of this book.

Very briefly, one view of sin is that it involves "falling short" of potentialities and demands; another view focuses on intentional harm done to others and/or oneself. In either case, we authors see sin as a condition unique to humans—even though pain and depredation are not. Recent insights into the brain/mind do not change this conclusion, but they may provide some new perspectives for unbundling it.

To function optimally, the brain/mind must constantly perform various tasks of balancing and integrating. The various sectors of the brain have somewhat different biochemical characteristics, as explained in an earlier chapter. Yet they must function together. We submit that, if these systems do not work well together, the result is likely to be the behaviors we have identified as sin!

Many examples could be cited in a general sort of way. For example, if the reptilian brain is activated with little reference to either left-brained reason or limbic-system love, some frightening behaviors are likely to result. One thinks of the goose-stepping parades of Hitler's Nazis, and their horrifying behavior toward those defined as outsiders. City street gangs and members of organized crime seem also to fit this cold-blooded mold. There is raw power without real relatedness.

But a limbic system without reference to reason or goals may also lead to damaging behavior. Think of parents whose attachment to children is so unyielding that the new generation can hardly progress into the independence of adulthood. Consider abusiveness resulting from the need to control a "loved one," because the abuser is terrified of losing a relationship.

Reason without emotion is similarly problematic. Emotion can provide an important guide to motivation. It attracts us humans to each other and propels us into the future. Without it, we may be unable to act, stuck in a "paralysis of analysis." Or we may act "reasonably," but in a way so coldly logical that we miss the point of what *really* matters.

To complicate matters, the brain also needs to strike a balance between different states associated with calmness or arousal. Embedded in our neuroendocrine system are two opposing sets of responses that help the body to deal with varying situations in the environment. One set equips the mind and body to deal with situations perceived as dangerous; the other adapts to conditions of safety. Both sets of responses involve changes in the brain and nervous system, as they regulate such bodily functions as heartbeat, breathing, blood pressure, and digestion, and also mood and reaction time.

There is also a cascade of hormonal variations. As a result, when danger is perceived, heartbeat and breathing speed up, blood is diverted away from the digestive tract and toward muscles used for striking and running, fighting or fleeing, freezing or fainting, and elements are released that make the blood clot more readily in case of injury. In many situations such responses are adaptive. People do need, at times, to fight, or to run quickly from an aggressor, or to respond with intense vigilance. In current urban life, however, the continual pressure for such responses may also lead to such illnesses as heart attacks and high blood pressure.[13]

Opposing these stress responses is an opposite set of responses that equips the body to function optimally regardless of the times. Under the influence of this set of responses, blood pressure decreases, digestion resumes, the blood clots normally, and a person experiences feelings of well-being. Psychologist Paul Gilbert terms these responses associated with stress and calm the "defense system" and the "safety system," respectively (see tables 8.1 and 8.2).[14]

The Defense System

While the defense system (table 8.1) is often useful, it may lead to psychological as well as physical maladaptation. Under conditions of anxiety in the mind and stress in the body (and anxiety/stress are two sides of a single reality),

---

Table 8.1——— The Defense System

FUNCTION:	To alert animal to danger. Designed to defend and/or protect. Involves the focus of signal analyzers on sensory information and passing it on to various appraisal systems for evaluating "meaning" of sensory data.
STIMULI:	1. Nonsocial (predator and physical injury) 2. Social (breeding; territorial and group living)
PSYCHOBIOLOGY:	1. Increase in arousal (e.g. startle, alert), priming go-stop options. 2. Increased activity in various psychobiological systems (e.g. sympathetic/parasympathetic; hippocampus in control mode) to mobilize resources for defense and protection activity.

RESPONSE (PSYCHOMOTOR) OPTIONS

	Go	Stop/Demobilize
ANTI-PREDATOR, NONSOCIAL, INJURY	Fight/Flight Active avoidance Distress (alarm) call	Freeze/Faint Camouflage Passive avoidance
TERRITORIAL CONSPECIFIC	Ritualistic agonistic behavior Flee from occupied territory Ritualistic guarding (homesite, mate, etc.)	Yielding subroutine Helplessness
GROUP LIVING (AGONISTIC)	Signaling dominance by gesture Retreat, avoidance Reverted escape	Signaling submission by gesture (appeasement) Brace readiness high but undischarged arousal

Note: The stop/demobilization responses of the antipredator system are short-term, whereas yielding and help-lessness are longer-lasting changes in state. The short-term responses are dependent on sensory data, whereas it is social behavior that triggers the dominance and yielding routines.

Based on Paul Gilbert, *Human Nature and Suffering.* Hillsdale, N.J.: Lawrence Erlbaum Associates, 1989, 84. By permission of Erlbaum (UK) Taylor & Francis and the author.

---

people tend to fall back on limited and restricting ways of being in the world.[15] When the defense system alerts a person to potential danger, curiosity and exploration may collapse into protectiveness; opposition and aggression tend to erupt. People fight or flee or freeze or faint depending on their appraisal of the situation and their resources for coping with the perceived threat.

As a result, memory, perception, and reasoning become restricted in their ability to serve human needs.[16] In theological terms such an emergency mentality may be termed eschatological apocalypticism. This is a pessimistic expectation that the end of the world, especially one's own psychic and physical world, is at hand.[17] Psychologically, the experience is that of catastrophe.

Taken "hostage" by such forces,[18] the brain may fail to take account of what it needs for adaptive resolution of intrapersonal and interpersonal difficulties. Concentration on survival reactions tends to preclude long-range planning and weighing options. Instead of adaptive engagement, people experience reactive panic, thereby eroding the constructive possibilities in the situation. The brain is unable to arrive at a direction that takes account of crucial information.

To make the best decisions, all parts of the brain must contribute to perception, classification, and understanding of situations. Instead, one's estimate of a situation may be off base, or even grossly distorted, as in psychosis. To the extent that one misunderstands, one will act inappropriately. The psyche is deprived "of its more advanced phylogenetic possibilities . . . and shifts the balance to impulsivity, i.e., away from integration."[19] In other words, people may lose the ability to become centered. The different modules of the brain no longer act in concert. Various parts are at odds with other parts.

Malicious behavior thus arises out of a misguided effort at self-preservation. Such behavior may be person-to-person. It may be built into the very structures of society itself—sexism, classism, racism, ethnocentrism, homophobia. For those caught up in such behavior, other people exist only to be exploited. They are eliminated for the sake of one's own survival.

Theologian Edward Farley identifies ambiguity and vulnerability as basic to the human condition.[20] Anxiousness accompanies vulnerability. People "defend against" anxiety, and thus against the truth of their finitude and mortality. There is a tendency to hide from such hard truths. In the imagery of the Garden of Eden story of the human condition, humanity "hides" from the presence of Yahweh God (Genesis 3:7–24).

Vulnerability may take center stage at any point in life. It can begin before birth with a pregnant mother engaging in substance abuse. That damages the effective development of an infant's nervous system. Or an infant or child may be abused or abandoned, triggering survival reactivity in later situations. In the preadolescent period, before the corpus callosum has matured, an observing ego or self has not yet solidified, and stress gives rise to erratic swings of emotion. Vulnerability can result from the grinding oppressiveness of poverty, helplessness, hopelessness, discrimination. For most of us, at some point, serious illness will underscore our real human vulnerability.

Whatever its origin, loss of integration can result in humans sinning against others and against themselves. It can cause us to do evil.

The Safety System

The safety system (table 8.2) promotes integration and well-being regardless of circumstances.

Table 8.2—— The Safety System

	Go (Active)	No-Go (Passive)
FUNCTION:	1. To alert animal to safety "no-threat cues." 2. Signal analyzers scan environment for stimuli leading to positive reinforcement.	
STIMULI:	1. Nonsocial: cues in the physical environment prompting exploration. 2. Social: attachment, affiliative and cooperative cues, presence of supportive others.	
PSYCHOBIOLOGY	1. Reduce defensive arousal, maintain low fluctuating arousal. 2. Deactivate (if necessary) biological defense responses. Defense against conspecifics not necessary.	
RESPONSE (PSYCHOMOTOR) OPTIONS		
	Go (Active)	No-Go (Passive)
PHYSICAL ENVIRONMENT	Appetitive, explorative	Relaxation, calm, sleep (related to low arousal, not psychomotor braking)
ATTACHMENT	Mutual reinforcing exchanges; cooing, smiling, exploring; intimate sharing. Proximity control (although may also be controlled by evaluation of threat)	As above but in the presence of attachment object
GROUP LIVING	Joint action; friendship, cooperation seeking, sharing, helping, seeking to contribute, group rather than egotistical goals. Close proximity; reassuring signaling, deactivating (defensive) braced readiness.	As above, but in the presence of other conspecifics.

Note: The hedonic safety system promotes health by maintaining defensive arousal at a low level. This is achieved by rendering the social environment safe (by reassurance signals) rather than a source of potential aversive stimulation as in agonic groups.

Based on Paul Gilbert, *Human Nature and Suffering* (Hillsdale, N.J.: Lawrence Erlbaum Associates, 1989), 86. By permission of Erlbaum (UK) Taylor & Francis and the author.

It is promoted by neurohormonal responses to perceptions of safety, and it acts in opposition to the defense system. When the safety system is predominant, it may seem easier to be "good." As Gilbert describes it, the safety system promotes mutually reinforcing behaviors, joint activities, and social rather than egocentric goals. It is the basis of cooperation and social support. It drives the imagination in every "flow" experience, according to psychologist Mihaly Csikszentmihalyi.

The delicate interbalancing of defense and safety systems depends on biochemical processes. It roots the workings of the brain-mind in the laws of physics and chemistry.[21]

Bottom-Up and Top-Down

A casual reading of such data could lead to the conclusion that we humans run on the basis of a bottom-up, reductionistic determinism: we are what our hormones and neurotransmitters make of us. However, a more careful examination of the facts points to influence from *both* a bottom-up nonconscious entry into the nervous system *and* a top-down conscious entry: our values and decisions and understandings influence the outcome as well.

A thoughtful observer will point out that some persons have endured the most wretched catastrophes without falling apart. Some men and women manage to maintain integrity in times of threat or loss. They do not let malice take over. They seem to consider the good of all, even in the face of death. Attaining such integrity may be the project of a lifetime. Although it may be supported by strong nurturing in early life, it may also be attained by those whose beginnings were not so ideal. One test of religious convictions and practices may be their contributions to such integrity—their "fruits."

Intentionality is still the core of humanity. Jesus is a prime exemplar of how even terminal suffering may be borne with nobility. Throughout his Passion, his actions were governed by his knowledge that his life had a purpose that outweighed the circumstances at hand. He was aware that he was playing a central role in a drama intimately connected to the past and the future. Yet even Jesus himself faltered a little in the face of pain and abandonment.

In daily life we encounter those who do not become aggressive or selfish in the face of dread. They may break down from time to time, but they maintain their basic integration. They do not transgress the boundaries and integrity of others. In fact, they may even continue to focus on what others need, whether that be affirmation, empathy, freedom, food, shelter, or security.

Neuroscience is making clear that our brains are made for meaning and for relatedness. Evidence is accumulating that the humanizing brain is a "healing" brain.[22] It develops and is organized to maintain the physical and psychic health of the human organism, even in "sin" and "sickness" and "suffering"—or, in the parlance of neuroscience, during "social-spiritual disturbance" and "bio-chemical-psychic disturbance." Within the nervous system's core is an inherently adaptive system that is "physiologically geared to process information to a state of mental health."[23] This, we suggest, is the neurological correlate of the view of the goodness of creation in Genesis 1.

GOD AS ALL-IN-ALL

This book has consistently taken the view that the human brain-mind, as part of the universe, partakes of the character of that universe. The laws of the universe affect the brain; the brain-mind provides clues to the nature of the cosmos. In the words of Alfred North Whitehead, "It is a false dichotomy to think of Nature *and* Man. Mankind is that factor in Nature that exhibits in its most intense form the plasticity of Nature."[24] There is no way we can understand humanity without its biophysical base, and no way we can understand nature without including human presence.

Faith emerges as an expression of the "fit" between the universe or context in which humanity finds itself and the only resource it has with which to engage that context, namely, the human brain. The study and understanding of the brain is fascinating in and of itself. However, we authors have taken an added step. We regard the brain as a primary lens with which to study and understand the cosmos and its dynamic source, namely, God.

Because we view the human mind as a prime connection between humanity and the universe of which it is a part, we ourselves regard the brain as both metaphor and analogue. When the brain is driven by fear and anxiety, its state suggests "increasing entropy." The "center does not hold"; brain functions are not optimally integrated. Except in situations where fight-or-flight is truly appropriate, such a brain is unlikely to promote the well-being of its owner or its neighbors. In contrast, when the brain is integrating and complexifying, it seems to echo the complexifying course of the emerging universe. The brain may then be seen as a metaphor of an emerging God—even though it is not God. Thus we have developed a way to move from examination of the working brain to identification of clues to God's ways of being God.

It is true that not all brain-minds are identical. For example, there seem to be gender differences in the brain, which apparently affect the ways in which men and women typically process information. Brains also differ from one individual to another—even in gross appearance, brains differ as much as faces do. Among our companions are some who can accomplish mental feats that others only dream of.

Any attempt to discern ultimate reality must employ the abilities of both hemispheres, the inclinations of both sexes, and the talents of all sorts of persons.[25] All these human variations may be seen as evolutionary "strategies" that help us humans to compensate for our finitude. Through our various abilities we collectively cast a wider net in our search for the "really real."[26]

We have used Paul MacLean's descriptions of the triune brain—a brain of three minds—as ways of glimpsing the self-organizing dynamics of the world as we know it. Our analysis has pointed to a God who attends to concrete reality and to a God of emotion—a loving, nurturant God, but also one who has been characterized as wrathful, jealous, and sometimes even playful. It has echoed a universe that has proven to be amazingly predictable through the use of left-brain analysis, including mathematics. The God underlying this universe has appeared to be a left-brained logician, a creator and sustainer of infinite subtlety. Prophetic writers have discerned a God who "holds the whole world in his hands," all at once and in context, rather as the right brain discerns all at once. Finally, the frontal lobes, with their empathic abilities, their ability to set goals and prioritize, echo familiar references to a God who has a plan, who has purposes, and who empathically interacts with the world and all that is therein.

The various views of God evoked by the human brain are in fact familiar. The theological insights are not new. All that may be new here is an analysis that finds in the human brain a mirror of all these *imagines Dei*—all these images of God—and thus may suggest further ways of comprehending them.

GOD AS INTEGRATING AND EMERGING

This concluding chapter has traced the ways in which the brain-mind is one. The substance of the brain and the processes of the mind—all interact, derive from one another, are inseparable. It is becoming increasingly clear, in fact, that the genetic knowledge of the old brain and the cultural knowledge of the new brain coevolve, as Ralph Burhoe and a few other prophets perceived some three decades ago.[27] These insights make meaning seeking understandable in new ways.

This chapter has also traced the ways in which the processes of the mind, losing integration under stress, may lose the ability to pursue the true good of the self and the good of others—two goals that actually are inseparable. It has thus alluded to sin and evil, although we have only begun to scratch the surface of these problems.

We humans are "fearfully and wonderfully made," as the psalmist put it (39:14), potential cocreators of the good, and potential perpetrators of evil. In the words of neuroscientist Antonio Damasio:

> Perhaps the most indispensable thing we can do as human beings, every day of our lives, is *remind ourselves and others of our complexity, fragility, finiteness, and uniqueness.* And this is of course the difficult job . . . : to move the spirit from its nowhere pedestal to a somewhere place, while preserving its dignity and importance; to recognize its humble origin and vulnerability, yet still call upon its guidance.[28]

Nature, as psychologist William Bevan has observed, is "orderly in its complexity rather than lawful in its simplicity."[29] A hidden wisdom permeates the universe. New things are being disclosed, emerging out of the covert informedness in which we dwell (cf. Isaiah 48:6–7).

God is continually creating the place in which we live, and we are ever renovating the world of which we are a part. The gradual but insistent emergence of the new has a basic impact on us humans; we join the "conversation" as we grope for our response. Our universe is in the hands of the whole-making, integrating, emerging God! May we, as cocreators, work also toward whole-making.

– Notes –

FOREWORD

1. Buber 1988.
2. Köhler [1938] 1976.
3. For a sense of the intellectual scope and larger stakes of earlier historical efforts in this direction, especially in the interwar German context, see my book, *Reenchanted Science: Holism in German Culture from Wilhelm II to Hitler* (Harrington 1996).
4. The poem from which this line is taken is worth enjoying in full:

> The Brain—is wider than the Sky—
> For—put them side by side—
> The one the other will contain
> With ease—and You—beside—
>
> The Brain is deeper than the sea—
> For—hold them—Blue to Blue—
> The one the other will absorb—
> As Sponges—Buckets—so—
>
> The Brain is just the weight of God—
> For—Heft them—Pound for Pound—
> And they will differ—if they do—
> As Syllable from Sound—

(Poem 632. Reprinted by permission of the publishers and the Trustees of Amherst College from *The Poems of Emily Dickinson*, Thomas H. Johnson, ed. Cambridge, Mass.: The Belknap Press of Harvard University Press, copyright © 1951, 1955, 1979, 1983 by the President and Fellows of Harvard College.)

PREFACE

1. Kauffman 1995, 4–5, 302.
2. Damasio 1994, 259.
3. Damasio 1994, 251.
4. Damasio 1994, 252, emphasis added.
5. Kauffman 1995, 47–48.
6. Burhoe 1981; see Breed 1990–1992, 1992.

INTRODUCTION: TOWARD A NEUROBIOLOGY OF MEANING

1. Cited by Taylor 1979, 17–19.
2. Cacioppo 1992; Cacioppo and Tassinary 1990; Cacioppo and Berntson 1992; Tillich 1963.
3. Gewertz 1995.
4. Schmitz-Moormann 1995.
5. Campbell 1974; Burhoe 1981.
6. Davies [1987] 1989.
7. Luria 1987.
8. Fleming 1974.
9. Rolston 1990, 85.
10. Augustine 1991, 4, Bk. 1, Ch. 3, emphasis added.
11. Whyte 1973.
12. Einstein 1954, 293.
13. Simmons 1993, 127, quoted by Gold 1995, 74, emphasis added.
14. Tillich 1948a, xiii.
15. E.g., Davies 1992; Barbour 1990; Hefner 1993.
16. Davies [1987] 1989, 203, emphasis in original. Here, and in excerpted material throughout our book, the reader will find forms of the word "man" or the masculine pronoun that are intended to refer to all human beings. We have opted not to mark such appearances with "*sic*" because of the distraction created by overusing this device.
17. Paul Davies describes patterns, novelty, creativity, and uncertainty as part of the "propensity for self-organization" at every level of the universe. He rejects the term *predestinist* because of its assumption of "inevitable outcome of the operation of the laws of nature." Instead, he prefers the term *predisposition*: "nature has a predisposition to progress along the general lines it has . . . [which includes] the existence of complexity and organization at all levels, including human consciousness." "Creation is not instantaneous; it is an ongoing process. The universal has a life history . . . [like an unfolding flower] a pre-existing plan or project which the universe is realizing as it develops," a "cosmic blueprint," if you will (Davies [1987] 1989, 201, 203, 200).
18. We caution the reader that by complexification we do not mean a process by which the world necessarily gets "better and better." It is a morally neutral process whose outcome *can be affected* by moral agents.
19. The word *symbol* comes from a Greek word meaning "to throw a token." We throw out symbols as tokens of larger ideas. They thereby point beyond themselves toward a greater structure in which they participate. The word *metaphor* also comes from the Greek and means "to transfer." Metaphors are images that bridge different meanings by showing a likeness between them. That transfers meaning from one object to another, thereby suggesting new and different understanding (Pearce 1992, 155).

20. We are indebted to Professor Rachel M. Caldwell, Director of the Division of Arts and Humanities, Rogers State College, for the phrase "the humanizing brain."

21. Augustine 1991, 201, Bk. 10, Ch. 26, emphasis added.

22. Augustine 1955, n. 28, 224.

23. Augustine 1991, 183, Bk. 10, Ch. 6.

24. Edelman 1992, 68, 112.

25. Sperry 1991.

26. Feindel 1975, xxvi.

27. Barbour 1974, 1990; Pannenberg 1976; Rolston 1987; Breed 1992; Gilkey 1993; Jones 1994.

28. Arbib and Hesse 1986; Gerhart and Russell 1984; Hefner 1993.

29. Like every generalization, broad categories such as "neuroscience" and "religion" obscure as much as they clarify. Our reference to neuroscience graphically illustrates the case of saying too much and informing too little. As a reflection of the accelerating importance of neuroscience research, the United States Congress declared the 1990s to be the "Decade of the Brain." During this era, research has emerged in a range of disciplines from molecular biology to behavioral analysis to consideration of consciousness. While we recognize the basic importance of a cellular and molecular approach to the function of the nervous system (for instance, Changeux 1985; Nicholls, Martin, and Wallace 1992) in which an understanding of neurons, synapses, neurotransmitters, and their properties are basic to understanding higher brain functions, our competence and interest are directed more to "the new cognitive neuroscience" (for instance, Gardner 1985; LeDoux and Hirst [1986] 1990; Kosslyn and Koenig 1992) in which attention is directed to how the brain thinks and perceives, to "cognitive psychology" (for instance, Medin and Ross 1990), functions of the mind (for instance, Trevarthen 1990), neuropsychology (for instance, Kolb and Whishaw [1981] 1985), to "the neuropsychology of consciousness" (for instance, Milner and Rugg 1992) and "the psychology of consciousness" (for instance, Farthing 1992), and to language itself (for instance, Lakoff 1987; Pinker 1994) as "a human instinct, hard-wired like web spinning in spiders."

30. Tillich 1959, 131–32.

31. Kaufman 1993, 424.

32. Kaufman 1993, 424–25.

33. Kaufman 1993, 418.

34. Kaufman 1993, 424.

35. Guthrie 1993, 62–90.

36. Cf. Hefner 1993.

37. MacLean 1985a, 1987.

38. Winnicott 1965, 1971.

1. A NEUROBIOLOGY OF FAITH

1. Diamond 1988.

2. Gazzaniga 1985, 65–73, 88–91.

3. Johnson 1994.

4. Gazzaniga 1967; Ornstein 1977, 30.

5. Gazzaniga 1985.

6. See Hewstone 1983; Harvey and Weary 1985.

7. Hellige 1990, 69.

8. Kauffman 1995, emphasis added.

9. Perecman 1984.

10. Gazzaniga 1992, 37–38.

11. See Diamond 1988.

12. Cited by Mecacci 1991, 273.

13. Jastrow 1981, 65–66.

14. Jastrow 1981, 66–67.

15. Mecacci 1991, 274–75, emphasis added.

16. Mecacci 1991, 275–76.

17. Arnheim 1969, 23; Guthrie 1993, 45, 47.

18. Gross 1992; Bruce et al. 1992.

19. Gross 1992; Rolls 1992; Perrett et al. 1992.

20. Bloom and Lazerson [1985] 1988, 110.

21. Gross 1992, 6.

22. Wiesel 1981, 267–77.

23. Bowlby 1969, 1973, 1980; Stern 1985; MacLean 1990a.

24. Freedman 1974, 28–30.

25. National Advisory Mental Health Council 1995, 840.

26. C. Jirari 1970; cited by Freedman 1974, 30–31.

27. Johnson and Morton 1991, 33, 106.

28. Johnson and Morton 1991, 141.

29. Freedman 1974, 31.

30. Berlyne 1958a, 1958b.

31. Freedman 1974, 31.

32. Berelson and Steiner 1964, 249.

33. Kolb and Whishaw [1980] 1985, 218.

34. Kolb and Whishaw [1980] 1985, 557.

35. Cohen-Levine et al. 1988.

36. Medin and Ross 1992.

37. Guthrie 1993.

38. Kauffman 1995, 42.

39. Davies [1987] 1989, 21.

40. Kauffman 1995, 45.

41. Harvey 1964, 146–48; Richardson and Bowden 1983, 338–39.

42. Chomsky 1986.

43. Bandler and Grinder 1975.

44. Research is detailing more precisely the neural structures serving language. For instance, Antonio and Hanna Damasio believe three interacting sets of structures process language (1992). First is a collection of neural systems in each cerebral hemisphere representing nonlanguage interactions between the body and its environment. These interactions are mediated by varied sensory and motor systems. The brain categorizes these nonlanguage representations and also creates another level of representation organizing the classification. These successive layers of symbolic expression "form the basis for abstraction and metaphor." Second is a smaller number of neural systems, mostly in the left hemisphere, representing syntactic rules for combining words. These systems assemble word forms and generate sentences. A third set of structures, also mostly in the left hemisphere, mediates between the first two systems. It can take a concept and stimu-

late words, or it can receive words and evoke concepts. The Damasios hypothesize "embodied ensembles of neurons within the brain's many 'convergence' regions." Here there are feedforward and feedbackward projections, firing simultaneously and reconstructing previous patterns of mental activity. They conclude that "because the brain categorizes perceptions simultaneously along many different dimensions, symbolic representations such as metaphor can easily emerge from the architecture." "The brain uses different neural systems to represent entities that differ in structure or behavior or entities that a person relates to in different ways."

45. Pinker 1994.
46. Korzbyski 1933.
47. Jones 1991, 129.
48. Jones 1991, 127–35.
49. Smith 1977, 44, 36–38.
50. Eccles 1989, 203.
51. Holmes 1991, 13.

2. "MIND" AS BRIDGE BETWEEN RELIGION AND NEUROSCIENCE

1. MacLean 1990a, 570.
2. Davies 1992, 16, 24.
3. Guthrie 1993, 4.
4. Tillich 1968, 63, 68.
5. James [1890] 1904, 8.
6. Pinker 1994, 430.
7. Pinker 1994, 430, emphasis added.
8. Prigogine and Stengers 1984, 47, 22, 49.
9. Prigogine and Stengers 1984, xxx, 36, 303, 310.
10. Prigogine and Stengers 1984 ,82.
11. Prigogine and Stengers 1984, 309.
12. E.g., Prigogine and Stengers 1984; Davies [1987] 1989, 1992; Barton 1994; Kauffman 1995.
13. Kauffman 1995, 20, 24, 25; emphasis added.
14. Guthrie 1993, 10–38.
15. Feuerbach 1957, 19, emphasis in original.
16. Feuerbach 1957, Ch. II, 10–11.
17. Feuerbach 1957, 65.
18. Greenberg and Mitchell 1983; Mitchell 1988; Merkur 1990.
19. Winnicott 1963, 94, quoted by Spero 1992, 188.
20. Although Jesus as the Christ symbolizes—incarnates—the eternal God for Christians, the New Testament witnesses to the rejection of that absolutizing by virtue of the crucifixion. Tillich (1957) contends that precisely because Jesus gave up the claim to ultimacy we have a criterion of ultimacy. In the Fourth Gospel, Jesus declares: "Who believes in me *believes not in me* but in him who sent me" (John 12:44, emphasis added).
21. Rizzuto 1979; McDargh 1983; Meissner 1984.
22. Geertz 1973, 90.
23. Geertz 1973, 87–125; cited by Guthrie 1993, 27.
24. Geertz 1973, 112.
25. Geertz 1973, 120.

26. Frankl 1978.

27. In contrast to Geertz's position, in the early 1980s anthropologist Victor Turner confessed to the limitation of anthropological axioms that "express the belief that all human behavior is the result of social conditioning" ([1983] 1993).

28. Geertz 1973, 140–41.

29. Laughlin, McManus, and d'Aquili 1990, xii.

30. Guthrie 1993, 90, emphasis added.

31. Guthrie 1993, 158–61.

32. MacLean 1990a, 570.

33. Guthrie 1993, 140.

34. MacLean 1990a, 570; Burhoe 1981.

35. MacLean 1990a, 545–52.

36. Vandervert 1988, 321, quoted by MacLean 1991, 20.

37. Davies 1992, 158.

38. Davies 1992, 170, 198.

39. Spero 1992, 187.

40. Barbour 1994, 6.

41. For instance, "we see in wildflowers only those patterns reflecting light visible to humans, that is, that between infrared and ultraviolet, and we assume we see all there is to see about flowers. In contrast insects, whose view of flowers is privileged by highly evolved relations with them, see flower patterns visible by ultraviolet as well" (Guthrie 1993, 81).

42. Quoted by Feindel 1975, xxvi.

43. MacLean 1992, 57.

44. MacLean 1992, 66.

45. Davies 1992, 136.

46. Rolston 1987, 45–47.

47. Waldrop 1992, 145, 253, and passim.

48. Waldrop 1992, 160.

49. Hobson 1994.

50. Jeans 1931, 137, quoted by Davies 1992, 203.

51. Davies 1992, 16.

52. Hefner 1993, 85.

53. Tillich 1968, 63, 68.

54. Cited by Davies 1992, 182.

55. Ashbrook 1958, 1991b, 1992a.

56. Gen. 1:28; note Metzger and Murphy 1991, 3.

57. Schussler Fiorenza 1994, 131.

58. Kuhn 1970.

59. Geertz 1973, 141.

60. Sperry 1991, 243; see also Sperry 1993.

61. Sperry 1991, 247.

62. Sperry 1991, 240.

63. Sperry 1991, 247.

64. Barbour 1994, 7.

65. The poet-painter William Blake (1757–1827) followed Michelangelo's lead in his own memorable image of God in *The Ancient of Days* in which the muscular figure, using his left hand

rather than his right, symbolically represents the Lord as the Architect of the Universe (Janson 1967, 467–68).

66. Fleming 1974, 191–94.

67. Quoted by Fleming 1974, 194.

68. Janson 1967, 360.

69. Janson 1967, 360.

70. Miller and Christensen 1991, 1111.

71. See Schüssler Fiorenza 1994.

72. Meshberger 1990, 1841.

3. THE UPPER BRAIN STEM, ATTENDING, AND AN EVER-PRESENT GOD

1. Einstein 1954, 292.

2. MacLean 1970; 1978, 1990a.

3. MacLean 1949, 350.

4. MacLean 1949, 351.

5. MacLean 1970; [1975] 1993, 24.

6. See Ashbrook 1993.

7. E.g., Rodriguez 1993; Trevarthen 1988, 93, 142; Pribram 1984. MacLean assumes an upward extension of the three main sections of the brain, reflecting three mentalities in an emergent and developmental progression. In assuming this extension, however, he indicates interconnections between the regions. Paleoneurologist Harry J. Jerison stresses the appearance of intelligence as a biological process. That means he traces distinct changes in the relation of brain size and body size. This is technically known as encephalization and reflects "the rapidity and recency of the increase . . . in the hominid lineage" (Jerison 1976). These changes required "new ways of encoding neural information," specifically, "translating spatial information [olfaction] into a temporal [audition] code." That culminated in the human capacity for imagery, language, and culture. In contrast, evolutionary linguist Terrence W. Deacon argues for a view that distinguishes "three distinct evolutionary processes: brain evolution, language evolution, and brain-language coevolution" (Deacon 1992). This view emphasizes "feedback" of the emergent functions more than a paleoneurological thrust upward and forward (Holmes 1995, 10). Deacon focuses particularly on the structural, functional, and neurologically unique features of vocal communication. Most crucial is the evolutionary shift from stereotypic cell repertoires to prefrontal intentional control of vocalization.

8. Augustine 1991, 127, Bk. 7.16.

9. We reject the implied Platonic view voiced by Augustine of something that is permanent, unchangeable, and fixed. Instead, we hold to a prototypical view of knowledge in which generalized abstract categories of "things" are conceivable because they are based on various examples or exemplars, some better "fits" than others. But the abstract generalization or category is *not* an "unchangeable" entity.

10. MacLean 1990a, 9.

11. MacLean 1990a, 9.

12. MacLean 1978, 318.

13. MacLean 1982b, 194.

14. Carr 1963, 128.

15. Carr 1963, 136, 157–67.

16. MacLean 1990a, 233–34.

17. MacLean 1982b, 200.

18. MacLean 1982b.

19. MacLean 1978, 321.

20. MacLean 1990a, 231.

21. Ardrey 1968, 3.

22. Ardrey 1968, 337.

23. Jones 1991. "1. Sovereign equality of states; 2. Territorial integrity and political independence of states; 3. Equal rights and self-determination of peoples; 4. Nonintervention in the internal affairs of states; 5. Peaceful settlement of disputes between states; 6. Abstention from the threat or use of force; 7. Fulfillment in good faith of international obligations; 8. Cooperation with other states; 9. Respect for human rights and fundamental freedoms" plus two additional principles: "Creation of an equitable international order/Protection of the environment" (xii).

24. Penfield 1975, 83.

25. Gardner 1985.

26. Bruce 1994.

27. Hobson 1994, 86–88.

28. Hobson 1994, 87–88.

29. MacLean 1976, 206.

30. Fox 1986, 38.

31. Ashbrook 1992a, 36.

32. Eccles 1983, xv; Fox 1986, 38.

33. Ashbrook 1992a, 41.

34. Hobson 1994, 15–16.

35. Hobson 1994, 14–15.

36. Hobson 1994, 88.

37. MacLean [1975] 1993, 24.

38. Ashbrook 1989b.

39. See Wilken 1993.

40. In a personal conversation with Ashbrook, Rabbi Herman E. Schalmann suggested that a proper translation of the Hebrew is not "jealous" but "zealous."

41. These categories reflect a Platonic realm of unchangeability, a characterization that we reject in terms of both theology and physics. We live in an open, dynamic universe, an emergent reality, not a static one.

42. Ruether 1983.

43. Ardrey 1968, 26.

44. See Will 1994, 49; Kauffman 1995.

45. McFague 1987.

46. Whitehead 1978, 222, cit. by Will 1994, 23.

47. Will 1994, 23.

48. Cirlot [1964] 1974, 285–90.

49. MacLean 1990a, 231–32.

50. Carr 1963, 165.

51. Gilbert 1989, 224.

52. Gilbert 1989, 224–33.

53. See, for instance, Jeremiah 20:7.
54. MacLean 1990a, 237.
55. MacLean 1978, 21–22.
56. MacLean 1990a, 237–38.
57. This was a line of permanent fortifications built by the French along their eastern border. Because of its inflexibility, the German armies easily bypassed it in their conquest of France.
58. Csikszentmihalyi 1993, 240.
59. Burhoe 1981.
60. Ashbrook 1984c, 1984d, 1985a.
61. Csikszentmihalyi 1993, 259.
62. Turner 1986.
63. Harlow 1972, 403.
64. Harlow 1972, 401.
65. Klivington 1989, 186; Ader, Felten, and Cohen 1990.
66. Stevens 1986, 23.
67. Pannenberg 1993, 156, emphasis added.
68. MacLean 1990a, 244.

4. THE LIMBIC LOBES, RELATING, AND A NURTURING GOD

1. Bronowski and Mazlish 1960, 228.
2. Barrett 1986, 14–20; Bronowski and Mazlish 1960, 220–29; Gregory 1987, 189–90. Ironically and paradoxically, Descartes's vision of mathematical physics as the basis and explanation of reality came to him in a dream and depended on "an omnipotent, benevolent, and non-deceiving God" (Gregory 1987, 189).
3. The claw image seems to imply that the limbic system is devoid of cortex. This implication is misleading. The great nineteenth-century neuroanatomist Paul Broca was the first to use the term *limbic,* describing what he called the limbic lobe in an 1878 paper. Broca's great limbic lobe is enveloped by an older (simpler) form of cortex.
4. MacLean popularized the term *limbic system* in his 1952 paper.
5. MacLean 1952; LaPlante 1993.
6. See, for example, Klivington 1989, 197.
7. Bloom and Lazerson [1985] 1988, 213.
8. Trevarthen [1986] 1993; Bowlby 1969, 1973, 1980.
9. Lazarus 1991.
10. Leeper 1970, 156–7, quoted by Lazarus 1991, 180.
11. MacLean 1990a, 314.
12. Tillich 1952.
13. Freud [1930] 1958, [1920] 1959, 93.
14. Quoted by Freud [1922] 1960, 41.
15. Freud [1927] 1957, 11.
16. Tillich 1948, 154–55.
17. Tillich 1948, 158–59.
18. MacLean 1990a, 314, 380.
19. Carrington 1963, 146.
20. Carrington 1963, 146–47.

21. Ploog 1992, 3–4.

22. Ploog 1992, 10.

23. Bradshaw and Rogers 1993, 248.

24. Bradshaw and Rogers 1993, 277. The use of tools and symbolic communication are not exclusive to *Homo sapiens*; "both can be studied in wild and captive chimpanzee populations." However, cultural and artistic developments "coincided with the arrival of anatomically modern people in Europe" (Bradshaw and Rogers 1993, 277).

25. Konner [1982] 1983, 246–52.

26. Csikszentmihalyi 1993, xii–xiii.

27. Turner [1983] 1993, 95–96, 94.

28. MacLean 1985a, 413.

29. Carrington 1963, 147–50.

30. Carrington 1963, 147–50.

31. Trevarthen [1986] 1993, 1990b.

32. MacLean 1985a, 1990a.

33. Carrington 1963, 146.

34. Carrington, 1963, 147.

35. Carrington 1963, 146.

36. Levy 1985.

37. Refers to the young Jewish person's arrival at religious and legal maturity and the occasion that formally recognizes and celebrates that event, usually the first Sabbath after his or her thirteenth birthday. The service for girls was not found before the nineteenth century and is not celebrated as often as bar mitzvah for boys.

38. Although originally part of the baptismal ritual, since the sixteenth century it has come to be a later ratification by a young person of the vows associated with her or his baptism in infancy.

39. Adult baptism was the norm of the early church and presupposed a process of instruction in the faith. While Baptist churches since the seventeenth century have insisted on the baptism of adults only and, therefore, a regenerate church membership—a gathering of believers—the rite is associated with a profession of faith as an intentional and freely chosen act.

40. Klivington 1989, 150.

41. Bloom and Lazerson [1985] 1988, 64.

42. Cohen 1988, 170.

43. Trevarthen 1990a, 5.

44. Klivington 1989, 152–53.

45. Klivington 1989, 22; Diamond 1988, 54.

46. Giovacchini 1993, 222–23.

47. Ashbrook 1993, 303, quoted from Winnicott 1971, 112.

48. Spitz 1945, 1946, cited in Giovacchini 1993, 39.

49. Giovacchini 1993, 38–39.

50. Trevarthen [1986] 1993.

51. Harlow and Harlow 1971, 70–73.

52. Harlow and Harlow 1971, 73.

53. Harlow and Harlow 1971, 73–74.

54. Begley 1997, 32.

55. Stern 1985, 72.

56. Stern 1985, 128, citing the work of Trevarthen and Hubley 1978.
57. Stern 1985, 128–32.
58. Whitehead 1933, 226.
59. Whitehead 1947, 230.
60. Will 1994, 7–32.
61. Whitehead 1926, 16, 59, cited by Will 1994, 20–21.
62. Hartshorne 1948, 27.
63. Hartshorne 1948, 28–29.
64. Hartshorne 1948, xv.
65. Hartshorne 1948, xv.
66. Hartshorne 1948, xv.
67. Schmitz-Moormann 1995.
68. Whitehead 1933, 213.
69. Whitehead 1933, 105
70. Whitehead 1933, 214.
71. Case-Winters 1990.
72. Hartshorne 1948, 142.
73. Whitehead 1933, 221.
74. Whitehead, quoted by Armstrong 1994, 384.
75. Whitehead 1933, 105–6.
76. Whitehead 1947, 297.

5. THE LIMBIC SYSTEM, REMEMBERING, AND A MEANING-MAKING GOD

1. Lazarus 1991.
2. Leeper 1970, 156–57, quoted by Lazarus 1991, 180.
3. Squire 1987, 152–74.
4. Squire 1987, 160, 169–70; Schacter and Tulving 1994.
5. Scoville and Milner 1957.
6. Mishkin and Appenzeller 1987, 4.
7. Squire 1987, 194; Lynch and Baudry 1988.
8. Schacter and Tulving 1994.
9. Winson [1985] 1986, 12.
10. Squire 1987, 176–77.
11. Squire 1983, 491.
12. Ashbrook 1992a.
13. Augustine 1991, 194, Bk. Ten, Ch. 17.
14. Augustine 1873, 93. The following material is taken from Ashbrook 1992a with minor changes.
15. Oates 1948, 766.
16. Morgan 1932, 127.
17. Oates 1948, 794; Augustine 1873, 254, 256, 354.
18. Augustine 1991, 231–32, Bk. 11, Ch. 15.
19. Augustine 1991, 200, Bk. 10, Ch. 25; 1, Bk. 1, Ch. 1.
20. Augustine 1991, 185, Bk. 10, Ch. 8.
21. Browning 1987, 23.

178 Notes to Pages 93–96

22. Scoville and Milner 1957.

23. Winson [1985] 1986, 30–34, 201–2; Fox 1986.

24. Eichenbaum, Otto, and Schottler, 1991.

25. Mishkin and Appenzeller 1987, 10.

26. Squire 1987, 194; Fox 1986, 35–37.

27. Squire 1987, 170.

28. Squire 1987, 162–63.

29. Squire 1987, 242.

30. Olton 1983.

31. Squire 1987, 169, 173.

32. Loftus and Yuille 1984, 168.

33. Neisser 1988, 357.

34. Spence 1982.

35. Neisser 1988, 365–66.

36. Barclay and DeCooke 1988, 91–92; see Barsalou 1984.

37. Antonovsky 1987; Squire 1987, 223.

38. Erikson 1968.

39. Barclay and DeCooke 1988, 120.

40. Winograd 1988, 17.

41. Weingartner and Parker 1984.

42. Spear and Mueller 1984, 116.

43. Kolb and Whishaw [1980] 1985, 481–94; Winson [1985] 1986, 10–17.

44. Kleitman 1969; Kripke 1982; Rossi [1986] 1993, 154. The original elements of the BRAC hypothesis—stomach contractions and waking activity—"are untenable." Further, nothing phylogenetically old or teleologically basic has been found. Several cycles—psychologic, physiologic, and hormonal—have been found. "The wealth of phenomena that have been uncovered in pursuit of the BRAC hypothesis should console any investigator troubled that the hypothesis remains controversial. Dramatic behavioral cycles have been discovered . . . fantasy, hemispheric dominance, and perceptual processing . . . [e]pisodic hormonal secretion . . . related to the REM cycle. . . . the pituitary['s responsivity] to intermittent releasing hormone stimulation . . . the most plausible revision of the BRAC hypothesis is to theorize that that same oscillatory process that is expressed during sleep in the REM-nonREM cycle may also be expressed in certain oscillatory phenomena during the day" (Kripke 1982, 336).

45. Rossi 1991.

46. Brown and Graeber 1982.

47. What dreams people are able to recall from non-REM sleep are reality-oriented rather than of the bizarre nature of REM dreams.

48. Hobson 1988.

49. Fiss 1979, 22–26.

50. Hauri 1979, 256.

51. Hobson 1988, 218 (emphasis in original), 169, 194.

52. Hobson 1988, 271.

53. Winson 1990.

54. Fiss 1979, 26.

55. Hauri 1979.

56. Winson [1985] 1986, 34.

57. Klein and Armitage 1978.

58. Ashbrook 1992a.

59. Morgenstern 1962; Andreasen 1978.

60. Ashbrook 1988a, 159–69.

61. Burhoe 1973, 417.

62. Squire, Cohen, and Nadel 1984, 188.

63. Eccles 1983, xv; Fox 1986, 35.

64. Fox 1986, 38.

65. Winograd 1988, 17.

66. Ornstein [1972, 1977] 1986.

67. Squire, Cohen, and Nadel 1984, 206.

68. Dourley 1975, 55.

69. Some of the following material is adapted from Ashbrook 1994.

70. Horton et al. 1988.

71. Winnicott 1971.

72. Winnicott 1971, 2.

73. Winnicott 1971, 14.

74. Cohen 1988, 170.

75. Cohen 1988, 170, citing Kaplan and Saddock 1980.

76. Diamond 1988, 91–114.

77. Werner and Smith 1982, 159, quoted by Kagan 1996, 902.

78. Tracy 1975, 105.

79. Tracy 1975.

80. McFague 1987.

81. Hefner 1994.

82. Hefner 1994, 508, emphasis in original.

83. Paraphrased by Hefner 1994, 527.

84. Tillich 1948, 162, emphasis in original.

85. d'Aquili [1983] 1993, 50.

86. d'Aqulli [1983] 1993, 61–62, emphasis in original.

87. d'Aquili [1983] 1993, 67.

88. d'Aqulli [1983] 1993, 63, emphasis in original.

89. Lex 1979.

90. Hess 1925.

91. Lex 1979; d'Aquili [1983] 1993, 68–69.

92. Turner [1983] 1993, 88.

93. Turner [1983] 1993, 89.

94. Augustine 1955, Bk. X, viii, 210.

95. Rossi [1986] 1993; see also Johnson 1987.

96. Trevarthen [1986] 1993.

97. Taylor 1979.

98. Taylor 1979, 17–19.

99. Lakoff 1987; Johnson 1987.

100. Burrell 1979, 31.

101. Aquinas 1945, Vol. 1, 6 (1.1.1).

102. Rumelhart et al. [1986] 1987.

103. Sellers 1962.
104. d'Aquili [1983] 1993, 72.
105. MacLean 1985b, 221.
106. MacLean 1982a.
107. Paterson and Moran 1988.
108. Burhoe 1981.
109. Hartshorne 1975, 92.
110. Wolf 1984, 119.
111. MacLean 1985a, 417.

6. THE NEOCORTEX, ORGANIZING, AND A VERSATILE GOD

1. Livingston 1981; Gregory 1987, 347–53. Since the 1980s, technologies for obtaining images of brain activity have become widely available. These include: Computed Tomography, or CT, which generates X-ray images of tissue density; Magnetic Resonance Imagery, or MRI, which provides information based on the magnetic properties of the atoms in the individual molecule; and Positron Emission Tomography, or PET, which provides an image of the distribution of radioactivity in specific planes through the tissue (Gregory 1987, 347–53).

2. See, e.g., Benson and Zaidel 1985; Liddon 1989.

3. Arguelles 1975, 6–15; Ashbrook 1985b.

4. Ashbrook 1984a, 1984c.

5. Penfield 1975, 28–29, 37–48.

6. By the late 1970s, the explanation of overall integrative processes was being acknowledged as "more tentative than has heretofore generally been admitted.... Nonetheless, there are certain general principles that can be recognized as contributing to sensory processing in systematic ways: spontaneous activity, localization of stimulus maxima, lateral inhibition, parallel processing, feedback loops for the hierarchal coordination of such systems, central control of sensory receptors, and central sensory transmission, plus a few useful neurophysiological metaphors: gate theories, ideals of corollary discharge, and notions of holographic images" (Livingston 1978, 30). In short, overall explanation of integrative processes is extremely complicated and uncertain (cf. Damasio 1994).

7. Livingston 1978, 82–83.

8. Livingston 1978, 3.

9. Rose 1994, emphasis in original.

10. Kolb and Whishaw [1980] 1985, 161.

11. Kolb and Whishaw [1980] 1985, 160–62.

12. Livingston 1978, 15–17.

13. Penfield 1975, 28.

14. Mountcastle 1976, 38–41.

15. Sperry 1995.

16. Gazzaniga 1970, 133; Bloom and Lazerson [1985] 1988, 53–85.

17. Livingston 1981, 9–12, 15–20; Lakoff 1987.

18. Hellige (1993, 136–67) has reviewed research on "Behavioral and Brain Asymmetries in Nonhuman Species." Accumulating evidence since the early 1980s "has made it clear that behavioral and biological asymmetries are ubiquitous in nonhumans" (136). Asymmetries have been observed in motor performance, the production and perception of vocalizations, visuospatial

processes, and motivation and emotion. Some of these "bear a striking resemblance to asymmetries seen in humans," though the search for such asymmetries "has been guided by what is already known about humans" (163). In examining "the evolution of lateral asymmetries, language, tool use, and intellect," Bradshaw and Rogers conclude that "human beings are at most quantitatively, not qualitatively, different from other vertebrate genera in nearly all behaviors, except just possibly art and esthetics; nor, indeed, are they unique in their lateral asymmetries" (Bradshaw and Rogers 1993, 388). Geshwind and Galaburda identify the adaptive survival capacities of human asymmetry and conclude, "Humans are not unique in the possession of lateral functions, but they may well be endowed with the most extensively asymmetrical brains." "Recent studies have suggested to us . . . that there may in fact be a continuous sequence from asymmetry in the spin of the neutrino all the way to human cerebral dominance" (Geshwind and Galaburda 1987, 20, 223; Davidson and Hugdahl 1995).

19. Hellige 1993, 335–36.

20. Luria 1970, 66–78; Kinsbourne 1978.

21. Harrington 1987; Robert Young [1970]1990; Davidson and Hugdahl 1995.

22. Geschwind 1974; Geschwind and Levitsky 1968; Galaburda 1995.

23. Witelson 1977; Wada 1977; Lemay and Culebras 1972; Blakemore, Iverson, and Zangwill 1972.

24. Gazzaniga 1974, 378; Gazzaniga and LeDoux 1978, 92; Coren 1992.

25. Browne 1993.

26. Cassirer 1946; Corballis and Beal 1972, 65–73; Pinker 1994; Deacon 1996.

27. Penfield 1975, 18–20.

28. Dimond 1972, 108–10, 194.

29. Geschwind 1972.

30. Heilman 1978; Wada 1977, 372.

31. Milner 1974.

32. "The quest for a fundamental dimension of hemispheric asymmetry has been unsuccessful . . . it is rarely the case in the intact brain that one hemisphere can perform a task normally whereas the other hemisphere is completely unable to perform the task at all. Instead, both hemispheres often have some ability to perform a task, but they may go about it in different ways and one is sometimes better than the other. Consequently, for many complex activities (e.g., language or face recognition), both hemispheres play a role, and these roles are often complementary. . . . Even simple tasks consist of [a] number of specific subprocesses, and there is no guarantee that hemispheric asymmetry for one subprocess involved in a task is the same as that for another subprocess that is also involved in that task" (Hellige 1993, 64).

33. Galaburda 1995, 52.

34. Sperry 1962, 43.

35. Gazzaniga 1967.

36. For a responsible and fascinating reporting of medical research showing how a scar on the temporal lobe of the brain can trigger strange aggressive or sexual behavior as well as the creative imagination, see LaPlante 1993.

37. Springer and Deutsch [1981] 1989, 29–32.

38. Geschwind 1965; Sperry 1982.

39. Gazzaniga 1970, 131; Levy 1974; A. Smith 1974; Springer and Deutsch [1981] 1989, 27–71.

40. Benson and Zaidel 1985.

41. Broadbent 1974.

42. Levy 1985.

43. Hellige 1993, 206.
44. Hellige 1993, 252, 259.
45. Jackson 1932.
46. Harrington 1987.
47. Harrington 1995, 8–9.
48. Harrington 1995, 11–15.
49. Watts [1963] 1969; Needham [1973] 1978.
50. Geschwind 1972. Some scientists have argued for a narrow localization of cerebral function, which means that speech is exclusively located in the left hemisphere. In contrast, others have argued for an antilocalization of function, namely, the entire cortex is responsible for all mental activity. This group has been known for its holistic view. Battles have been fought as to whether the whole brain is involved or only specific parts. The gestalt-oriented group emphasized that everything did everything; the localizers stressed that most cortical cells performed specific functions. The controversy suggests how hemispheric "leading" must be taken as a qualified generalization. The localizers have tended to work with older individuals; the generalizers with children less than ten. Exceptions, of course, are many. A concept of "overlapping" fields of control is more adequate to account for recovery of function after injury or deficit than the general theory of equipotentiality (Kolb and Whishaw [1980] 1985, 164–66). For an informed critique of a literal and dichotomized view of hemisphere specialization, see Efron 1990.
51. Levy 1974, 180.
52. Nebes 1974.
53. Gazzaniga 1970, 1985, 1988, 1992.
54. Levy and Trevarthen 1976.
55. Penfield 1975, 52.
56. Pinker 1993.
57. Broadbent 1974.
58. Gazzaniga and LeDoux 1978, 97.
59. Tillich 1957, 36.
60. Levy-Agresti and Sperry 1968.
61. Gazzaniga 1970, 1988.
62. Gazzaniga and LeDoux 1978, 146.
63. Pribram 1971, 51.
64. Levy 1974, 180–82.
65. Luria 1973, 229–30.
66. Springer and Deutsch [1981] 1989, 48–51.
67. Gazzaniga 1970, 105.
68. Harrington 1987.
69. Jackson 1932, 142.
70. Nebes 1974, 163.
71. Gazzaniga and LeDoux 1978; Gardner [1974] 1976, 321–22; Kimura 1973.
72. Nebes 1974, 8–10.
73. Harris 1978.
74. Nebes 1978.
75. There is evidence that the more this structure is understood (as by professional musicians), the more it is processed in the left hemisphere.

76. Levy 1974, 180; Nebes 1974, 13; 1978, 121.

77. Kimura 1973.

78. Personal communication by Dirac to John Albright, Tallahassee, Fla.

79. Springer and Deutsch [1981] 1989.

80. Hellige 1990, 1993.

81. Davidson and Hugdahl 1995.

82. Springer and Deutsch [1981] 1989, 284.

83. Ashbrook 1996c.

84. Ornstein [1972] 1986.

85. Sperry 1982, 1992; Trevarthen 1990a.

86. Jaynes 1976.

87. Cf. Harrington 1992b, 237.

88. Ornstein [1972] 1977, 37.

89. Ashbrook 1984d, 8–9.

90. Stevens 1982, 247–75; 1986.

91. Springer and Deutsch [1981] 1989, 285.

92. Liederman 1995, 482–83.

93. Banich 1995, 447.

94. Banich 1995.

95. Graber and Petersen 1991, 267–69.

96. Ashbrook 1988a, 1989a, 1992b, 1996a, 1996b.

97. MacLean 1996. MacLean links "a sense of 'responsibility' . . . with the maternal instinct to feed her young and . . . [with] such a sense generalized psychologically to include others and become what we call 'conscience.'" Attachment, empathy, and altruism, he suggests, are primarily mediated through the female of the species. He speculates that from an emergent evolutionary perspective, "thanks in large part to the attitudes of women, we are witnessing for the first time . . . the development of beings with a concern for the suffering and dying not only of their own kind but also for all living things" (MacLean 1996, 437).

98. E.g., Waber 1976, 1979; Levy 1980; Springer and Deutsch [1981] 1989.

99. Banich 1995, 437.

100. Ricoeur 1978.

101. Tracy 1981.

102. Ashbrook 1984d, 261.

103. Ashbrook 1988a.

104. Hawking 1988, 141.

105. Davies [1987] 1989, 1992.

106. MacKay 1977, 62.

107. Buttrick 1954, s.v. Acts 17:28.

108. We have focused on the cognitive rather than the biochemical. We realize that much of the excitement in brain research these days centers in molecular biology, with its tremendous promise for ameliorating the tragic consequences of diseases such as Alzheimer's and Parkinson's. Beyond the scope of our inquiry are issues of the cell nucleus, the electrical messages that travel down the nerve's axon, and the chemical messages that cross the synaptic gaps (see, for instance, Churchland 1986; Bloom and Lazerson [1985] 1988; Kosslyn and Koenig 1992; Edelman 1992).

109. MacLean 1976, 206.

7. THE FRONTAL LOBES, INTENDING, AND A PURPOSEFUL GOD

1. Damasio 1994, 3–33.
2. Harrington 1991, 215.
3. Damasio 1994, 12.
4. Damasio 1994, 17.
5. Damasio 1994, 61.
6. See Damasio 1994.
7. Begley 1995b, 77.
8. Deacon 1996.
9. Deacon 1996, 637–38.
10. Deacon 1996, 639.
11. Mirsky 1978.
12. Gazzaniga 1970, 131.
13. Damasio 1994, 262.
14. d'Aquili [1983] 1993.
15. Restak [1994] 1995, 133.
16. Teilhard 1959, 44.
17. An older view of physics traced four fundamental forces: the electromagnetic force, the strong force, the weak force, and the gravitational force. The latest view conflates the four forces into three.
18. Huxley 1959, 13.
19. Kauffman 1995, 47–48.
20. It is important to keep in mind that Teilhard's use of the term *complexity*, while prophetically suggestive of current complexity theory, is not precisely the same as present usage.
21. Teilhard 1959, 243–44; emphasis added.
22. Waldrop 1992, 124.
23. We are indebted to Timothy Staveteig for this illustration.
24. Waldrop 1992, 145.
25. See Gell-Mann 1994.
26. Waldrop 1992, 145.
27. Cobb and Griffin 1976, 100.
28. Kaufman 1992, 388.
29. Campbell 1976.
30. Waldrop 1992, 145–47.
31. Volk 1995, 192.
32. Goodenough 1996.
33. Sperry 1988, 3.
34. Sperry 1991, 247.
35. Sperry 1988, 4.
36. Peacocke 1993, 255.
37. Shakespeare, *The Tempest*, II, 1, 261.
38. Kauffman 1995, 69.
39. Buber 1937.
40. Bonhoeffer [1953] 1956.
41. Polkinghorne 1991, 233.
42. Polkinghorne 1991, 232.

CONCLUSION: THE MIND-PRODUCING BRAIN AND GOD AS ALL-IN-ALL

1. Damasio 1994, 260.

2. Penfield and Rasmussen [1950] 1957, 14.

3. Pinker 1994, 410.

4. Pinker 1994, 427.

5. Researchers like Gazzaniga surmise that the observing, interpreting left hemisphere is the source of a constructed and conventionalized sense of "I." It manages separate cognitive entities by means of a vigilance that explains what it observes (Gazzaniga 1985, 1988, 1992). Several contrasting positions on the functional center of consciousness itself exist: Penfield's integrative cortex (Penfield 1975), Eccles's left frontal cortex (Eccles 1970, 1989), and Mountcastle's association cortex (Mountcastle 1976).

6. Gilbert 1989, 197; MacLean 1985a, 1985b.

7. Deacon 1992, 77.

8. Trevarthen [1986] 1993, 148–49.

9. Holmes 1995, 5.

10. Frankl 1978.

11. Boyce 1988.

12. Kauffman 1995.

13. See Selye 1976.

14. Gilbert 1989, 79–100.

15. Selye 1976; Benson 1979; Borysenko 1987; Rossi [1986] 1993; Ornstein and Sobel 1987; Ornstein and Swencionis 1990; Shapiro 1995; Ashbrook 1995b.

16. Hampden-Turner 1981, 84.

17. Richardson and Bowden 1983, 183–86; 280–29.

18. McEwen and Schmeck 1994.

19. Gilbert 1989, 92–93.

20. Farley 1990.

21. Hobson 1994, 210.

22. Ornstein and Swencionis, 1990.

23. Shapiro 1995, 13.

24. Quoted by Kaufman 1993, 96.

25. Most evidence suggests that male brains tend to be more lateralized than female brains (Levy 1980; Springer and Deutsch [1981] 1989, ch. 7; Ashbrook 1992b; Hellige 1993, 232–39). Eighty percent of females but 95 percent of males have linguistic processes more prevalent in the left hemisphere than the right. In such processing, most males draw on the left brain by itself, whereas most females utilize both hemispheres (Kimura 1985).

26. Ashbrook 1989a; Ruether 1983; Johnson 1992; Begley 1995a.

27. Burhoe 1973, 1981; Hefner 1993.

28. Damasio 1994, 252, emphasis added.

29. Cited by Cacioppo and Berntson 1992.

– A Glossary for Religion –

ANALOGICAL: a way of referring to God using concepts and inferences drawn from the empirical world.

ATTRIBUTES OF GOD: characteristic ways of referring to the nature of God.

CHRISTOLOGY: the part of Christian doctrine that focuses on the meaning of God's revelation in Jesus Christ.

COSMOLOGY: the study of the structure and evolution of the universe; also, the "doctrine of the world," or that theological inquiry which focuses on the origin and nature of the universe.

CREATION: the view that all things are ultimately dependent on God as the one transcendent reality.

DUALISM: a philosophical view which argues that matter and mind are two separate and irreducible substances.

EMPIRICAL: an inductive approach to knowledge that deals with concrete data and experience and that in theology involves inferences about God drawn from "tangible facts" in the public domain.

EMPIRICAL THEOLOGY: an approach to theology on the bases of human experience and scientific knowledge.

EPISTEMOLOGY: the sources, scope, and criteria of knowledge with special attention to the power of human reason to grasp basic truth.

ESCHATOLOGY: that part of Christian doctrine dealing with the final end and purpose of life in God.

ETERNAL: that which is not subject to time and space.

FAITH: one's basic orientation to life; the centrality of a total response of unconditional trust, ultimately, only in relationship to God.

HEURISTIC: an interpretive tool for understanding.

LOGOS: the Greek word for reason and order. The early church used the notion of "Word" or mind of God to identify and understand God's action in Christ.

MANIFESTATION: the pattern of beliefs disclosing wonder, power, and mystery preverbally in and through natural and symbolic expressions.

METAPHORICAL: a way of thinking that focuses on surplus meaning in language and by so doing identifies basic similarities among referents even as it starts from dissimilarities.

NATURAL THEOLOGY: an approach to understanding God apart from special revelation and on the basis of the general revelation found in experience and reason. In medieval times it meant the faculty of reason; in the era of the brain it refers to both rational cortical processes and nonrational subcortical processes.

ONTOLOGY: inquiry into the rational, coherent, and necessary nature of the universe.

PHENOMENOLOGY: a way of understanding that is based on identifying the basic structures given in the phenomena of experience and that brackets assumptions as to causal factors.

POSTMODERNISM: in the humanities and social sciences, a view that rejects determinism as an essential element of the description of nature and questions human ability to gain reliable knowledge of any kind because there is no single vantage point from which to view the world; therefore all knowing must take account of a particular perspective and a particular context. In the terminology of physics, "postmodern" thinking is called "modern," and "modern" thinking is called "classical."

PROCLAMATION: the pattern of beliefs centering on the spoken Word, instructions, and imperatives.

PROPHETIC-HISTORICAL: the pattern of beliefs that deals with practical transforming action and that calls into question existing institutions and ideologies.

REDEMPTION: God's action to save or restore the relationship that has been broken because of humanity's sin and rebellion.

SACRAMENTAL: the view that God is present in and through the concrete world.

SYMBOL: a concrete or tangible image or object that bears or creates special meaning without being literal and limited.

THEOLOGY: most generally, a way of thinking about the nature and meaning of ultimate reality that is both rational and systematic; more particularly, the attempt to discover, define, defend, and share the truth implied by the experiences of faith of the Christian church.

– A Glossary for Science –

ACETYLCHOLINE: the neurotransmitter sending signals to many target cells, using the autonomic nervous system and the skeletal muscles to mediate inhibitory and excitatory activities.

ADAPTATION: any beneficial modification of an organism necessary to meet environmental demands.

AMYGDALA: the almond-shaped structures in the limbic system related to active emotions involving survival of the self, such as aggression, fight-flight-freeze, and the struggle for food.

ANTERIOR: that portion of the cortex situated toward the front of the cerebral cortex, as opposed to posterior.

APHASIA: a group of disorders affecting the ability to translate experiences into words.

AROUSAL: the physiological condition of being alert; activated by the sympathetic adrenal response of the fight-flight-freeze pattern of the autonomic nervous system.

ASSOCIATION CORTEX: those parts of the brain that are neither sensory nor motor but have the function of associating or integrating incoming sensations with outgoing actions.

ASYMMETRY: refers to structural or functional differences between the left and right hemispheres.

AUTONOMIC NERVOUS SYSTEM: a part of the nervous system somewhat independent of the central (voluntary) nervous system and so somewhat independent of conscious control. It includes both the sympathetic and the parasympathetic systems, which regulate breathing, heart rate, blood pressure, unintentional movement, and hormone secretions.

AXON: the long fiber of a neuron that carries signals to other cells by connecting with dendrites at the synaptic gaps.

BILATERAL: a brain arranged so that a function is distributed across both hemispheres, in contrast to being confined to one.

BRAIN STEM: the enlarged bulbous area of the upper part of the spinal cord that carries sensory information from the body to the thalamus and, in turn, motor information from the cerebral cortex to motor centers in the stem and spinal cord. It encases the reticular activating system, which is associated with wakefulness and attention and may also provide a constant input of stimulation to maintain the resting potential just below the critical threshold of consciousness.

BROCA'S AREA: the area in the left frontal cortex associated with articulate or spoken speech.

CENTRAL NERVOUS SYSTEM: those parts of the brain and spinal cord that respond to conscious or deliberate intentions.

CEREBELLUM: the region of the brain tucked under the cerebrum and next to the spinal cord; it is mainly responsible for coordinated movement based on the fundamental repertoire of learned motor responses and some calculating and memory functions.

CEREBRAL CORTEX: the outer, convoluted gray matter of the two hemispheres necessary for higher cognitive activity and constituting the top 80 percent of the human brain.

CEREBRAL HEMISPHERES: the two large halves of the brain that rest on top of the brain stem and are separated by a cleft (fissure) running lengthwise between them.

CEREBRUM: the largest part of the brain, which, in humans, perceives sensory input, organizes thought and memory, and controls voluntary activity. Another name for the *cerebral cortex.*

CHAOTIC PROCESSES: processes that are deterministic at root but whose behavior is unpredictable in any practical sense.

CHOLINERGIC SYSTEM: the group of neurons that uses the neurotransmitter acetylcholine and is thought to mediate information coming from the peripheral parasympathetic nervous system.

CINGULATE GYRUS: one of the three main subdivisions of the limbic system, associated with caregiving, empathy, and creative social behavior.

COGNITIVE PROCESS: the mental representational activity of perceiving, conceiving, reasoning, remembering, and judging.

COMMISSURES: the neural connections between the corresponding areas in the right and left hemispheres, the largest being the corpus callosum.

COMPLEXITY: the result of a system in which many agents, acting in parallel, continually adapt to one another in a process that promotes self-organization. This process is also known as autocatalysis. Situations that support self-organization have both orderly, predictable features and disorganized, unpredictable elements. The products of self-organization are *emergent.*

CORPUS CALLOSUM: the largest group of nerve fibers connecting the two hemispheres; it sends information back and forth and coordinates their processes.

CORRELATES: in terms of the brain, biological events that change as behavior changes; in terms of the mind, cognitive processes that accompany sociopsycho-cultural activities.

COSMOLOGY: the study of the structure and evolution of the universe; also, the "doctrine of the world," or that theological inquiry which focuses on the origin and nature of the universe.

DENDRITE: the bushy structure of a neuron that receives signals from other cells.

DOPAMINE: a neurotransmitter thought to regulate movement, modulate the more extreme symptoms of schizophrenia, and facilitate some pleasurable sensations.

ELECTROENCEPHALOGRAM (EEG): a recording of electrical changes in large groups of nerves, produced by attaching electrodes to the surface of the scalp.

EMERGENCE: a product of self-organization that could not be predicted from its precursors. See also *complexity.*

ENTROPY: a measure of the degree of randomness or disorder in a system.

EPILEPSY: a disturbance of the nervous system in which a damaged area in the brain (usually the temporal lobe) produces electrical discharges (like a thunderstorm) that can result in seizures or convulsions by spreading across the corpus callosum throughout the brain.

FOREBRAIN: the two cerebral hemispheres and the thalamus and hypothalamus; characteristic of mammalian brains.

FORNIX: a large bundle of fibers (right and left) that makes up a major output pathway of the hippocampus to subcortical structures.

FRONTAL LOBES: the front part of the cerebrum where initiating, planning, executing, and evaluating behavior originates.

GANGLIA: a group of nerve cells or cell bodies that form a kind of nerve center; some lie outside the brain and spinal cord and others make up the mass of gray matter within the brain or cord.

HEMISPHERE: half of the cerebral cortex.

HINDBRAIN: the stalk-like structures, including the cerebellum and brain stem, that form the major pathways the forebrain uses to send and receive signals from the spinal cord and peripheral nervous system; critical for survival.

HIPPOCAMPUS: the large curved structures (right and left) in the limbic system that look like a small marine seahorse and are thought to contribute to memory.

HOLISTIC: involving the simultaneous processing of information in terms of a pattern or configuration of information that is more than the sum of the separate parts.

HPAC: the hypothalamic-pituitary-adrenal-cortical system (HPAC), which probably sets up long-term states of "defensive stop" so as to minimize or avoid negative situations that cannot be controlled. Such situations include low expectations of success, expectations of defeat, low self-esteem, and depression.

HYPOTHALAMUS: a small structure near the base of the brain that serves as the master gland mediating mind-body communication by regulating hormonal activity, hunger, thirst, temperature, sleep, sex, and autonomic integration.

LIMBIC SYSTEM: part of the cerebral hemispheres, including the amygdala, the septum, and the thalamocingulate. Evolutionarily the oldest part of the cerebral cortex, the limbic system is found in all mammals; in humans it adds emotional content and valuation to experience.

MIDBRAIN: the portion of the brain developed from the middle part of the primitive brain, lying under and surrounded by the cerebral cortex; provides relay stations for monitoring and regulating information.

NEOCORTEX: the outer layer of the cerebrum, which contributes to what is the uniquely human or rational mind and is capable of symbolization, intellect, and imagination.

NEURON: the single cell that forms the basis of cortical tissue; it includes the cell body, the dendrites, and the axon. Neurons can be classified as sensory, motor, or connecting.

NEUROTRANSMITTERS: powerful chemical substances, secreted in small amounts at the synapses, that play the central role in controlling the flow of information throughout the nervous system; they amplify, block, inhibit, or lessen the microelectric signals passing on patterns of complexity that provide the physical basis of mind.

NOREPINEPHRINE: a neurotransmitter thought to activate emotional arousal.

OCCIPITAL LOBES: the back part of the cerebral cortex that processes visual information.

OLFACTORY LOBES: the sensory parts of the brain that process smell and are an extension of the cerebrum.

PALEOMAMMALIAN BRAIN: the middle region of the brain dealing with emotional and motivational behaviors.

PARASYMPATHETIC: one of the two subdivisions of the autonomic nervous system; associated with rest, relaxation, and renewal.

PARIETAL LOBES: the top middle part of the cerebral cortex; processes general sensory input from the body itself.

PERIPHERAL NERVOUS SYSTEM: the parts of the nervous system apart from the central nervous system that are in contact with the environment.

PHOTON: the elementary package of energy for light.

POSTERIOR: situated toward the back of the cortex, as opposed to anterior or "toward the face."

REPTILIAN BRAIN/R-COMPLEX: the oldest part of the forebrain; rests on top of the brain stem and involves instinctual behavior necessary for survival.

RETICULAR ACTIVATING SYSTEM: the system in the brain stem that sends messages to the thalamus and on to the cortex, resulting in wakefulness and attention. It continually provides a constant input of stimulation to maintain the resting potential of the nervous system just below the critical threshold of consciousness. It is essential to organizing, breathing, and control of the heart and blood pressure; it is concerned with waking and sleeping, with relaxation, and also with vigilance and arousal.

SELF-ORGANIZATION. See *complexity.*

SENSORY AREAS: the regions in the middle of the cerebrum directly involved in receiving sensory information—hearing, seeing, smelling, sense of touch.

SEPTUM: the hedgelike structures (right and left) in the limbic system thought to motivate behaviors related to the preservation of the species such as grooming, sociability, and cooperating.

SEROTONIN: a neurotransmitter thought to inhibit arousal and induce quietness and sleep.

SPECIALIZATION: the location of specific cognitive functions in either the left or the right hemisphere.

SPLIT BRAIN OPERATION: the severing of the nerve fibers of the corpus callosum that carry information between the two hemispheres.

SPLENIUM: the large posterior area (back) of the corpus callosum that communicates visual and auditory information to each hemisphere.

SUBCORTICAL: concerning deep regions or areas of the brain below the cerebral cortex, including the limbic system and the brain stem, that regulate cortical activity, complex information processing, transfer of information among cortical units, motivation, and other functions.

SUBSYMBOLIC: processed by an area of the brain that does not operate through conventional symbol systems, such as language or mathematics, and is the mental correlate of the brain's subcortical processing.

SYMPATHETIC: one of the two divisions of the autonomic nervous system, which is activated during arousal, tension, and stress for the purpose of appropriate action.

SYNAPSE: the junction or gap between axon and dendrite where chemical signals cross from one side to the other by means of neurostransmitters.

TACHISTOSCOPE: an instrument that presents visual material for fractions of a second to one or the other eye. A subject looks at a dot in the center of the visual field and the device permits images to be presented to only one hemisphere.

TEMPORAL LOBE: one of the four major subdivisions of each hemisphere of the cerebral cortex; plays the major role for perception of sound in mammals and for speech in humans; also critical for visual and spatial discrimination.

THALAMOCINGULATE: a division of the limbic system thought to motivate behavior related to the maintenance of familial patterns such as maternal nurturing, communication between offspring and caregiver, and play.

THALAMUS: a portion of the midbrain that serves as a relay station for almost all information coming into and out of the forebrain.

UNCOMMITTED CORTEX: the newly evolved areas of the cerebral cortex that are not specifically prewired or "committed" to sensory or motor functions.

ULTRADIAN CYCLE: the 90- to 120-minute rhythm of activity throughout the day and night that consists of a peak of alertness (about 90 minutes) followed by a period of fatigue or a "break" (about 20–30 minutes) contributing to renewal and healing. It is dramatically apparent in the deep stages of sleep followed by rapid-eye-movement (REM) dreaming.

— Bibliography —

Ader, R., D. Felten, and N. Cohen, eds. 1990. *Psychoneuroimmunology.* 2d ed. San Diego: Academic Press.

Andreasen, Niels-Erik. 1978. *Rest and Redemption: A Study of the Biblical Sabbath.* Berrien Springs, Mich.: Andrews University Press.

Antonovsky, Aaron. 1987. *Unravelling the Mystery of Health: How People Manage Stress and Stay Well.* San Francisco: Jossey-Bass.

Aquinas, Thomas. 1945. *Basic Writings of Saint Thomas Aquinas.* Vols. 1 and 2. Edited and annotated, with an introduction by Anton C. Pegis. New York: Random House.

Arbib, Michael A., and Mary B. Hesse. 1986. *The Construction of Reality.* Cambridge: Cambridge University Press.

Ardrey, Robert. 1968. *The Territorial Imperative: A Personal Inquiry into the Animal Origins of Property and Nations.* Drawings by Berdine Ardrey. New York: Atheneum.

Arguelles, Jose A. 1975. *The Transformative Vision: Reflections on the Nature and History of Human Expression.* Boulder, Colo.: Shambhala Publications.

Armstrong, Karen. 1994. *A History of God: The 4000-Year Quest of Judaism, Christianity, and Islam.* New York: Alfred A. Knopf.

Arnheim, Rudolf. 1969. *Visual Thinking.* Berkeley: University of California Press.

Asbury, Beverly Allen. 1996. "Recent Perspectives on the Holocaust." *Religious Studies Review* 13, no. 3: 197–207.

Ashbrook, James B. 1958. "The Functional Meaning of the Soul in the Christian Tradition." *Journal of Pastoral Care* 12, no. 1: 1–16.

————. 1984a. "Juxtaposing the Brain and Belief." *Journal of Psychology and Theology* 12, no. 3: 198–207.

————. 1984b. "Ambiguity in Neuropsychology: A Response to Wong." *Journal of Psychology and Theology* 12, no. 4: 314–19.

————. 1984c. "Neurotheology: The Working Brain and the Work of Theology." *Zygon: Journal of Religion and Science* 19, no. 3 (September): 331–50.

————. 1984d. *The Human Mind and the Mind of God: Theological Promise in Brain Research.* Lanham, Md.: University Press of America.

————. 1985a. "Brain, Mind, and God." *Christian Century* (19–26 March): 295–98.

————. 1985b. "Half Brains and Split-Minds." *Pastoral Psychology* 34, no. 1 (fall): 9–20.

————. 1988a. *The Brain and Belief: Faith in Light of Brain Research.* Bristol, Ind.: Wyndham Hall Press.

————. 1988b. *Paul Tillich in Conversation.* With contribution by James B. Ashbrook. Bristol, Ind.: Wyndham Hall Press.

————. 1989a. "Ways of Knowing God: Gender and the Brain." *Christian Century* (4–11 Jan.): 14–15.

————. 1989b. "The Whole Brain as the Basis for the Analogical Expression of God." *Zygon: Journal of Religion and Science* 24 (March): 65–81.

————. 1989c. "The Human Brain and Human Destiny: A Pattern for Old Brain Empathy with the Emergence of Mind." *Zygon: Journal of Religion and Science* 24 (September): 335–57.

————. 1991a. "The Seat of the Soul: Where Religion and the Neurosciences Intersect." *Insights: The Magazine of the Chicago Center for Religion and Science* 3, no. 1: 6–10.

————. 1991b. "Soul: Its Meaning and Its Making." *Journal of Pastoral Care* 45, no. 2 (summer): 159–68.

————. 1992a. "Making Sense of Soul and Sabbath: Brain Processes and the Making of Meaning." *Zygon: Journal of Religion and Science* 27, no. 1 (March): 31–60.

————. 1992b. "Different Voices, Different Genes: Male and Female Created God Them." *Journal of Pastoral Care* 46, no. 2 (summer): 174–83.

————. 1993. *Brain, Culture, and the Human Spirit: Essays from an Emergent Evolutionary Perspective,* edited by James B. Ashbrook. Lanham, Md.: University Press of America.

————. 1994. "The Cry for the Other: The Biocultural Womb of Human Development." *Zygon: Journal of Religion and Science* 29, no. 3 (September): 297–314.

————. 1996a. *Minding the Soul: Pastoral Counseling as Remembering.* Minneapolis: Fortress.

————. 1996b. "A Rippling Relatedness in Reality." *Zygon: Journal of Religion and Science* 31, no. 3 (September): 469–82.

————. 1996c. "Interfacing Religion and the Neurosciences: A Review of Twenty-five Years of Exploration and Reflection." *Zygon: Journal of Religion and Science* 31, no. 4 (December): 545–82.

Ashbrook, James B., and Paul W. Walaskay. 1977. *Christianity for Pious Skeptics.* Nashville: Abingdon Press.

Augustine, Saint. 1873. *On the Trinity.* Vol. 7. Edited by Marcus Dods. Translated by Arthur West Hadden. Edinburgh: T. & T. Clark.

————. 1955. *Confessions and Enchiridion.* Translated and edited by Albert Cook Outler. Philadelphia: The Westminster Press.

————. 1991. *Saint Augustine Confessions*. Translated with an Introduction and Notes by Henry Chadwick. Oxford: Oxford University Press.

Bandler, Richard, and John Grinder. 1975. *The Structure of Magic I: A Book about Language and Therapy*. Palo Alto, Calif.: Science and Behavior Books.

Barclay, Craig R., and Peggy A. DeCooke. 1988. "Ordinary Everyday Memories: Some of the Things of Which Selves Are Made." In *Remembering Reconsidered: Ecological and Traditional Approaches to the Study of Memory*, edited by Ulric Neisser and Eugene Winograd, 91–125. Cambridge: Cambridge University Press.

Banich, Marie T. 1995. "Interhemispheric Processing: Theoretical Considerations and Empirical Approaches." In *Brain Asymmetry*, edited by Richard J. Davidson and Kenneth Hugdahl, 427–50. Cambridge: A Bradford Book/MIT Press.

Barbour, Ian. 1974. *Myths, Models, and Paradigms: The Nature of Scientific and Religious Language*. London: SCM Press.

————. 1990. *Religion in an Age of Science: The Gifford Lectures 1989–1991*. Vol. 1. San Francisco: Harper & Row.

————. 1994. "Response to Critiques of *Religion in an Age of Science*." Science and Theology Section, American Academy of Religion, Chicago, Nov. 20.

Barsalou, Lawrence W. 1988. "The Content and Organization of Autobiographical Memories." In *Remembering Reconsidered: Ecological and Traditional Approaches to the Study of Memory*, edited by Ulric Neisser and Eugene Winograd, 193–242. Cambridge: Cambridge University Press.

Barton, Scott. 1994. "Chaos, Self-Organization, and Psychology." *American Psychologist* 49, no. 1 (January): 5–14.

Begley, Sharon. 1995a. "Gray Matters: Science—New Technologies That Catch the Mind in the Very Act of Thinking Show How Men and Women Use Their Brains Differently." *Newsweek,* 27 March.

————. 1995b. "Lights of Madness: For the First Time, Researchers Isolate the Venues of Hallucination." *Newsweek,* 20 November.

————. 1997. "How to Build a Baby's Brain." *Newsweek,* Special Issue, Your Child.

Benson, D. Frank, and Eran Zaidel, eds. 1985. *The Dual Brain: Hemisphere Specialization in Humans*. New York: The Guilford Press.

Benson, Herbert. 1979. *The Mind/Body Effect*. New York: Simon & Schuster.

Berelson, Bernard, and Gary A. Steiner. 1964. *Human Behavior: An Inventory of Scientific Findings*. New York: Harcourt, Brace & World.

Berlyne, Daniel E. 1958a. "The Influence of Complexity and Novelty in Visual Figures in Orienting Responses." *Journal of Experimental Psychology* 55:289–96.

————. 1958b. "The Influence of the Albedo and Complexity of Stimuli on Visual Fixation in the Human Infant." *British Journal of Psychology* 49:315–18.

Bird, Phyllis. 1981. "'Male and Female He Created Them': Gen. 1:27b in the Context of the Priestly Account of Creation." *Harvard Theological Review* 74, no. 2: 129–59.

————. 1988. "Sexual Differentiation and Divine Image in the Genesis Creation Texts." In *Image of God and Gender Models*, ed. Kari E. Borreson. Oslo: Solum Forlag; Atlantic Heights, N.J.: Humanities Press.

Blakemore, C., S. D. Iverson, and O. L. Zangwill. 1972. "Brain Functions." *Annual Review of Psychology*, 433–35.

Bloom, Floyd E., and Arlyne Lazerson. [1985] 1988. *Brain, Mind, and Behavior.* 2d ed. New York: W. H. Freeman.

Bonhoeffer, Dietrich. [1953] 1956. *Letters and Papers from Prison.* Edited by Eberhard Bethge. Translated by Reginald H. Fuller. London: SCM Press.

Borysenko, Joan, with Larry Rothstein. 1987. *Minding the Body, Mending the Mind.* Foreword by Herbert Benson. Reading, Mass.: Addison-Wesley.

Bowlby, John. 1969. *Attachment.* Vol. 1. New York: Basic Books.

———. 1973. *Separation: Anxiety and Anger.* Vol. 2. New York: Basic Books.

———. 1980. *Loss: Sadness and Depression.* Vol. 3. New York: Basic Books.

Boyce, Richard Nelson. 1988. *The Cry to God in the Old Testament.* Atlanta: Scholars Press (Dissertation series/Society of Biblical Literature, no. 103).

Bradshaw, John, and Lesley Rogers. 1993. *The Evolution of Lateral Asymmetries, Language, Tool Use, and Intellect.* San Diego: Academic Press.

Breed, David R. 1992. *Yoking Science and Religion: The Life and Thought of Ralph Wendell Burhoe.* Foreword by Roger W. Sperry. Chicago: Chicago Center for Religion and Science/Zygon Books.

Broadbent, Donald. 1974. "Division of Function and Integration of Behavior." In *The Neurosciences: Third Study Program,* edited by F. O. Schmitt and F. G. Worden, 31–41. Cambridge: MIT Press.

Bronowski, J., and Bruce Mazlish. 1960. *The Western Intellectual Tradition: From Leonardo to Hegel.* New York: Harper & Brothers.

Brown, Frederick M., and R. Curtis Graeber, eds. 1982. *Rhythmic Aspects of Behavior.* Hillsdale, N.J.: Lawrence Erlbaum Associates.

Browne, Malcolm W. 1993. "'Handedness' Seen in Nature, Long Before Hands." *New York Times,* 15 June, B5, B7.

Browning, Don S. 1987. *Religious Thought and the Modern Psychologies: A Critical Conversation in the Theology of Culture.* Philadelphia: Fortress Press.

Bruce, Darryl. 1994. "Lashley and the Problem of Serial Order." *American Psychologist* 49, no. 2 (February): 93–103.

Bruce, V., A. Cowey, A. W. Ellis, and D. I. Perrett (organizers and editors). 1992. *Processing the Facial Image.* Proceedings of a Royal Society Discussion Meeting held on 9 and 10 July 1991. Oxford: Clarendon Press.

Buber, Martin. 1937. *I and Thou.* Translated by Ronald Gregor Smith. Edinburgh: T. & T. Clark.

———. 1988. *Hasidism and Modern Man.* Edited and translated by Maurice Friedman; new introduction by Martin S. Jaffee. Atlantic Highlands, N.J.: Humanities Press International.

Burhoe, Ralph Wendell. 1973. "The Concepts of God and Soul in a Scientific View of Human Purpose." *Zygon: Journal of Religion and Science* 8, nos. 3–4 (Sept.–Dec.): 412–42.

———. 1981. *Toward a Scientific Theology.* Belfast: Christian Journals Limited.

Burrell, David B. 1979. *Aquinas: God and Action*. London: Routledge & Kegan Paul.

Cacioppo, John T. 1992. "Social Psychological Contributions to the Decade of the Brain." *American Psychologist* 47, no. 8 (August): 1019–28.

Cacioppo, John T., and Gary G. Berntson. 1992. "The Principles of Multiple, Nonadditive, and Reciprocal Determinism: Implications for Social Psychological Research and Levels of Analysis." In *The Social Psychology of Mental Health: Basic Mechanisms and Applications*, edited by Diane N. Ruble, Philip R. Costanzo, and Mary Ellen Oliveri, 328–49. New York: Guilford Press.

Cacioppo, John T., and Louis G. Tassinary. 1990. "Inferring Psychological Significance from Physiological Signals." *American Psychologist* 45, no. 1 (January): 16–28.

Campbell, Donald T. 1974. "'Downward Causation' in Hierarchically Organized Biological Systems." In *Studies in the Philosophy of Biology/Reduction and Related Problems*, edited by Francisco J. Ayala and Theodosius Dobzhansky, 179–86. Berkeley: University of California Press.

———. 1976. "On the Conflicts between Biological and Social Evolution and between Psychology and Moral Tradition." *Zygon: Journal of Religion and Science* 9, no. 2 (June): 156–82. Originally printed in *American Psychologist* 30 (1975): 1103–26.

Capra, Fritjof, and David Steindl-Rast, with Thoma Matus. 1991. *Belonging to the Universe: Explorations on the Frontiers of Science and Spirituality*. New York: Harper Collins.

Carr, Archie. 1963. *The Reptiles*. Life Nature Library. New York: Time, Stonehenge Books.

Carrington, Richard. 1963. *The Mammals*. Life Nature Library. New York: Time, Inc.

Case-Winters, Anna. 1990. *God's Power: Traditional Understandings and Contemporary Challenges*. Louisville: Westminster/John Knox Press.

Cassirer, Ernest. 1946. *Language and Myth*. Translated by Susanne K. Langer. New York: Dover Publications, Inc.

Changeux, Jean-Pierre. [1983] 1985. *Neuronal Man: The Biology of Mind*. Translated by Laurence Garey. New York: Oxford University Press.

Churchland, Patricia Smith. 1986. *Neurophilosophy: Toward a Unified Science of the Mind-Brain*. Cambridge: A Bradford Book/MIT Press.

Cirlot, J. E. [1964] 1974. *A Dictionary of Symbols*. 2d ed. Translated by Jack Sage. Foreword by Herbert Read. New York: Philosophical Library.

Cobb, John, and David Ray Griffin. 1976. *Process Theology: An Introductory Exposition*. Philadelphia: Westminster Press.

Cohen, Gene D. 1988. *The Brain in Human Aging*. New York: Springer.

Cohen-Levine, S., M. T. Banich, and M. P. Koch-Weser. 1988. "Face Recognition: A General or a Specific Right Hemisphere Capacity?" *Brain and Cognition* 8:303–25.

Corballis, Michael C., and Ivan L. Beal. 1972. "On Telling Left from Right." In *Altered States of Awareness: Readings from Scientific American*, 65–73. San Francisco: W. H. Freeman.

Coren, Stanley. 1992. *The Left-Hander Syndrome: The Causes and Consequences of Left-Handedness*. New York: The Free Press.

Corsi, Pietro, ed. 1991. *The Enchanted Loom: Chapters in the History of Neuroscience.* New York: Oxford University Press.

Council, National Advisory Mental Health. 1995. "Basic Behavioral Science Research for Mental Health: A National Investment Emotion and Motivation." *American Psychologist* 50, no. 10 (October): 838–45.

Csikszentmihalyi, Mihaly. 1993. *The Evolving Self: A Psychology for the Third Millennium.* New York: HarperCollins.

Damasio, Antonio R. 1994. *Descartes' Error: Emotion, Reason, and the Human Brain.* New York: A Grosset/Putnam Book.

Damasio, Antonio R., and Hanna Damasio. 1992. "Brain and Language." *Scientific American* 267, no. 3 (September): 88–95.

d'Aquili, Eugene G. 1983/1993. "The Myth-Ritual Complex: A Biogenetic Structural Analysis." *Zygon: Journal of Religion and Science* 18, no. 4 (September): 247–69. In *Brain, Culture and the Human Spirit,* edited by James B. Ashbrook, 45–76. Lanham, Md.: University Press of America, 1993.

———. 1993. "Profile: Eugene G. d'Aquili." *Zygon: Journal of Religion and Science* 28, no. 2 (June).

d'Aquili, Eugene G., and Charles D. Laughlin Jr., eds. 1979. *The Spectrum of Ritual: A Biogenetic Structural Analysis.* New York: Columbia Univ. Press.

d'Aquili, Eugene G., and Andrew B. Newberg. 1993. "Religious and Mystical States: A Neuropsychological Model." *Zygon: Journal of Religion and Science* 28, no. 2 (June): 177–200.

Davidson, Richard J., and Kenneth Hugdahl, eds. 1995. *Brain Asymmetry.* Cambridge: A Bradford Book/MIT Press.

Davies, Paul. [1987] 1989. *The Cosmic Blueprint: Order and Complexity at the Edge of Chaos.* London: Penguin.

———. 1992. *The Mind of God: The Scientific Basis for a Rational World.* New York: Simon & Schuster.

Deacon, Terrence W. 1992. "Brain-Language Coevolution." In *The Evolution of Human Languages, Santa Fe Institute Studies in the Science of Complexity,* vol. 10, edited by John A. Hawkins and Murray Gell-Mann, 49–83. Reading, Mass.: Addison-Wesley.

———. 1996. "Why a Brain Capable of Language Evolved Only Once: Prefrontal Cortex and Symbol Learning." *Zygon: Journal of Religion and Science* 31, no. 4 (December): 635–69.

Diamond, Marian Cleeves. 1988. *Enriching Heredity: The Impact of the Environment on the Anatomy of the Brain.* New York: The Free Press.

Dimond, Stuart J. 1972. *The Double Brain.* London: Churchill-Livingstone.

Dourley, John P. 1975. *Paul Tillich and Bonaventure: An Evaluation of Paul Tillich's Claim to Stand in the Augustinian-Franciscan Tradition.* Leiden: E. J. Brill.

Eccles, John C. 1983. "Foreword." In *Neurobiology of the Hippocampus,* edited by W. Seifert, xiii–xvi. London: Academic Press.

———. 1989. *Evolution of the Brain: Creation of the Self.* London and New York: Routledge.

————. 1992 (1980). *The Human Psyche: The Gifford Lectures: 1978–1979.* New York: Routledge.

Edelman, Gerald M. 1992. *Bright Air, Brilliant Fire: On the Matter of the Mind.* New York: Basic Books.

Efron, Robert. 1990. *The Decline and Fall of Hemisphere Specialization.* Hillsdale, N.J.: Lawrence Erlbaum Associates.

Eichenbaum, Howard, Tim Otto, and Frank Schottler. 1991. "Hippocampus and Olfactory Discrimination Learning: Effects of Entorhinal Cortex Lesions on Olfactory Learning and Memory in a Successive-Cue Go-No-Go Task." *Behavioral Neuroscience* 105 (1):111–19.

Eimas, Peter D., and Albert M. Galaburda, eds. 1989. *Neurobiology of Cognition.* 2d ed. Cambridge: MIT Press.

Einstein, Albert. [1934] 1954. *Ideas and Opinions.* Based on *Mein Weltbild,* edited by Carl Seelig and others; new translation and revision by Sonja Bargmann. New York: Bonanza Books.

Erikson, Erik. 1968. *Identity, Youth, and Crisis.* New York: W. W. Norton.

Farthing, G. William. 1992. *The Psychology of Consciousness.* Englewood Cliffs, N.J.: Prentice Hall.

Feindel, William. 1975. "Discussion." In Wilder Penfield, *The Mystery of the Mind: A Cortical Study of Consciousness and the Human Brain,* xxiv–xxix. Princeton, N.J.: Princeton University Press.

Feuerbach, Ludwig. 1957. *The Essence of Christianity.* Edited and abridged by E. Graham Waring and F. W. Strothmann. New York: Frederick Ungar.

Fiss, Harry. 1979. "Current Dream Research: A Psychobiological Perspective." In *Handbook of Dreams: Research, Theories and Applications,* edited by Benjamin B. Wolman, 20–75. New York: Van Nostrand Reinhold.

Fleming, William. 1974. *Arts and Ideas.* New and brief edition. New York: Holt, Rinehart and Winston.

Fox, Robin. 1986. "The Passionate Mind: Brain, Dreams, Memory, and Social Categories." *Zygon: Journal of Religion and Science* 21, no. 1 (March): 31–46.

Frankl, Victor E. 1978. *The Unheard Cry for Meaning: Psychotherapy and Humanism.* New York: Simon & Schuster.

Freedman, Daniel G. 1974. *Human Infancy: An Evolutionary Perspective.* Hillsdale, N.J.: Lawrence Erlbaum Associates.

Freud, Sigmund. [1920] 1959. *Beyond the Pleasure Principle.* Translated by J. Strachey. Introduction by G. Zilboorg. New York: Bantam Books.

————. [1922] 1960. *Group Psychology and the Analysis of the Ego.* Translated by J. Strachey. Introduction by Franz Alexander. New York: Bantam Books.

————. [1927] 1957. *The Future of an Illusion.* Translated by W. D. Robson-Scott. Garden City, N.Y.: Doubleday Anchor Books.

————. [1930] 1958. *Civilization and Its Discontents.* Translated by J. Riviere. New York: Doubleday, Anchor Books.

Galaburda, Albert M. 1995. "Anatomic Basis of Cerebral Dominance." In *Brain Asym-*

metry, edited by Richard J. Davidson and Kenneth Hugdahl, 51–73. Cambridge: MIT Press.

Gardner, Howard. [1974] 1976. *The Shattered Mind: The Person after Brain Damage.* New York: Vintage Books.

———. 1985. *The Mind's New Science: A History of the Cognitive Revolution.* New York: Basic Books.

Gazzaniga, Michael S. 1967. "The Split Brain in Man." *Scientific American* (August): 24–29.

———. 1970. *The Bisected Brain.* New York: Appleton-Century-Crofts.

———. 1974. "Cerebral Dominance Viewed as a Decision System." In *Hemisphere Function in the Human Head,* edited by S. J. Dimond and J. G. Beaumont. New York: John Wiley & Sons.

———. 1985. *The Social Brain: Discovering the Networks of the Mind.* New York: Basic Books.

———. 1988. *Mind Matters: How the Mind and Brain Interact to Create Our Conscious Lives.* With a Foreword by Robert Bazell. Boston: Houghton Mifflin Company.

———. 1992. *Nature's Mind: The Biological Roots of Thinking, Emotions, Sexuality, Language, and Intelligence.* New York: Basic Books/HarperCollins.

Gazzaniga, Michael S., and Joseph LeDoux. 1978. *The Integrated Mind.* New York: Plenum Publishing Company.

Gazzaniga, Michael S., and R. W. Sperry. 1967. "Language after Section of the Cerebral Commissures," *Brain* 90:131–48.

Geertz, Clifford. 1973. *The Interpretation of Cultures: Selected Essays.* New York: Basic Books.

Gell-Mann, Murray. 1993. "Complex Adaptive Systems." Physics colloquium presentation, University of Chicago, November.

Geschwind, Norman. 1972. "Language and the Brain." *Scientific American* (April): 76–83.

———. 1974. "The Anatomical Basis of Hemisphere Differentiation." In *Hemisphere Function in the Human Head,* edited by S. J. Dimond and J. G. Beaumont, 7–24. New York: John Wiley & Sons.

Geschwind, Norman, and Albert M. Galaburda, eds. 1984. *Cerebral Dominance: The Biological Foundations.* Cambridge: Harvard University Press.

———. 1987. *Cerebral Lateralization: Biological Mechanisms, Associations, and Pathology.* Cambridge: A Bradford Book/MIT Press.

Geschwind, Norman, and W. Levitsky. 1968. "Human Brain: Left-Right Asymmetries in Temporal Speech Region," *Science* 161:186–87.

Gewertz, Ken. 1995. "Inquiring into Mind: Anne Harrington Translates Meaning and Metaphor into the Language of Science." *Harvard College Gazette* (fall): 3, 10.

Gibson, Kathleen R., and Anne C. Petersen, eds. 1991. *Brain Maturation and Cognitive Development: Comparative and Cross-Cultural Perspectives.* New York: Aldine de Gruyter.

Gilbert, Paul. 1989. *Human Nature and Suffering.* Hillsdale, N.J.: Lawrence Erlbaum Associates.

Gilkey, Langdon. 1993. *Nature, Reality, and the Sacred: The Nexus of Science and Religion.* Minneapolis: Fortress Press.

Giovacchini, Peter L. 1993. *Borderline Patients, the Psychosomatic Focus, and the Therapeutic Process*. Northvale, N.J.: Jason Aronson.

Gold, Ann Grodzins. 1995. "Magical Landscapes and Moral Orders: New Readings in Religion and Ecology." *Religious Studies Review* 21, no. 2 (April): 71–77.

Goldberg, E., and L. D. Costa. 1981. "Hemispheric Differences in the Acquisition and Use of Descriptive Systems." *Brain and Language* 14:144–73.

Goldstein, Arnold P. 1994. *The Ecology of Aggression*. New York: Plenum Press.

Goodenough, Ursula. 1996. "The Origin of Sex." Lecture in the Epic of Creation series, Chicago Center for Religion and Science, January 19.

Gordon, Harold W. 1990. "The Neurobiological Basis of Hemisphericity." In *Brain Circuits and Functions of the Mind: Essays in Honor of Roger W. Sperry,* edited by Colwyn Trevarthen, 249–65. Cambridge: Cambridge University Press.

Graber, Julia A., and Anne C. Petersen. 1991. "Cognitive Changes at Adolescence: Biological Perspectives." In *Brain Maturation and Cognitive Development: Comparative and Cross-Cultural Perspectives,* edited by Kathleen R. Gibson and Anne C. Petersen. New York: Aldine De Gruyter.

Greenberg, Jay R., and Stephen A. Mitchell. 1983. *Object Relations in Psychoanalytic Theory*. Cambridge: Harvard University Press.

Greenberg, N., P. D. MacLean, and J. L. Ferguson. 1979. "Role of the Paleostriatum in Species-Typical Display Behavior of the Lizard (*Anolis carolinensis*)." *Brain Research* 172:229–41.

Gregory, Richard L., ed. 1987. *The Oxford Companion to the Mind*. With the assistance of O. L. Zangwill. Oxford: Oxford University Press.

Gross, Charles G. 1992. "Representation of Visual Stimuli in Inferior Temporal Cortex." In *Processing the Facial Image*. Proceedings of a Royal Society Discussion Meeting held on 9 and 10 July 1991, organized and edited by V. Bruce, A. Cowey, A. W. Ellis, and D. I. Perrett, 3–10. Oxford: Clarendon Press.

Guthrie, Stewart Elliott. 1993. *Faces in the Clouds: A New Theory of Religion*. New York: Oxford University Press.

Harlow, Harry F., and Margaret Kuenne Harlow. 1971. "Social Deprivation in Monkeys." *Contemporary Psychology: Readings from Scientific American*. San Francisco: W. H. Freeman.

Harlow, Jules, ed. 1972. *Mahzor for Rosh Hashanah and Yom Kippur*. New York: The Rabbinical Assembly.

Harrington, Anne. 1987. *Medicine, Mind, and the Double Brain: A Study in Nineteenth-Century Thought*. Princeton, N.J.: Princeton University Press.

———. 1991. "Beyond Phrenology: Localization Theory in the Modern Era." In *The Enchanted Loom: Chapters in the History of Neuroscience,* edited by Pietro Corsi, 207–39. New York: Oxford University Press.

———, ed. 1992a. *So Human a Brain: Knowledge and Values in the Neurosciences*. Boston: Birkhauser.

———. 1992b. "Other 'Ways of Knowing': The Politics of Knowledge in Interwar German Brain Science." In *So Human a Brain: Knowledge and Values in the Neuro-*

sciences, edited by Anne Harrington, 229–44. Boston: Birkhauser.

———. 1995. "Unfinished Business: Models of Laterality in the Nineteenth Century." In *Brain Asymmetry,* edited by Richard J. Davidson and Kenneth Hugdahl, 3–27. Cambridge: A Bradford Book/MIT Press.

———. 1996. *Reenchanted Science: Holism in German Culture from Wilhelm II to Hitler.* Princeton, N.J.: Princeton University Press.

Harris, Lauren Julius. 1978. "Sex Differences in Spatial Ability: Possible Environmental, Genetic, and Neurological Factors." In *Asymmetrical Function of the Brain,* edited by Marcel Kinsbourne, 405–522. New York: Cambridge University Press.

Hartshorne, Charles. 1948. *The Divine Relativity: A Social Conception of God.* New Haven, Conn.: Yale University Press.

———. 1975. "Physics and Psychics: The Place of Mind in Nature." In *Mind in Nature,* edited by John B. Cobb Jr. and David Ray Griffin, 89–97. Washington, D.C.: University Press of America.

Harvey, John H., and Gifford Weary, eds. 1985. *Attribution: Basic Issues and Applications.* Orlando: Academic Press.

Harvey, Van. 1964. *A Handbook of Theological Terms.* New York: Macmillan.

Hauri, Peter. 1979. "What Can Insomniacs Teach Us about the Function of Sleep?" In *Frontiers of Sleep,* edited by Rene Drucker-Colin, Mario Shkurovich, and M. R. Sterman, 251–71. New York: Human Science Press.

Hawking, Stephen W. 1988. *A Brief History of Time: From the Big Bang to Black Holes.* New York: Bantam.

Hefner, Philip. 1993. *The Human Factor: Evolution, Culture, and Religion.* Foreword by Arthur Peacock. Minneapolis: Fortress Press.

———. 1994. "Can Nature Truly Be Our Friend?" *Zygon: Journal of Religion and Science* 29, no. 4 (December): 507–28.

Heilman, Kenneth M. 1978. "Language and the Brain: Relationship of Localization of Language Function to the Acquisition and Loss of Various Aspects of Language." In *Education and the Brain: The 77th Yearbook of the National Society for the Study of Education, Part I,* 143–68. Chicago: University of Chicago Press.

Hellige, Joseph B. 1990. "Hemispheric Asymmetry." In *Annual Review of Psychology* 41, edited by Mark R. Rosenzweig and Lyman W. Porter, 55–80. Palo Alto, Calif.: Annual Reviews, Inc.

———. 1993. *Hemisphere Asymmetry: What's Right and What's Left.* Cambridge: Harvard University Press.

Hess, W. R. 1925. *On the Relationship between Psychic and Vegetative Functions.* Zurich: Schwabe.

Hewstone, Miles, ed. 1983. *Attribution Theory: Social and Functional Extensions.* Oxford: Basil Blackwell.

Hobson, J. Allan. 1988. *The Dreaming Brain.* New York: Basic Books.

———. 1994. *The Chemistry of Conscious States: How the Brain Changes Its Mind.* Boston: Little, Brown.

Hollander, E., and D. J. Stein, eds. 1995. *Impulsivity and Aggression.* Chichester, Eng.: Wiley.

Holmes, Rodney. 1991. "Did *Homo religiosus* Emerge from the Evolution of the Brain?" *Insights: The Magazine of the Chicago Center for Religion and Science* 3, no. 1: 10–14.

———. 1995. "*Homo religiosus* and Its Brain: Reality, Imagination and the Future of Nature." A paper presented at the James B. Ashbrook Symposium, Garrett-Evangelical Theological Seminary, Evanston, Ill., Jan. 25.

Horton, Paul C., Herbert Gerwirtz, and Karole J. Kreutter, eds. 1988. *The Solace Paradigm: An Eclectic Search for Psychological Immunity.* Madison, Conn.: International Universities.

Hubel, David H. 1981. "Evolution of Ideas on the Primary Visual Cortex, 1955–1978: A Biased Historical Account." In *Les Prix Nobel,* 224–48. Stockholm: Almqvist & Wiksell International.

Huxley, Julian. 1959. "Introduction." In *The Phenomenon of Man,* by Pierre Teilhard de Chardin. New York: Harper & Row.

Jackson, J. Hughlings. 1932. "On the Duality of the Brain." *Medical Press* 1, 19. Reprinted in *Selected Writings of John Hughlings Jackson,* vol. 2, edited by J. Taylor. London: Hodder and Stoughton.

James, William. [1890] 1904. *The Principles of Psychology.* Vol. 1. New York: Henry Holt and Company.

Janson, H. W. [1962] 1967. *History of Art: A Survey of the Modern Visual Arts from the Dawn of History to the Present Day.* With Dora Lane Janson. Englewood Cliffs, N.J.: Prentice-Hall, and New York: Harry N. Abrams.

Jastrow, Robert. 1981. *The Enchanted Loom: Mind in the Universe.* New York: Simon & Schuster.

Jaynes, Julian. 1976. *The Origin of Consciousness in the Breakdown of the Bicameral Mind.* Boston: Houghton Mifflin.

Jeans, James. 1931. *The Mysterious Universe.* Cambridge: Cambridge University Press.

Jerison, Harry J. 1976. "Paleoneurology and the Evolution of Mind." *Scientific American* 234, no. 1 (January): 90–101.

Jirari, C. 1970. "Form Perception, Innate Form Preferences, and Visually Mediated Head-turning in Human Neonates." Unpublished doctoral dissertation, Committee on Human Development, University of Chicago.

Johnson, Elizabeth. 1992. *She Who Is: The Mystery of God in Feminist Theological Discourse.* New York: Crossroad.

Johnson, George. 1994. *The New York Times,* 27 April.

Johnson, Mark. 1987. *The Body in the Mind: The Bodily Basis of Meaning, Imagination, and Reason.* Chicago: University of Chicago Press.

Johnson, Mark H., and John Morton. 1991. *Biology and Cognitive Development: The Case of Face Recognition.* Oxford: Blackwell.

Jones, Dorothy V. 1991. *Code of Peace: Ethics and Security in the World of the Warlord States.* Chicago: University of Chicago Press.

Jones, James W. 1991. *Contemporary Psychoanalysis and Religion: Transference and Transcendence.* New Haven, Conn.: Yale University Press.

Kagan, Jerome. 1996. "Three Pleasing Ideas." *American Psychologist* 51, no. 9: 901–8.

Kaplan, H. I., and B. J. Saddock, eds. 1980. *Comprehensive Textbook of Psychiatry/IV.* Baltimore: Williams & Wilkins.

Kauffman, Stuart. 1995. *At Home in the Universe: The Search for Laws of Self-Organization and Complexity.* New York: Oxford University Press.

Kaufman, Gordon D. 1992. "Nature, History, and God: Toward an Integrated Conceptualization." *Zygon: Journal of Religion and Science* 27, no. 4 (December): 379–401.

————. 1993. *In Face of Mystery: A Constructive Theology.* Cambridge: Harvard University Press.

Kelly, Ronald R., and Kenneth D. Orton. 1979. "Dichotic Perception of Word-Pairs with Mixed Image Values." *Neuropsychologia* 17:363–71.

Kimura, Doreen. 1973. "The Asymmetry of the Human Brain." *Scientific American,* March, 72–73.

————. 1985. "Male Brain, Female Brain: The Hidden Difference." *Psychology Today,* November, 50–58.

Kinsbourne, Marcel, ed. 1978. *Asymmetrical Function of the Brain.* New York: Cambridge University Press.

Kinsbourne, M., and W. L. Smith, eds. 1974. *Hemisphere Disconnection and Cerebral Function.* Springfield, Ill.: Charles C. Thomas.

Klein, R., and R. Armitage. 1978. "Rhythms in Human Performance: One-and-a-Half Oscillations in Cognitive Styles." *Science* 204:1326–28.

Kleitman, Nathaniel. 1969. "Basic Rest–Activity Cycle in Relation to Sleep and Wakefulness." In *Sleep: Physiology and Pathology,* edited by A. Kales, 33–38. Philadelphia: Lippincott.

Klivington, Kenneth. 1989. *The Science of Mind.* Cambridge: MIT Press.

Köhler, W. [1938]1976. *The Place of Value in a World of Facts.* New York: Liveright.

Kolb, Bryan, and Ian Q. Whishaw. [1980] 1985. *Fundamentals of Human Neuropsychology.* 2d ed. New York: W. H. Freeman.

Konner, Melvin. [1982] 1983. *The Tangled Wing: Biological Constraints on the Human Spirit.* New York: Harper Colophon.

Korzybski, A. 1933. *Science and Sanity.* 4th ed. Lakeville, Conn.: The International Non-Aristotelian Library Publishing Company.

Kosslyn, Stephen M. 1992. "Cognitive Neuroscience and the Human Self." In *So Human a Brain: Knowledge and Values in the Neurosciences,* edited by Anne Harrington, 37–56. Boston: Birkhauser.

Kosslyn, Stephen M., and Olivier Koenig. 1992. *Wet Mind: The New Cognitive Neuroscience.* New York: The Free Press.

Kotulak, Ronald. 1996. *Inside the Brain: Revolutionary Discoveries of How the Mind Works.* Kansas City, Mo.: Andrews & McMeel.

Kripke, Daniel F. 1982. "Ultradian Rhythms in Behavior and Physiology." In *Rhythmic Aspects of Behavior,* edited by Frederick M. Brown and R. Curtis Graeber, 313–43. Hillsdale, N.J.: Lawrence Erlbaum Associates.

Kuhn, Thomas. 1970. *The Structure of Scientific Revolutions.* 2d ed. Chicago: University of Chicago Press.

Lakoff, George. 1987. *Women, Fire, and Dangerous Things: What Categories Reveal about the Mind.* Chicago: University of Chicago Press.

Lancaster, Brian. 1991. *Mind, Brain, and Human Potential: The Quest for an Understanding of Self.* Rockport, Mass.: Element.

LaPlante, Eve. 1993. *Seized: Temporal Lobe Epilepsy as a Medical, Historical, and Artistic Phenomenon.* New York: HarperCollins.

Laughlin, Charles D., Jr., John McManus, and Eugene G. d'Aquili. 1990. *Brain, Symbol, and Experience: Toward a Neurophenomenology of Human Consciousness.* Boston: New Science Library/Shambhala.

Lazarus, Richard S. 1991. *Emotion and Adaptation.* New York: Oxford University Press.

LeDoux, Joseph, and William Hirst, eds. [1986] 1990. *Mind and Brain: Dialogues in Cognitive Neuroscience.* Cambridge: Cambridge University Press.

Leeper, R. W. 1970. "The Motivational and Perceptual Properties of Emotions as Indicating Their Fundamental Character and Role." In *Feelings and Emotions: The Loyola Symposium,* edited by M. B. Arnold. New York: Academic Press.

LeMay, M., and A. Culebras. 1972. "Human Brain: Morphological Differences in the Hemispheres Demonstrable by Carotid Arteriography." *New England Journal of Medicine* 287:168–70.

Lettvin, J. Y., H. R. Maturana, W. S. McCullock, and W. H. Pitts.[1959] 1969 . "Che cosa l'occhio della rana communica al cervello della rana." ("What the Frog's Eye Tells the Frog's Brain.") In *La Fisica della Menta,* edited by V. Somenzi, 172–204. Turin: Boringhieri.

Levy, Jerre. 1974. "Psychobiological Implications of Bilateral Asymmetry." In *Hemisphere Function in the Human Head,* edited by S. J. Dimond and J. G. Beaumont. New York: John Wiley & Sons.

———. 1980. "Varieties of Human Brain Organization and the Human Social System." *Zygon: Journal of Religion and Science* 15 (December): 351–75.

———. 1985. "Interhemispheric Collaboration: Single-mindedness in Asymmetrical Brain." In *Hemisphere Function and Collaboration in the Child,* edited by Catherine T. Best, 11–31. Orlando: Academic Press.

Levy, Jerre, and Colwyn Trevarthen. 1976. "Metacontrol of Hemispheric Function in Human Split Brain Patients." *Journal of Experimental Psychology: Human Perception and Performance* 2:299–312.

Levy-Agresti, J., and R. W. Sperry. 1968. "Differential Perceptual Capacities in Major and Minor Hemispheres," *Proceedings of the National Academy of Science, U.S.A.* 61:1151 (abstract).

Lewis, David Warren, and Marian Cleeves Diamond. 1995. "The Influence of Gonadal

Steroids on the Asymmetry of the Cerebral Cortex." In *Brain Asymmetry,* edited by Richard J. Davidson and Kenneth Hugdahl, 32–50. Cambridge: A Bradford Book/ MIT Press.

Lex, Barbara. 1979. "The Neurobiology of Ritual Trance." In *The Spectrum of Ritual: A Biogenetic Structural Analysis,* edited by E. G. d'Aquili, Charles D. Laughlin, and John McManus. New York: Columbia University Press.

Liddon, Sim C. 1989. *The Dual Brain, Religion, and the Unconscious.* Buffalo: Prometheus Books.

Liederman, Jacqueline. 1995. "A Reinterpretation of the Split-Brain Syndrome: Implications for the Function of Corticocortical Fibers." In *Brain Asymmetry,* edited by Richard J. Davidson and Kenneth Hugdahl, 451–90. Cambridge: A Bradford Book/ MIT Press.

Livingston, Robert B. 1978. *Sensory Processing, Perception, and Behavior.* New York: Raven Press.

———. 1981. "Some Consequences of Brain Organization and Individuation." *Basic Medical Neurology,* 2 April, mimeographed.

Loftus, Elizabeth, and John C. Yuille. 1984. "Departures from Reality in Human Perception and Memory." In *Memory Consolidation: Psychobiology of Cognition,* edited by Herbert Weingartner and Elizabeth S. Parker, 163–83. Hillsdale, N.J.: Lawrence Erlbaum Associates.

Luria, Aleksandr Romanovich. 1970. "The Functional Organization of the Brain." *Scientific American,* March, 66–78.

———. 1973. *The Working Brain: An Introduction to Neuropsychology.* Translated by Basil Haigh. New York: Basic Books.

———. [1966] 1980. *Higher Cortical Functions in Man.* 2d ed., revised and expanded. Prefaces to the English edition by Hans-Lukas Teuber and Karl H. Pribram. New York: Basic Books.

———. 1987. "Reductionism in Psychology." In *The Oxford Companion to the Mind,* edited by Richard L. Gregory, with the assistance of O. L. Zangwell, 579–80. New York: Oxford University Press.

Lynch, Gary, and Michel Baudry. 1988. "Structure-Function Relationships in the Organization of Memory." In *Perspectives in Memory Research,* edited by Michael S. Gazzaniga, 23–91. Cambridge: MIT Press.

Mackay, Alan L., ed. 1977. *The Harvest of a Quiet Eye.* London: The Institute of Physics.

MacLean, Paul D. 1949. "Psychosomatic Disease and the 'Visceral Brain': Recent Developments Bearing on the Papez Theory of Emotion." *Psychosomatic Medicine* XI, no. 6, Nov.–Dec.: 38–53.

———. 1952. "Some Psychiatric Implications of Physiological Studies on Frontotemporal Portion of Limbic System (Visceral Brain)." *Electroencephalography and Clinical Neurophysiology* 4:407–18.

———. 1958. "The Limbic System with Respect to Self-preservation and the Preservation of the Species." *Journal of Nervous and Mental Disorders* 127:1–11.

———. 1967. "The Brain in Relation to Empathy and Medical Education." *Journal of Nervous and Mental Disorders* 144:374–82.

———. 1970. "The Triune Brain, Emotion, and Scientific Bias." In *The Neurosciences Second Study Program,* edited by F. O. Schmitt. New York: Rockefeller University Press.

———. 1975/1993. "On the Evolution of Three Mentalities." *Man-Environment Systems* 5:213–24. Reprinted in *Brain, Culture, and the Human Spirit,* edited by James B. Ashbrook, 3–44. Lanham, Md.: University Press of America, 1993.

———. 1976. "The Imitative-Creative Interplay of Our Three Mentalities." In *Astride the Two Cultures: Arthur Koestler at 70,* edited by Harold Harris. London: Hutchinson.

———. 1978. "A Mind of Three Minds: Educating the Triune Brain." In *Education and the Brain: The 77th Yearbook of the National Society for the Study of Education, Part 2,* edited by Jeanne S. Chall and Allan F. Mirsky, 308–42. Chicago: University of Chicago Press.

———. 1982a. "The Co-Evolution of the Brain and Family." In *Anthroquest: The L. S. B. Leakey Foundation News* 24, no. 1: 14–15.

———. 1982b. "Evolution of the Psychencephalon." *Zygon: Journal of Religion and Science* 17, no. 2 (June): 187–211.

———. 1985a. "Brain Evolution Relating to Family, Play, and the Separation Call." *Archives of General Psychiatry* 42 (April): 405–17.

———. 1985b. "Evolutionary Psychiatry and the Triune Brain." *Psychological Medicine* 15:219–21.

———. 1987. "The Midline Frontolimbic Cortex and the Evolution of Crying and Laughter." In *The Frontal Lobes Revisited,* edited by Ellen Perecman, 121–40. New York: IRBN Press.

———. 1990a. *The Triune Brain in Evolution: Role in Paleocerebral Functions.* New York: Plenum Press.

———. 1991. "Neofrontocerebellar Evolution in Regard to Computation and Prediction: Some Fractal Aspects of Microgenesis." In *Cognitive Microgenesis: A Neuropsychological Perspective,* edited by Robert Hanlon, 3–31. New York: Springer-Verlag.

———. 1992. "Obtaining Knowledge of the Subjective Brain ('Epistemics')." In *So Human a Brain: Knowledge and Values in the Neurosciences,* edited by Anne Harrington, 57–70. Boston: Birkhauser.

———. 1996. "Women: A More Balanced Brain?" *Zygon: Journal of Religion and Science* 31, no. 3 (September): 421–39.

McDargh, John. 1983. *Psychoanalytic Object Relations Theory and the Study of Religion: On Faith and the Imaging of God.* Lanham, Md.: University Press of America.

McEwen, Bruce S., and Harold M. Schmeck. 1994. *The Hostage Brain.* New York: Rockefeller University Press.

McFague, Sallie. 1987. *Models of God: Theology for an Ecological, Nuclear Age.* Philadelphia: Fortress Press.

———. 1993. *The Body of God: An Ecological Theology.* Philadelphia: Fortress Press.

Mecacci, Luciano. 1991. "Pathways of Perception." In *The Enchanted Loom: Chapters in the History of Neuroscience,* edited by Pietro Corsi, 272–88. New York: Oxford University Press.

Medin, Douglas L., and Brian H. Ross, eds. 1990. *Cognitive Psychology.* Fort Worth, Tex.: Harcourt Brace Jovanovich College Publishers.

Meissner, W. W. 1984. *Psychoanalysis and Religious Experience.* New Haven, Conn.: Yale University Press.

Meland, B. S., ed. 1969. *The Future of Empirical Theology.* Chicago: University Chicago Press.

Merkur, Daniel. 1990. "Freud's Atheism: Object Relations and the Theory of Religion." *Religious Studies Review* 16, no. 1 (January): 11–16.

Meshberger, Frank Lynn. 1990. "An Interpretation of Michelangelo's *Creation of Adam* Based on Neuroanatomy." *Journal of the American Medical Association* 264, no. 14 (10 October): 1837–41.

Metzger, Bruce M., and Roland E. Murphy, eds. 1991. *The Oxford Annotated Bible with Apocryphal/Deuteroncanonical Books: New Revised Standard Version.* New York: Oxford University Press.

Miller, Christina A., and Duane L. Christensen. 1991. Letter about Meshberger's *The Creation of Adam. Journal of the American Medical Association* 265, no. 9 (6 March): 1111.

Milner, A. D., and M. D. Rugg, eds. 1992. *The Neuropsychology of Consciousness.* New York: Academic Press.

Milner, Brenda. 1974. "Introduction;" "Hemisphere Specialization: Scope and Limits." In *The Neurosciences: Third Study Program,* edited by F. O. Schmitt and F. G. Worden, 3–4, 75–89. Cambridge: MIT Press.

Mirsky, Allan F. 1978. "Attention: A Neuropsychological Perspective." In *Education and the Brain: The 77th Yearbook of the National Society for the Study of Education, Part 2,* edited by Jeanne S. Chall and Allan F. Mirsky, 33–60. Chicago: University of Chicago Press.

Mishkin, Mortimer, and Tim Appenzeller. 1987. "The Anatomy of Memory." *Scientific American* (special report): 1–12.

Mitchell, Stephen A. 1988. *Relational Concepts in Psychoanalysis: An Integration.* Cambridge: Harvard University Press.

Morgan, James. 1932. *The Psychological Teaching of St. Augustine.* London: Elliot Stock.

Morgenstern, J. 1962. "Sabbath." In *The Interpreter's Dictionary of the Bible: R–Z,* George A. Buttrick, gen. ed., 135–41. New York: Abingdon Press.

Mountcastle, V. B. 1976. "The World Around Us: Neural Command Functions for Selective Attention." *Neurosciences Research Program Bulletin,* vol. 14, supplement (April).

Nathan, Peter. 1969. *The Nervous System.* Baltimore: Penguin Books.

Nebes, Robert D. 1974. "Dominance of the Minor Hemisphere in Commissurotomized Man for the Perception of Part-Whole Relationships." In *Hemisphere Disconnection and Cerebral Function,* edited by M. Kinsbourne and W. L. Smith. Springfield, Ill.: Charles C. Thomas.

————. 1978. "Direct Examination of Cognitive Function in the Right and Left Hemispheres." In *Asymmetrical Function of the Brain,* edited by Marcel Kinsbourne, 99–137. New York: Cambridge University Press.

Needham, Rodney, ed. [1973] 1978. *Right and Left: Essays on Dual Symbolic Classification.* Edited and with an introduction by Rodney Needham. Foreword by E. E. Evans-Pritchard. Chicago: University of Chicago Press.

Neisser, Ulric. 1988. "What Is Ordinary Memory the Memory Of?" In *Remembering Reconsidered: Ecological and Traditional Approaches to the Study of Memory,* edited by Ulric Neisser and Eugene Winograd, 356–73. Cambridge: Cambridge University Press.

Nicholls, John G., A. Robert Martin, and Bruce G. Wallace. 1992. *From Neuron to Brain: A Cellular and Molecular Approach to the Function of the Nervous System.* 3d ed. Sunderland, Mass.: Sinauer Associate.

Oakley, David A., ed. 1985. *Brain and Mind.* New York: Methuen.

Oates, Whitney J., ed. 1948. *The Basic Writings of St. Augustine: On the Trinity.* New York: Random House.

Olton, D. S. 1983. "Memory Functions and the Hippocampus." In *Neurobiology of the Hippocampus,* edited by W. Seifert, 335–73. London: Academic Press.

Ornstein, Robert E. [1972] 1977. *The Psychology of Consciousness.* 2d ed. New York: Harcourt Brace Jovanovich.

————. 1986. *The Psychology of Consciousness.* Completely revised and updated. New York: Penguin Books.

Ornstein, Robert E., and David Sobel. 1987. *The Healing Brain: Breakthrough Discoveries about How the Brain Keeps Us Healthy.* New York: A Touchstone Book.

Ornstein, Robert E., and Charles Swencionis. 1990. *The Healing Brain: A Scientific Reader.* New York: Guilford Press.

Pannenberg, Wolfhart. 1993. *Toward a Theology of Nature: Essays on Science and Faith.* Edited by Ted Peters. Louisville: Westminster/John Knox.

Papez, J. W. 1937. "A Proposed Mechanism of Emotion." *Archives of Neurology and Psychiatry* 33:725–43.

Passingham, R. E. 1993. *The Frontal Lobes and Voluntary Action: Oxford Psychology Series no. 21.* Oxford: Oxford University Press.

Paterson, Randolph J., and Greg Moran. 1988. "Attachment Theory, Personality Development, and Psychotherapy," *Clinical Psychology Review* 8:611–36.

Peacocke, Arthur. 1993. *Theology for a Scientific Age: Being and Becoming--Natural, Divine, and Human.* Minneapolis: Fortress Press.

Pearce, Joseph Chilton. 1992. *Evolution's End: Claiming the Potential of Our Intelligence.* San Francisco: Harper.

Penfield, Wilder. 1975. *The Mystery of the Mind: A Critical Study of Consciousness.* Princeton, N.J.: Princeton University Press.

Perecman, Ellen, ed. 1984. *Cognitive Processing in the Right Hemisphere.* New York: Academic Press.

Perrett, D. I., J. K. Hietanen, M. W. Oram, and P. J. Benson. 1992. "Organization and Functions of Cells Responsive to Faces in the Temporal Cortex." In *Processing the Facial Image.* Proceedings of a Royal Society Discussion Meeting held on 9 and 10 July 1991, organized and edited by V. Bruce, A. Cowey, A. W. Ellis, and D. I. Perrett, 23–30. Oxford: Clarendon Press.

Pinker, Steven. 1994. *The Language Instinct: How the Mind Creates Language.* New York: William Morrow.

Ploog, Detlev W. 1992. "Neuroethological Perspectives on the Human Brain: From the Expression of Emotions to Intentional Signing and Speech." In *So Human a Brain,* edited by Anne Harrington, 3–13. Boston: A Dibner Institute Publication/Birkhauser.

Polkinghorne, John. 1991. "The Nature of Physical Reality." *Zygon: Journal of Religion and Science* 26, no. 2 (June): 221–36.

Pribram, Karl H. 1971. *Languages of the Brain: Experimental Paradoxes and Principles of Neuropsychology.* Englewood Cliffs, N.J.: Prentice-Hall.

———. 1984. "Emotion: A Neurobehavioral Analysis." In *Approaches to Emotion,* edited by K. R. Scherer and P. Ekman, 13–38. Hillsdale, N.J.: Erlbaum.

Prigogine, Ilya, and Isabelle Stengers. 1984. *Out of Chaos: Man's New Dialogue with Nature.* Foreword by Alvin Toffler. New York: Bantam Books.

Restak, Richard M. [1994] 1995. *Receptors.* New York: Bantam Books.

Richardson, Alan, and John Bowden. 1983. *The Westminster Dictionary of Christian Theology.* Philadelphia: Westminster Press.

Ricoeur, Paul. 1978. "Manifestation and Proclamation." *Journal of the Blaisdell Institute* 12 (winter): 13–35.

Rizzuto, Anna-Maria. 1979. *The Birth of the Living God: A Psychoanalytic Study.* Chicago: University of Chicago Press.

Rodriguez, Ward A. 1993. "Societal, Cultural, and Biological Constraints on Neuroscience." Review of *So Human a Brain: Knowledge and Values in the Neurosciences,* edited by Anne Harrington. *Contemporary Psychology* 38, no. 10 (October): 1100–1101.

Rolls, Edmund T. 1992. "Neurophysiological Mechanisms Underlying Face Processing within and beyond the Temporal Cortical Visual Areas." In *Processing the Facial Image:* Proceedings of a Royal Society Discussion Meeting held on 9 and 10 July 1991, organized and edited by V. Bruce, A. Cowey, A. W. Ellis, and D. I. Perrett, 1992. 11–22. Oxford: Clarendon Press.

Rolston, Holmes, III. 1987. *Science and Religion: A Critical Survey.* New York: Random House.

Rose, Steven. 1974. *The Conscious Brain.* New York: Alfred A. Knopf.

Rossi, Ernest Lawrence, with David Nimmons. 1991. *The 20 Minute Break: Using the New Science of Ultradian Rhythms.* Los Angeles: Jeremy P. Tarcher.

———. [1986] 1993. *The Psychobiology of Mind-Body Healing: New Concepts of Therapeutic Hypnosis.* Rev. ed. New York: W. W. Norton.

Ruether, Rosemary Radford. 1983. *Sexism and God-Talk: Toward a Feminist Theology.* Boston: Beacon Press.

Rumelhart, David E., James L. McClelland, and the PDP Research Group. [1986] 1987. *Explorations in the Microstructure of Cognition: Computational Models of Cognition and Perception: 1: Foundations; 2. Psychological and Biological Models.* Cambridge: MIT Press.

Russell, Peter. 1979. *The Brain Book.* New York: Hawthorne Books.

Sanders, J. N. 1962. "The Word." In *The Interpreter's Dictionary of the Bible: R–Z,* George Arthur Buttrick, general editor, 368–72. New York: Abingdon Press.

Schacter, Daniel L., and Endel Tulving. 1994. *Memory Systems.* Cambridge: MIT Press.

Schleiermacher, Friedrich. 1928. *The Christian Faith.* Edited by H. K. Mackintosh and J. S. Stewart. Edinburgh: T. & T. Clark.

Schmitz-Moormann, Karl. 1995. "The Future of Teilhardian Theology." *Zygon: Journal of Religion and Science* 30, no. 1 (March): 117–29.

Schüssler Fiorenza, Elisabeth. 1994. *Jesus: Miriam's Child, Sophia's Prophet—Critical Issues in Feminist Christology.* New York: Continuum.

Scoville, W. B., and B. Milner. 1957. "Loss of Recent Memory after Bilateral Hippocampal Lesions." *Journal of Neurological Neurosurgical Psychiatry* 20:11–21.

Sellers, O. R. 1962. "Heart." In *The Interpreter's Dictionary of the Bible: E–I,* George Buttrick, gen. ed., 549–50. New York: Abingdon Press.

Shapiro, Francine. 1995. *Eye Movement Desensitization and Reprocessing: Basic Principles, Protocols, and Procedures.* New York: Guilford Press.

Sherrington, Sir Charles. [1940] 1941. *Man on His Nature: The Gifford Lectures 1937–38.* New York: Macmillan.

Simmons, I. G. 1993. *Interpreting Nature: Cultural Constructions of the Environment.* New York: Routledge.

Smith, A. 1974. "Dominant and Nondominant Hemispherectomy." In *Hemisphere Disconnection and Cerebral Function,* edited by M. Kinsbourne and W. L. Smith, 7–17. Springfield, Ill.: Charles C. Thomas.

Smith, Hewstone, ed. 1983. *Attribution Theory: Social and Function Extensions.* Oxford: Basil Blackwell.

Smith, Wilfred Cantwell. 1977. *Belief and History.* Charlottesville, Va.: University Press of Virginia.

Spear, Norman E., and Christian W. Mueller. 1984. "Consolidation as a Function of Retrieval." In *Memory Consolidation: Psychobiology of Cognition,* edited by Herbert Weingartner and Elizabeth S. Parker, 111–47. Hillsdale, N.J.: Lawrence Erlbaum Associates.

Spence, D. P. 1982. *Narrative Truth and Historical Truth: Meaning and Interpretation in Psychoanalysis.* New York: W. W. Norton.

Spero, Moshe Halevi. 1992. *Religious Objects as Psychological Structures: A Critical Integration of Object Relations Theory, Psychotherapy, and Judaism.* Chicago: University of Chicago Press.

Sperry, R. W. 1962. "Some General Aspects of Interhemispheric Integration." In *Interhemispheric Relations and Cerebral Dominance,* edited by V. B. Mountcastle. Baltimore: Johns Hopkins University Press.

————. 1969. "A Modified View of Consciousness." *Psychological Review* 76, no. 6: 532–36.

————. 1981. "Some Effects of Disconnecting the Cerebral Hemispheres." In *Les Prix Nobel,* 209–19. Stockholm: Almqvist & Wiksell International.

————. 1982. "Some Effects of Disconnecting the Cerebral Hemispheres." *Science* 217:1223–26.

————. 1985. "Changed Concepts of Brain and Consciousness: Some Value Implications." *Zygon: Journal of Religion and Science* 20, no. 1 (March): 41–57.

————. 1988. "Sperry on Consciousness." *Caltech News* 22, no. 5 (October): 3–4.

————. [1988]1993. "Psychology's Mentalist Paradigm and the Religion/Science Tension." *American Psychologist* 43, no. 8 (August): 607–13. In *Brain, Culture, and the Human Spirit,* edited by James B. Ashbrook, 109–27. Lanham, Md.: University Press of America.

————. 1991. "Search for Beliefs to Live by Consistent with Science." *Zygon: Journal of Religion and Science* 26 (June): 237–58.

————. 1992. "Paradigms of Belief, Theory, and Metatheory." *Zygon: Journal of Religion and Science* 27, no. 3 (September): 245–59.

————. 1993. "The Impact and Promise of the Cognitive Revolution." *American Psychologist* 48, no. 8 (August): 878–85.

————. 1995. "The Future of Psychology." *American Psychologist* 50, no. 7 (July): 505–6.

Spitz, R. 1945. "Hospitalism: An Inquiry into the Genesis of Psychiatric Conditions in Early Childhood." *Psychoanalytic Study of the Child* 1:53–72.

————. 1946. "Anaclitic Depression." *Psychoanalytic Study of the Child* 2:313–42.

Springer, Sally P., and Georg Deutsch. [1981] 1989. *Left Brain, Right Brain.* 3d ed. New York: W. H. Freeman.

Squire, Larry R. 1983. "The Hippocampus and the Neuropsychology of Memory." In *Neurobiology of the Hippocampus,* edited by W. Seifert, 491–511. New York: Oxford University Press.

————. 1987. *Memory and Brain.* New York: Oxford University Press.

————. 1992. "Memory and the Hippocampus: A Synthesis from Findings with Rats, Monkeys, and Humans." *Psychological Review* 99:195–231.

Squire, Larry R., Neal J. Cohen, and Lynn Nadel. 1984. "The Medial Temporal Region and Memory Consolidation: A New Hypothesis." In *Memory Consolidation: Psychobiology of Cognition,* edited by Herbert Weingartner and Elizabeth S. Parker, 185–210. Hillsdale, N.J.: Lawrence Erlbaum Associates.

Stead, Christopher. 1983. "Logos." In *The Westminster Dictionary of Christian Theology,* edited by Alan Richardson and John Bowden, 339–40. Philadelphia: Westminster Press.

Stern, Daniel N. 1985. *The Interpersonal World of the Infant: A View from Psychoanalysis and Developmental Psychology.* New York: Basic Books.

Stevens, Anthony. 1982. *Archetypes: A Natural History of the Self.* New York: William Morrow.

————. 1986. "Thoughts on the Psychobiology of Religion and the Neurobiology of Archetypal Experiences." *Zygon: Journal of Religion and Science* 21, no. 1 (March): 9–30.

Taylor, Gordon Rattray. 1979. *The Natural History of the Mind.* New York: E. P. Dutton.

Teilhard de Chardin, Pierre. [1955] 1959. *The Phenomenon of Man.* Translated by Bernard Wall. New York: Harper & Row.

Tillich, Paul. 1948a. *The Protestant Era.* Translated and with a concluding essay by James Luther Adams. Chicago: University of Chicago Press.

————. 1948b. *The Shaking of the Foundations.* New York: Charles Scribner's Sons.

————. 1951. *Systematic Theology, Vol. I: Reason and Revelation, Being and God.* Chicago: University of Chicago Press.

————. 1952. *The Courage to Be.* New Haven, Conn.: Yale University Press.

————. 1954. *Love, Power, and Justice: Ontological Analyses and Ethical Applications.* New York: Oxford University Press.

————. 1957. *Systematic Theology, Vol. 2: Christ and Existence.* Chicago: University of Chicago Press.

————. 1959. *Theology of Culture,* edited by Robert C. Kimball. New York: Oxford University Press.

————. 1963. *Systematic Theology, Vol. 3: Life and the Spirit; History and the Kingdom of God.* Chicago: University of Chicago Press.

————. 1968. *A History of Christian Thought,* edited by Carl E. Braaten. London: SCM Press.

Tracy, David. 1975. *Blessed Rage for Order: The New Pluralism in Theology.* Minneapolis: Winston-Seabury Press.

————. 1981. *The Analogical Imagination: Christian Theology and the Cultural of Pluralism.* Chicago: University of Chicago Press.

Trevarthen, Colwyn. [1986]1993. "Brain Sciences and the Human Spirit." *Zygon: Journal of Religion and Science* 21, no. 2 (June): 161–200. In *Brain, Culture and the Human Spirit,* edited by James B. Ashbrook, 129–82. Lanham, Md: University Press of America.

————, ed. 1990a. *Brain Circuits and Functions of the Mind: Essays in Honor of Roger W. Sperry.* Cambridge: Cambridge University Press.

————. 1990b. "Growth and Education in the Hemispheres." In *Brain Circuits and Functions of the Mind: Essays in Honor of Roger W. Sperry,* edited by Colwyn Trevarthen, 334–63. Cambridge: Cambridge University Press.

Trevarthen, Colwyn, and P. Hubley. 1978. "Secondary Intersubjectivity: Confidence, Confiders and Acts of Meaning in the First Year." In *Action, Gesture and Symbol,* edited by A. Lock. New York: Academic Press.

Turner, Victor. [1983]1993. "Body, Brain, and Culture." *Zygon: Journal of Religion and Science* 18, no. 3 (September): 221–45. In *Brain, Culture, and the Human Spirit,* edited by James B. Ashbrook, 77–108. Lanham, Md.: University Press of America.

————. 1986. "My Career." *Zygon: Journal of Religion and Science* 21, no. 1 (March): 3.

Vandervert, L. R. 1988. "Systems Thinking and a Proposal for a Neurological Positivism." *Systems Research* 5:313–21.

Varela, Francisco J., Evan Thompson, and Eleanor Rosch. [1991] 1993. *The Embodied Mind: Cognitive Science and Human Experience.* Cambridge: MIT Press.

Volauka, Jan. 1995. *Neurobiology of Violence.* Washington, D.C.: American Psychiatric Press.

Volk, Tyler. 1995. *Metapatterns: Across Space, Time, and Mind.* New York: Columbia University Press.

Waber, D. P. 1976. "Sex Differences in Cognition: A Function of Maturation Rate?" *Science,* May, 572–73.

————. 1979. "Cognitive Abilities and Sex-related Variations." In *Sex-related Differences in Cognitive Functioning: Developmental Issues,* edited by H. A. Wittig and A. C. Peterson. San Francisco: Academic Press.

Wada, John A. 1977. "Pre-Language and Fundamental Asymmetry of the Infant Brain." In *Evolution and Lateralization of the Brain* 299, edited by Stuart J. Dimond and David A. Blizard, 370–79. New York: Annals of the New York Academy of Sciences.

Waldrop, M. Mitchell. 1992. *Complexity: The Emerging Science at the Edge of Order and Chaos.* New York: Simon & Schuster.

Watts, Alan W. [1963] 1969. *The Two Hands of God: The Myths of Polarity.* Toronto: Collier.

Weingartner, Herbert, and Elizabeth S. Parker, eds. 1984. *Memory Consolidation: Psychobiology of Cognition.* Hillsdale, N.J.: Lawrence Erlbaum Associates.

Werner, E. E., and R. L. Smith. 1982. *Vulnerable but Invincible.* New York: McGraw-Hill.

Whitehead, Alfred North. 1926. *Religion in the Making.* New York: The Macmillan Company.

————. 1933. *Adventures of Ideas.* New York: The Macmillan Company.

————. 1947. *Science and the Modern World: Lowell Lectures 1925.* New York: The Macmillan Company.

————. 1978. *Process and Reality.* Corrected, edited by David Ray Griffin and Donald W. Sherburne. New York: The Free Press.

Whyte, Lancelot. 1973. *Contemporary Psychology* 18 (July): 330.

Wiesel, Torsten N. 1981. "The Postnatal Development of the Visual Cortex and the Influence of the Environment." In *Les Prix Nobel,* 261–99. Stockholm: Almqvist & Wiksell International.

Wilken, Robert L. 1993. *The Land Called Holy: Palestine in Christian History and Thought.* New Haven, Conn.: Yale University Press.

Will, James E. 1994. *The Universal God: Justice, Love, and Peace in the Global Village.* Louisville: Westminster/John Knox Press.

Winnicott, D. W. 1963. "Morals and Education." In *The Maturational Processes and the Facilitating Environment,* 93–105. New York: International Universities Press, 1965 reprint.

————. 1965. *The Maturational Processes and the Facilitating Environment.* New York: International Universities Press.

————. 1971. *Playing and Reality.* New York: Basic Books.

Winograd, Eugene. 1988. "Continuities between Ecological and Laboratory Approaches to Memory." In *Remembering Reconsidered: Ecological and Traditional Approaches to the Study of Memory,* edited by Ulric Neisser and Eugene Winograd, 11–20. Cambridge: Cambridge University Press.

Winson, Jonathan. [1985] 1986. *The Brain and Psyche: The Biology of the Unconscious.* New York: Vintage Books.

————. 1990. "The Meaning of Dreams." *Scientific American,* November, 86–96.

Witelson, Sandra F. 1977. "Anatomic Asymmetry in the Temporal Lobes: Its Documentation, Phylogenesis, and Relationship to Functional Asymmetry." In *Evolution and Lateralization of the Brain* 299, edited by Stuart J. Dimond and David A. Blizard, 328–54. New York: Annals of the New York Academy of Sciences.

Wolf, George. 1984. "The Place of the Brain in an Ocean of Feelings." In *Existence and Actuality: Conversations with Charles Hartshorne,* edited by John B. Cobb Jr. and Franklin I. Gamwell, 167–84. Chicago: University of Chicago Press.

Young, Robert M. [1970] 1990. *Mind, Brain, and Adaptation in the Nineteenth Century: Cerebral Localization and Its Biological Context from Gall to Ferrier.* New York: Oxford University Press.

Zaidel, Dahlia W. 1991. "Long-term Semantic Memory in the Two Cerebral Hemispheres." In *Brain Circuits and Functions of the Mind: Essays in Honor of Roger W. Sperry,* edited by Colwyn Trevarthen, 266–80. Cambridge: Cambridge University Press.

— Subject Index —

– Scriptural Index –

Genesis

1	96, 117, 163
1:1	25
1:1–2	150
1:28	64
1:31–2:3	96–97
2	96
2:7	23
2:9a	106
2:9b	106
2:15	23
2:19	120, 140
2:19–20	23
3:7–24	160
9:1–11	30
11:1–2	150
11:1–9	27

Exodus

20:3–5	63
20:8	97–98
29:11	96

Leviticus

19:18	108

Numbers

21:6	65

Deuteronomy

4:23–24	63
5:12–15	96

Psalms

7:17	63
8	24
9:2	63
11:1	63
27:7–9	26
39:14	165
46:4	63
47:2	63
57:2	63
73:11	63
83:18	63
99:3	xxviii
104:27–30	26

Isaiah

2:8	xxxi
48:6–7	165
58:11	147

Jeremiah

31:33	106

Matthew

5:43	108
6:26	63
10:29–31	63
19:19	108
22:39	108

Mark

12:31	108

Luke

1:52–53	64
4:9–12	144
10:27	108
12:6–7	63
22:19	98

John

1	117
1:1	25
1:1–4	24
1:1–14	24
15:8–11, 15	64

Acts

2:1–3	30
2:6, 11	28

Romans

7:21–24	65
8:28	144
13:9	108

1 Corinthians

11:24	98
14:40	128

Galatians

5:14	108

Ephesians

1:8b–10	42
2:8	xviii

Philippians

2:5–8	64

Colossians

1:16–18	xxviii

Hebrews

11:1	145
12:1a	xvii
13:8	63

James

2:8	108
3:16	65
4:1	65

1 John

3:2	64
4:16b–19	151

Revelation

20:15	98

DATE DUE

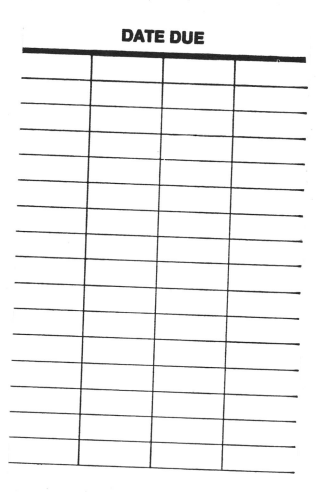